Standards
for Day and
Resident Camps

Standards for Day and Resident Camps

1990 Edition, Revised 1993

Accreditation Programs of the
American Camping Association®

Photo credits. Appreciation is extended to the following for the use of the photos in this book: Camp Puh'tok, Salvation Army Boys Clubs, Maryland; Girl Scout Council of St. Louis (by Amelia Brazell); YMCA of the Ozarks, Missouri; Boys Clubs of Metro Detroit, Michigan; and Belvoir Terrace, Massachusetts.

Previously published as *Camp Standards with Interpretations for the Accreditation of Organized Camps.*

© 1972, 1975, 1984, 1990 by American Camping Association, Inc. Revised 1993. Earlier editions 1935, 1941, 1956, 1960, 1966, 1972, 1978, 1984.

Printed in the United States of America on recycled paper.

American Camping Association, Inc.
5000 State Road 67 North
Martinsville, IN 46151-7902
317/342-8456 American Camping Association National Office
800/428-CAMP American Camping Association Bookstore & Publications Office
317/342-2065 FAX

Library of Congress Cataloging-in-Publication Data

American Camping Association.
    Standards for day and resident camps: the accreditation programs
  of the American Camping Association.
        p. cm.
    ISBN 0-87603-123-8: $17.95 — ISBN 0-87603-124-6 (Organizer):
$49.95
    1. Camps — United States — Accreditation.   I. Title
GV198.A38A4 1990a
796.54'0973 — dc20   90-1012
                                                          CIP

Acknowledgements

These Standards reflect the cooperative effort of many . . .

The Members . . . who share ideas, suggestions, and yes — complaints. But all of this provides input for improvement. Members write, call, field test, and tell us what they want. These **Standards** exist for them, and because of them!

The Delegates . . . who spend countless hours listening, reflecting, suggesting, voting, and sharing in the dynamic process of creating change and improvement.

The Section Standards Personnel . . . visitors, instructors, Standards chairs and committee members whose incredible efforts accomplish close to 1000 visits over a ten week period of time . . . in the summer . . . when they are the busiest, for they, too, are camp directors!

The National Standards Board . . . a small group of dedicated volunteers whose commitment to excellence in standards causes all of us to stretch. A list of the Board members who have served during this revision is below.

The Staff of the American Camping Association . . . and not just the staff of the Standards Department, but the whole group who share in the work, provide understanding support, and work together to accomplish what no one Department could accomplish alone.

To all of these we give our thanks.

National Standards Board Members, 1986-1990

Connie Coutellier, Chair (1988-1992)
Camp Fire, Inc., Missouri

Stuart Mace, Chair (1982-1988)
Easter Seal Society, Illinois

Ed Andrews, Maine
Mary Faeth Chenery, Washington
Coral Cotten, California
Cindy Moore, California
Dale Roth, Pennsylvania
Wes Stevens, North Carolina
George Sudduth, Massachusetts
Wes Voigt, South Carolina

Jani Brokaw, New York
Ed Cohen, Maryland
Sally Horner, California
Bob Rick, Minnesota
Barry Royce, New York
Miles Strodel, New Hampshire
Kathy Trotter, Indiana

National Standards Staff

Pat Hammond, Assistant Director
Fran McQueary, Administrative Assistant
Marge Scanlin, Division Director, Member and Camp Services

Disclaimer

The purpose of these standards is to educate camp directors and camp personnel regarding practices and procedures followed generally within the camp industry. That purpose is furthered to the extent that the standards provide a basis for accreditation of camps by the American Camping Association, Inc. It should be recognized that each part of every standard may not be applicable to all camps. Further, it is not the intention of the American Camping Association, Inc. to attempt to include every practice or procedure that might be desirable for or implemented by a camp since conditions, facilities, and the goals or objectives of all camps are not identical or uniform.

The accreditation programs of the American Camping Association are designed to be applied only to those camp programs that are consistent with the stated definitions and eligibility requirements of the identified designations. Programs outside of these definitions or criteria are not subject to our standards and are not considered for accreditation.

In developing and applying these standards in the accreditation process, the American Camping Association, Inc. and its sections do not undertake to verify the continuous adherence by those camps or directors to every applicable standard or guideline. Nor does the Association warrant, guarantee, or insure that compliance with these standards will prevent any or all injury or loss that may be caused by or associated with any person's use of facilities, equipment, or other items or activities that are the subjects of these standards; nor does the Association assume any responsibility or liability for any such injury or loss.

Further, the American Camping Association, Inc. hereby expressly disclaims any responsibility, liability or duty to affiliated camps, directors, camp personnel, and to campers and their families, for any such liability arising out of injury or loss to any person by the failure of such camps, directors, or camp personnel to adhere to these standards.

Accreditation Logos of The American Camping Association

The American Camping Association Accredited Camp and Approved Site logos are registered trademarks. Any use of the ACA signs, seals, and logos is a privilege reserved for camps that are currently accredited and sites that are currently approved. Such symbolism represents to the public that a camp has met the criteria for the accreditation designation displayed.

It is inappropriate for camps to advertise or imply that accreditation has been applied for or earned until notification has been received from the American Camping Association, Inc. indicating that all accreditation requirements have been met and verified by an on-site visit.

Any improper use of accreditation symbols or statements should be reported to ACA's national office and is subject to prosecution to the full extent of the law.

ACA Exemplary Ethical Practices for Camp Directors/Owners

The members of the American Camping Association recognize and support the concept that custody of others' lives and welfare as well as the earth and its living things, calls for reverence for such life, in dedication and commitment to a higher good. Whatever form such a dedication and commitment may take, it must be essentially moral in nature.

The members further:

a. recognize and support the objectives that the well-being of the camper is primary.

b. recognize and support the concept that a camp is necessarily a total community within the society with significant impact upon its inhabitants' capacity to learn, grow, develop, assimilate values, create and relate to other persons and the earth.

c. accept, respect and will be responsive to the rich diversity of our society.

d. recognize and support the concept of an ecological conscience that a thing is right when it tends to preserve the integrity, stability and beauty of the biotic community.

The association recognizes the camp director/owner as the primary professional person assuming the greatest responsibility for actual camping practices. Therefore, the association shall ask the person assuming this responsibility to subscribe to the following, to the extent permitted by law.

I shall endeavor to provide an environment conducive to promoting and protecting the physical and emotional well-being of the campers and staff.

I shall seek to instill in my staff and campers not only a reverence for the land and its waters and all living things, but also an ecological conscience which reflects the conviction of individual responsibility for the health of that environment.

I shall maintain a camp membership enrollment policy without regard to religious affiliations (unless my camp is operated either by or in behalf of an established church or for bona fide religious purposes), national origin, or race.

I shall follow equal employment opportunity practices in hiring, assigning, promoting and compensating staff. I shall endeavor to employ persons based upon factors necessary in the performance of the job and the operation of the camp, without discriminating because of religious affiliation (unless my camp is operated either by or in behalf of an established church or for bona fide religious purposes), race, national origin, gender, age, marital status or disability.

I shall be truthful and fair in representing my camp and other camps by whatever medium of communications.

(continued)

I shall be truthful and fair in securing and dealing with campers and staff.

I shall strive to conduct my camp in such a way as to build good will not only for my camp but also for the camping movement.

I shall strive to be responsible and sensitive to the local community influenced by the presence of my camp.

I shall provide a written enrollment policy for all applicants including fees, payment schedules, discounts, dates of arrival and departure, together with clearly stated refund policy.

I shall provide for each staff member a written job description and contract including period of employment, compensation, benefits and exceptions.

I shall tell parents my procedures for promptly notifying them in the event their child is hospitalized or suffers accident or illness.

I shall maintain in professional confidence camper and staff information, observation, or evaluation.

I shall promptly consult with parents or guardians as to the advisability of removing a child from camp should it be clear that the child is not benefiting from the camp experience.

I shall refrain from actively recruiting any camper or staff member known by me to be currently enrolled or employed at another camp.

I shall honor my financial commitments to parents, staff, vendors and others.

I shall maintain the proper membership classification and pay the proper camp service fee as defined by the National Board of Directors.

I shall use the ACA seals of accreditation only in accordance with policies of the ACA Standards Program.

I shall abide by ACA requirements and respect ACA guidelines for my profession.

ADOPTED BY THE COUNCIL OF DELEGATES MARCH 5, 1976, MARCH 2, 1978, FEBRUARY 16, 1980, MARCH 6, 1987, MARCH 4, 1989

Table of Contents

Part 1

Introduction

Introduction

THE AMERICAN CAMPING ASSOCIATION

The American Camping Association (ACA) is a private, nonprofit educational organization with members in all 50 states and several foreign countries. Its members represent a diverse constituency of camp and conference owners and directors, executives, educators, clergy, business representatives, consultants, staff members, volunteers, students, retirees and others associated with the operation of conference/retreat centers or camps for children and adults.

The association defines camping as:

A sustained experience which provides a creative, recreational and educational opportunity in group living in the outdoors. It utilizes trained leadership and the resources of the natural surroundings to contribute to each camper's mental, physical, social, and spiritual growth.

The mission of the American Camping Association is to serve organized camps, affiliated programs, and the public by promoting better camping for all. To accomplish this mission, ACA:

Goals

- Educates camp personnel to create positive growth experiences for children, teens, and adults, using the outdoors responsibly as a program environment;

- Protects the public by promoting health and safety practices and effective management through accreditation, certification, and education programs;

- Promotes advocacy of issues affecting camps; and

- Communicates the value of camp experiences to the public and encourages camp opportunities for all.

The programs of the association are administered through 32 local sections. Section and national officers are elected by the membership and serve without pay. The organization is supported primarily by the dues and contributions of its members. Other support comes from convention fees, the sale of publications, project grants, and fees for services.

Members belong to the national organization and to a local section responsible to deliver services including the accreditation programs. In addition to the two accreditation programs described in this book, ACA also offers an accreditation program for conference/retreat centers. This program is fully described in a separate publication, *Standards for Conference and Retreat Centers*.

Services of ACA include educational programs and conferences, accreditation services, networking through activities in local sections, monitoring of legislation at the federal and state levels, *Camping Magazine*, public relations efforts, certification programs, and mail order bookstore services providing the largest selection of books related to camping, conferencing, and outdoor education to be found.

ACA serves as a consultant and advisor to many state and federal agencies related to the field of camping and to colleges and universities in the fields of outdoor education and recreation.

THE ACCREDITATION PROGRAMS OF THE AMERICAN CAMPING ASSOCIATION

Purpose

The main purpose of the ACA accreditation programs is to educate camp owners and directors in the administration of key aspects of camp operation, particularly those related to program quality and the health and safety of campers and staff. The standards establish guidelines for needed policies, procedures, and practices. The camp, then, is responsible for on-going implementation of those policies.

A second purpose of the ACA accreditation programs is to assist the public in selecting camps which meet industry-accepted and government-recognized standards. While standards focus on health and safety practices, accreditation is not a guarantee that the camper will be absolutely free from harm.

Accreditation does, however, indicate to the public that the camp administration has voluntarily allowed its practices to be compared with the standards established by professionals in the camping industry. At least once every three years an outside team of trained camping professionals visits the camp to verify compliance with the standards.

Unlike inspections by state licensing bodies, ACA accreditation is voluntary. ACA does not have the authority to close or otherwise penalize an entity not meeting its accreditation criteria, except for the removal of the accreditation status. Licensing focuses on the enforcement of minimum standards. Accreditation focuses on education and evaluation of one's operation using standards that go beyond the minimum requirements of licensing.

ACA standards identify practices considered basic to quality camping. They do not, however, require all programs to look alike. The ACA accreditation programs serve a broad range of facilities and programs: some primitive, some rustic, others highly developed. Each will have addressed in its own way the concerns identified by the standards.

Many types of programs seek ACA Camp Accreditation such as day and resident camps, travel and trip camps, school camps and environmental education centers, and camps with special program emphases (e.g. sports, academic, therapeutic, religious). ACA Site Approval is also sought by conference and retreat centers who specialize in offering facilities and services to other program operators.

▌ Camp Accreditation

Eligibility

"American Camping Association Accredited Camp" describes the operation of the site and the program of a camp by an owner/director. This designation may be sought by a camp operating on its own property or on the property belonging to someone else. The visitation requires establishing compliance with standards related to the camp's site, program, and operation, and it must occur while the camp is in full operation.

To be eligible for *Camp Accreditation*, an operation must:

1. Operate a program consistent with ACA's definition of camping (see page 3).
2. Submit an Annual Application and Statement of Compliance indicating the camp's compliance with applicable laws, regulations, and permit requirements; and the continued compliance with all applicable mandatory standards and other criteria for accreditation as noted at the time of the visit.
3. Pay appropriate dues and services fees as determined by ACA.
4. Have an operating season consisting of sessions a majority of which are at least 5 consecutive days in length if a resident camp; or, if a day camp, at least 5 consecutive days in length or five days in not more than 14 days.
5. Be visited by ACA-certified visitors for accreditation on a typical camp program day.

Generally, the Accredited Camp designation extends only to the program visited (e.g. summer youth camp program). In some instances a camp may offer an additional session or sessions at some other time of year. To be considered accredited, that separate program must:

1. Be at least five days in length;
2. Be represented by the camp owner/director to be in compliance with the standards;
3. Be under the same supervision as the summer program;
4. Be operated under the same camp name as the visited program; and
5. Have the same health care, staffing and program pattern as the visited program.
6. In addition, the accreditation of the visited program must still be in effect.

In order to become an Accredited Camp, the camp must be in full compliance with all applicable mandatory standards. Furthermore, a score of at least 80% must be achieved in each applicable section of the standards, and the camp must pass the applicable "specialized activities" sub-sections.

▌ Site Approval

"American Camping Association Approved Site" describes the facilities and services offered to another camp director or program director. This designation is only applicable to camps that rent or lease their facilities to other groups who retain the primary responsibility for their own program. An Approved Site meets standards specific to site operation and to those services furnished by the site owner/operator.

To be eligible for *Site Approval*, an operation must:

1. Provide a facility whose operation enables programs to be carried out that are consistent with the definition of camping as set forth by the American Camping Association (see page 3).

2. Submit an Annual Application and Statement of Compliance indicating the site's compliance with applicable laws, regulations, and permit requirements; and the continued compliance with all applicable mandatory standards and other criteria for Site Approval as noted at the time of the visit.
3. Pay appropriate dues and service fees as determined by ACA.
4. Lease, rent, or otherwise make available its site and/or facilities to other program operators or sponsors.
5. Agree to follow the applicable ACA standards with all groups using the Approved Site; and
6. Provide a site which makes possible the use of the resources of the natural setting.

In order to become an Approved Site, the site must be in full compliance with all applicable mandatory standards. Furthermore, a score of at least 80% must be achieved in each applicable section of the standards.

Content of the Standards

Accredited Camps and Approved Sites are responsible not only for state and local laws, but also for those requirements defined by the standards. Those requirements include:

■ Camp Accreditation
Site and Facility standards including food service, provision of adequate sleeping quarters in resident camps, toilet and handwashing facilities, and fire and law enforcement protection.

Administration standards including safety regulations, emergency procedures, and risk management planning.

Administration of Transportation and Vehicles standards including driver qualifications and training, vehicle maintenance, and safety procedures.

Personnel standards including qualifications, training, and supervision of camp staff.

Program standards including activity leadership qualifications, safety regulations, and procedures for conducting activities.

Health care standards including supervision of health care practices, availability of first aid equipment and personnel, the use of health histories and health examination forms, health care procedures, and the availability of emergency transportation.

Activity standards in aquatics, horseback riding and trip/travel camping including staff qualifications, and the conduct of these activities.

■ Site Approval
Site standards including fire protection, toileting and handwashing areas, sleeping quarters, bathing facilities, and food service.

Administration standards including transportation, health care, risk management planning, and personnel concerns.

Activity standards when such activities are provided including aquatics and horseback riding.

The use of the American Camping Association Camp Accreditation and Site Approval signs, seals, and logos is a privilege reserved for camps that are currently accredited and sites that are currently approved. Such symbolism represents to the public that a camp has met the criteria for accreditation. All indications of ACA Accreditation and Approval are protected by U.S. patent and copyright laws. Any improper use of symbols should be reported to ACA National Headquarters and may be prosecuted to the full extent of the law.

Symbols Protected

Since the formation of the Camp Directors' Association in 1910, the leadership of organized camping in the United States has directed many of its efforts toward health and safety concerns affecting camps. Following mergers with regional and specialized camping organizations, the name American Camping Association was adopted in 1935. In this same year, a listing of "Suggested Tentative Standards" was adopted. These standards were in addition to those being developed independently by individual agencies such as the Young Men's Christian Association, the Girl Scouts, and the Boy Scouts.

History and Development of Standards

The Executive Committee of the ACA in 1940 decided that the existing formulations of standards should be assembled, examined, and worked into a composite form that might represent a consensus of the camping movement. Grants from Kellogg and Chrysler foundations enabled this project to go forward, and in 1948 the first set of Camp Standards was officially adopted at ACA's National Convention.

At subsequent conventions, additional standards and/or concepts related to standards were adopted:

1950   Personnel and program standards adopted.
1954   Methods of establishing compliance with the standards were instituted.
1956   Day camp standards adopted.
1961   Travel and family camp standards adopted.
1965   A standards program that consolidated all the previous sets of standards was put in place, and the concept of prerequisite (necessary for accreditation irrespective of other scores) was adopted.
1968   A Standards Rewrite Committee was formed to thoroughly study the standards, utilizing research conducted over the previous few years with the assistance of Pennsylvania State University and the Fund for Advancement of Camping.
1972   The recommendations of the Standards Rewrite Committee were approved by the Council of Delegates.
1974   With the cooperation of the National Easter Seal Society, standards for the physically disabled were adopted.
1980   With input from state associations for mentally retarded persons, standards for the mentally retarded were adopted.
1982   With input from the American Diabetes Association, standards for camps serving persons with diabetes were adopted.
1984   A complete revision of standards for Camp Accreditation and Site Approval was adopted, consolidating all recently adopted revisions into the core document. The National Standards Board agreed to maintain this set of standards in place for six years if at all possible.
1990   A revised set of standards focusing on health and safety issues was adopted. In Camp Accreditation, items reflecting good business practice were placed in a separate Self-Assessment document.

ADMINISTRATION OF THE STANDARDS PROGRAM

The National Standards Board is responsible to develop and administer the Standards Program of the association. Its members are selected according to defined criteria and operate within specific guidelines and procedures approved by the National Board of Directors of the American Camping Association.

The scheduling of visits and assigning of visitors is handled by ACA's geographical units called "sections." These sections are chartered by the Association on an annual basis and are held responsible for the orderly local administration of the accreditation programs under the supervision of the National Standards Board and the staff of the Standards Department in the national office.

Responsibility to accredit

The American Camping Association camp accreditation programs are national programs that utilize the local section as the implementing agency within the ACA structure. The minimum criteria for accreditation are established and monitored by the National Standards Board.

Sections schedule and conduct visitations. They also approve accreditation for camps that meet the mandatory standards and the minimum score percentages established by the National Standards Board, and reject accreditation for camps that have not met at least the minimum criteria.

Sections do not have the authority to waive either the established mandatory standards or the specified minimum score percentages established for compliance. If a section deems that it is highly desirable to waive such criteria, such request must be made to the National Standards Board according to the procedure set forth by that board.

Preparing for the visit

Step One — Apply by completing appropriate membership and accreditation application forms, and signing the Statement of Compliance that will be sent when ACA receives the application.

Step Two — Remit service fees as described in current membership materials.

Step Three—Attend the Basic Standards Course, offered by the local section, which explains the process and describes the requirements for accreditation. At the time of the accreditation visit, there must be an individual on the campsite who has completed the Basic Standards Course and has participated in the development of materials for the visit.

Step Four — Prepare materials and written documentation required by the standards. Review and evaluate each area of camp operation utilizing the guidelines in the standards, and, in Camp Accreditation, the "Self-Assessment of Additional Professional Practices" document found on page 177.

Step Five—Participate in the visit by a team of ACA-trained visitors who will spend a full day observing the camp and working with the director in the scoring process. This visit must occur when the camp is in full operation, as compliance with the standard is determined by observations made on the day of the visit. Results of the visit will be reported no later than November 10 for camps visited in the summer.

▮ The Visitor

Visitors are volunteers. They are persons with a background in camp administration who have completed at least twenty-one hours of training prior to conducting visits for ACA. They have also completed an "apprenticeship" with an experienced visitor.

Many visitors are camp directors themselves. They understand the importance of accreditation and the scope of laws, regulations, and procedures of camps.

▮ The Visit

Accreditation visits occur on a typical camp program or site operation day (not the opening or closing day of a camp session), and generally require a full day. Visitors often arrive at camp during or shortly after breakfast and spend the morning touring, observing, and learning about the camp.

During the visitation process, visitors will observe living areas including sleeping accommodations for campers and staff; food preparation and dining areas; aquatic activity areas; health care areas; garbage, sewage and rubbish disposal areas; maintenance and fuel storage areas; and other activity areas. At the end of each standard in this book a *Compliance Demonstration* statement defines the minimum recommendation for observation and discussion necessary for the visitor to score that standard.

During this observation, visitors should have an opportunity to interview staff and campers and observe program activities in action.

Once this thorough tour of the camp is complete, the visitors will meet with the camp director to determine compliance with each standard that applies to the camp. Written documentation required by the standards will also be observed by the visitors at this time.

The visitors will score the standard based on compliance as observed at the time of the visit.

If, during the visit, the visitors note that the camp is not in compliance with a mandatory standard, the *Immediate Corrective Action* policy will be instituted. Applicable only to mandatory standards, the Immediate Corrective Action policy requires a camp to immediately correct the deficiency, and document that correction within 10 days or accreditation will be immediately withdrawn (if previously accredited) or denied.

▮ Criteria for Accreditation

In order to achieve accreditation (or reaccreditation), the camp must fully comply with each of the applicable mandatory standards, attain scores of at least 80% in each applicable category of standards, and, in Camp Accreditation, pass the applicable "specialized activities" sub-sections by missing no more than one scoreable item in any activity subset scored.

Conduct of the visit

**Evaluation
of the Visit**

■ Notification of the Accreditation Decision

Camps visited in the summer will be notified between September 1 and November 10 of the results of the visit. Camps visited at other times of the year will be notified between six and eight weeks following the receipt of the score form at the national office. While a camp may be visited for accreditation during its first season of operation, accreditation is not achieved until action by the Section Board confirms that all accreditation criteria are met. The "accreditation year" is November 1 through October 31.

■ Review and Appeal

If a camp fails to meet the accreditation criteria, it has the right to a review by the section in order to question either the overall accreditation decision or the scoring of a particular standard. Ultimately, this review may be appealed to the National Standards Board. The decision of the National Standards Board is final.

The review process will include the opportunity for a hearing before the Section Standards Committee and full consideration of all issues affecting the accreditation status of the camp. These due process rights are fully described in "The Camp Director's Guide to Review and Appeal." Copies of this document are available from the section or national office.

Procedures for Revisitation

A camp may be revisited at any time as determined by the section board of directors. Reasonable notice must be provided to the camp in order to have opportunity to update any written documents required for the visit.

A camp visit is scheduled when:
1. Three years have passed since the last visit,
2. The camp was not accredited following the previous year's visit,
3. The camp is a new applicant for accreditation; or

A camp may be revisited at the section's discretion when:
1. The camp moves to a new site.
2. There is a new owner,
3. There is a new on-site camp director, or
4. Other factors related to accreditation criteria indicate to the Board that a revisit is called for.

Removal of Accreditation

Accreditation may be removed from a camp by the section board of directors under the following circumstances:

1. The camp refuses to schedule an accreditation visit by the section when required by the procedures identified above, or
2. The camp is visited, but failed to meet the minimum criteria established for accreditation, or
3. For reasons as described in the current Statement of Compliance (see Appendix A, page 195).

The camp retains the right of appeal to the National Standards Board in such circumstances.

USING THIS BOOK

The ACA accreditation programs are designed to be applicable to all types of camps, whether day or resident; church, private-independent, or agency sponsored; large or small; conducted using a decentralized or centralized program philosophy; male, female or coed; or focusing on a program specialty.

To enhance the value of the accreditation program as an educational process, it is strongly recommended that the camp administration involve the staff in the preparation of materials for the visit, and in the visit itself. It is suggested that the person in charge of each program area conduct the evaluation of his or her own program as preparation in this process.

Format of the Standards

The standard in bold type should be distinguished from both the *Interpretation* and the *Compliance Demonstration*. For the purposes of scoring, the camp is responsible to meet the requirement identified in bold type, the standard.

There are two designations that may appear at the beginning of individual standards. The first of these is used to designate *MANDATORY* standards and appears as an asterisk (*) prior to the standard number and the word **MANDATORY** following the standard number. Sometimes an entire standard is mandatory (see standard *A-8), while other times only one part of a standard is mandatory (see *D-19, part D). Compliance with standards marked "* MANDATORY" is required for Camp Accreditation or Site Approval to be granted, regardless of scores achieved in other areas of the standards. A full list of the mandatory standards can be found on pages 196 and 198 in the Appendix.

The second designation is a *DNA* (does not apply) statement which may also appear at the beginning of a standard (see A-2), at the beginning of a part of a standard (see A-ll, B), or prior to a group of standards such as food service (see the introduction preceding A-24).

It will be noted that some standards have *numbered* subparts (such as A-2, page 16). *Numbered* subparts are to be scored as an aggregate. This will require all the criteria in the standard to be met in order to comply with the standard.

Other standards have *lettered* subparts (such as A-7, page 18). Each *lettered* subpart will be scored independently. It is, therefore, possible for a lettered subpart to be **mandatory** such as A-11, parts A, C, and D. In this example, only part B is not mandatory.

Additional Items Included with the Standard

At the end of each standard, two additional items may appear. The first is an *Interpretation.* This will provide camp administrators and visitors assistance in applying the terminology of the standard consistently and in understanding the intent of the standard as written.

The *Compliance Demonstration* identifies for directors and visitors the minimum expectation of the National Standards Board as to how compliance with the standard should be determined. General guidelines for the Compliance Demonstration include the following:

1. Written procedures/documents must be seen by the visitor when specified by the standard.
2. Written procedures/documents shall be evaluated by the visitor to see that they contain the specifics required by the standard.
3. Written plans require that all materials specified by the standard be together in one place as a single document.

4. Procedures or policies <u>not specified in the standard to be in writing</u> may be described by the camp administration or staff.

5. The visitors' tour around the property will give informal opportunity to observe the implementation of policies and procedures in camp program in selected areas. It is recognized that all activities may not be occurring on the day of the visit due to scheduling and weather conditions. In such circumstances, visitors should discuss the standard's requirements with appropriate staff and score the standards accordingly.

6. Standards required to be "in practice" or "rehearsed" are to be verified by the visitor through discussion or observation to ascertain that implementation has occurred.

In the area next to each standard is the *Director's Pre-Visit Evaluation* and room for notes. The Pre-Visit Evaluation helps the director conduct a self-evaluation on the standard while preparing for the visit. However, it should be noted that it is the visitor's analysis of compliance with the standard during the observation portion of the visit that is represented on the actual score form.

Additional Items Included in this Book

The *Glossary* (see page 169) contains definitions of terms used throughout the document. The standards are intended to be applied within the framework of the definitions as stated in this book.

The *Self-Assessment of Additional Professional Practices* (see page 177) contains business practices and other items included in previous editions of *Standards*. One standard for Camp Accreditation (B-1) requires camp administrators to complete a self-evaluation process using this tool for planning and self-study.

The *Appendix* (see page 193) contains examples or outlines of materials to be included in various documents, or further instructional helps. Information under each standard will direct the reader to the Appendix if such information can be found there.

Part 2

Standards for Camp Accreditation

Standards for Camp Accreditation

INTRODUCTION

American Camping Association Accredited Camp describes a day or resident camp operating on its own property or on the property belonging to someone else. The visitation requires establishing compliance with standards related to the camp site, program, and overall operation, and it must occur while the camp is in full operation.

The Camp Accreditation standards include:

Core Standards that are applied to all camps seeking Camp Accreditation:

A — Site and Facilities
B — Administration
BT — Administration of Transportation and Vehicles
C — Personnel
D — Program
E — Health Care

Activity Standards that are applicable only if these activities are offered:

F — Aquatics
G — Trip/Travel
H — Horseback Riding

SECTION A — SITE and FACILITIES

The physical setting of the camp operation is an integral part of the total camp experience. While personnel and program are key to meeting objectives for camper development in a healthy atmosphere, the importance of the site and its facilities cannot be overlooked. They make an important contribution to the overall experience.

Whether the camp owns, rents, or leases its site, the camp administration should be certain that provision has been made for the items in this section.

The standards in the Site section are NOT scored for camps which are exclusively TRIP camps and/or TRAVEL camps (with no permanent base camp). Site concerns for these two specialized types of camps are found in Section G (Trip/Travel). Also, DAY CAMPS that meet each day on a different site and do not have a base camp are not scored on the Site standards.

When a camp seeking accreditation is using or renting/leasing from an ACA-Approved Site, the Site standards DO NOT need to be scored again. However, information must be provided on the score form identifying the camp whose accreditation or approval is being relied upon. All other applicable sections of the standards must be scored specifically for the camp seeking its own accreditation.

DNA A-1 through A-29 **ONLY IF** camp is:

1) a trip or travel camp with no established base camp, or
2) a day camp that meets at different sites daily, or
3) a camp using an Approved Site.

A-1

Director's Pre-Visit Evaluation

☐ Yes ☐ No

To provide for the protection of the camp, has contact been made in writing with local fire and law enforcement officials to notify them of the dates of camp operation and the numbers of participants in the camp program? Yes No

Interpretation: Due to possible changes in personnel or districts, local officials should be notified annually in the case of year-round operations. Seasonal camps should make such contact just prior to the operating season.

In situations where the site is automatically covered by municipal fire and police service, the camp should still notify those officials of camp operation dates and number of persons on the site.

Compliance Demonstration: Visitor observation of letters to or from local officials.

A-2

Director's Pre-Visit Evaluation

☐ Yes ☐ No ☐ DNA

DNA if the camp is operated on a site without facilities.

Does the camp administration implement a system to have annual examination(s) conducted by qualified person(s) of the following fire equipment and areas:

1. **Smoke detectors and other detection devices — availability and location,**
2. **Fire extinguishers — type, location and readiness,**
3. **Fireplaces and chimneys,**
4. **Storage and use areas for flammable materials and fuel,**
5. **Open fire areas, and**
6. **Cooking areas?** **Yes No**

Interpretation: A "site without facilities" includes sites that do not have buildings used for permanent sleeping quarters and sites that do not have substantial capital investment in structures which would constitute a significant loss in the event of fire.

"Qualified persons" include fire fighting professionals or equipment distributors, insurance underwriters, and other forest/fire officials who have recognized expertise in fire safety inspections. Camp staff with appropriate training and/or experience also may be qualified.

Compliance Demonstration: Director/staff description of system to conduct evaluation annually.

A-3

DNA if on a community (public) water supply.

Is there written confirmation that all water sources used for drinking or food preparation purposes meet state guidelines for approval and have been tested:

1. **If a seasonal water supply, within 30 days preceding the first use by campers or staff, or**
2. **If a continuously used water supply, within the past three months (quarterly); and**
3. **If initial test results do not meet state guidelines, there is evidence that specific recommendations of local health officials are being implemented to correct the problem?** **Yes No**

Interpretation: This standard applies to water which comes from the camp's own wells or reservoir system, not to water provided by a municipal or other water authority responsible for its own testing.

The Environmental Protection Agency periodically updates rules affecting water testing requirements. The rules vary based on the source of water (ground, surface, or both) and are also subject to modification by state authorities. Testing frequency requirements range from weekly to annually. Directors are advised to contact local health authorities to confirm local test requirements.

"Continuously used" means the water supply is used throughout the calendar year. "Seasonal water supply" means the water supply is in use for only a portion of the year.

In a situation where the state or local authorities require testing after occupancy or in some other time period not in conformity with the 30 day requirement of the standard, the camp must have a test completed by another qualified laboratory within the timeframe specified by the standard to be in compliance with the standard.

Compliance Demonstration: Visitor observation of dated test results; director verification of recommended corrective steps (if applicable).

A-4

DNA if no utilities on site.

For the purpose of safety in an emergency, are blueprints, charts, or physical descriptions indicating the location of all electrical lines and cutoff points, gas lines and valves, and water cutoff points:

1. **Available on site, or**
2. **In the case of a non-owned site, does the on-site camp director have a written telephone number of the individual or agency to contact in case of problems?** **Yes No**

Interpretation: Camp staff should have information immediately available to enable them to locate cutoff points in the event of an emergency, as well as for routine maintenance. Charts or descriptions should be available for immediate access when needed.

Compliance Demonstration: Visitor observation of charts, blueprints, etc.; OR for non-owned sites, telephone number of contact person.

A-5

DNA if no electrical service on site.

Does the camp administration require that an electrical evaluation be conducted annually by (a) qualified person(s)?   Yes   No

Interpretation: Evaluations should be conducted in all facilities with electrical service including the swimming pool, water pumps, living areas for campers and staff, program buildings or areas, food service and storage areas, maintenance areas, and dining halls.

The evaluation should include at least a visual observation of areas and facilities to check for such things as damaged or loose wires or fixtures, electrical equipment needing repair or replacement, face plates and panel fronts in place, correct-sized fuses and circuit breakers, and appropriately grounded receptacles.

Particular attention should be paid to facilities which have little or no use during some seasons, where damage from rodents or weather may have occurred.

"Qualified persons" could include camp staff, maintenance personnel, persons identified as qualified by local statute/regulation, or other persons with training and/or experience in basic electrical evaluation, as well as electricians or other licensed persons.

Compliance Demonstration: Director description of procedures and personnel used to conduct the annual evaluation.

A-6

Is the camp free from observable evidence of a sewage disposal problem, or is there evidence that specific recommendations of local health officials are being implemented to correct the problem?   Yes   No

Compliance Demonstration: Visitor observation of septic system areas; demonstrated implementation of health department recommendations where applicable.

A-7

Is there evidence that a systematic maintenance routine is in effect throughout the camp that results in:

    A. Buildings (including toilets), paths, and activity locations maintained in good repair?   Yes   No

    B. Clean and sanitary conditions?   Yes   No

Interpretation: Part A includes all buildings and program areas in camp. Railings, porches, floorboards, screens, and doors are examples of items that should show signs of regular maintenance and repair.

Part B includes garbage and rubbish disposal areas, kitchen garbage disposal systems and area, toilet areas, program areas and buildings. In addition to being "in repair" (part A), there should be signs of regular cleaning, garbage/trash collection, and regular activity to keep the area free of accumulated dirt, grease, mildew, etc. Campers or staff may be involved in such routines.

On a non-owned site, only the areas in immediate use and for which the camp program has jurisdiction need to be evaluated for part B. For example, litter control may be the only level of jurisdiction allowed for a camp using a public park. Such camps are still scored on part A of this standard.

Compliance Demonstration: Visitor observation of camp facilities and areas; director/staff description of maintenance procedures.

* A-8 MANDATORY

DNA if firearms or ammunition are not stored in camp.

Are all firearms and ammunition in camp stored under lock?   **Yes   No**

Director's Pre-Visit Evaluation
☐ Yes   ☐ No   ☐ DNA

Interpretation: This standard applies to firearms used in program activities as well as to personal weapons of staff. It is recommended that all firearms be stored and locked in locations separate from ammunition. Also see page 61 for standards on target sports, where the storage of non-firearms is included.

This standard is not intended to be applied to homes or buildings on camp property that are used solely as private residences of staff, are designed for the exclusive use of the individual staff and/or families who live there, and are not accessible to campers and staff. Guns stored in the back of trucks, however, that are accessible to campers and other persons on the property must be locked to meet the requirement of the standard.

Compliance Demonstration: Visitor observation of firearm and ammunition storage.

*A-9 MANDATORY

DNA if no flammable, explosive, or poisonous materials are used or stored on site.

Is there implementation of policies requiring that gas and liquid flammables, explosives, and poisonous materials be:

Director's Pre-Visit Evaluation
☐ Yes   ☐ No   ☐ DNA

1. **Stored in covered, safe containers that are plainly labeled as to contents,**
2. **Handled only by persons trained or experienced in their safe use, and**
3. **Stored in locations separate from food?**   **Yes   No**

Interpretation: Liquid flammables include gasoline, kerosene and other liquid fuels. Poisonous materials include bleach, many cleaning agents, insecticides, weed killers, or other substances labeled as poisonous.

Camp Directors may want to check with local officials for other recommendations concerning storage and handling of flammable or poisonous substances.

Campers who are under the direct supervision of trained personnel while learning to use materials are in compliance with the standard.

Compliance Demonstration: Visitor observation of storage and handling of listed substances; director/staff description of handling procedures.

A-10

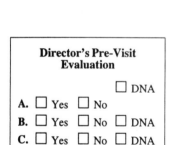

DNA if power tools are not used.

Is there a camp policy in practice requiring that power tools:
 1. **Be provided with necessary safety devices,**
 2. **Be in good repair, and**
 3. **Be operated only by those persons trained and experienced in their use?**   **Yes   No**

Interpretation: This standard applies to tools utilized in program activities as well as in maintenance.

Compliance Demonstration: Visitor observation of power tools and their use, where possible; or director/staff description of policy and practices.

*A-11 Parts A and C MANDATORY

DNA if campers and staff never stay overnight in buildings.

Are all buildings used by campers or staff for sleeping constructed or equipped with the following safety features:

 *A. At least one emergency exit in addition to the main door or entrance?
                                                           Yes   No

DNA B if 30% or more of the wall area is screened or open.

 B. Smoke detection equipment in working order?   **Yes   No**

DNA C if all sleeping quarters are at ground level.

 *C. A direct means of emergency exit to the outside from each sleeping floor that does not have a ground level entrance?   **Yes   No**

Interpretation: The concern of this standard is protection of human life. The entire standard applies ONLY to sleeping quarters located in buildings. "Buildings," for the purposes of this standard, are permanent, enclosed structures that remain intact regardless of season. Tents and adirondack shelters are not considered buildings for the purposes of this standard.

In part A, emergency exits should be located opposite from entrances so that they could be used if the main entrance is blocked. "Emergency exit" does not imply a particular structure or evacuation device, but means a quick, safe, accessible alternative exit. Approval of state or local fire officials or insurance underwriters provides guidance to acceptable escape plans. Windows with screening could be considered emergency exits if occupants are informed of procedures for exit and could easily and safely escape through them.

Ground level entrances should be accessible without the use of lifts or elevators to facilitate easy access and quick evacuation for all persons. In split level buildings that have ground level access on only one side, emergency exits from upper level sleeping quarters must facilitate quick, safe evacuation of all persons in case the ground level exit is blocked.

In part B, it is not suggested or implied that fire detection and alarm devices are inappropriate in all structures not included in this definition of buildings. However, due to the wide diversity of such shelters, these devices are not required universally.

In part C, "...to the outside" means that either the escape is on the outside of the building or an enclosed stairway exits directly to the outside when it reaches ground level.

While camp owners should be concerned about the provision of safety in all sleeping quarters on the property, it is not the intent of this standard to require observation by visitors of private, permanent residences of year-round staff.

Compliance Demonstration: Visitor observation of randomly selected sleeping areas, particularly those facilities with sleeping floors that do not have ground level entrances.

A-12

DNA if no hot water available.

To prevent scalding, is there a system in practice for regulating the hot water temperature other than by individual adjustment at the taps of bathing, showering and handwashing facilities used by campers? **Yes No**

Interpretation: Temperatures may be regulated by:

    a. thermostatically controlled temperature regulating valves,
    b. water heater thermostats, or
    c. properly adjusted mixing valves (provided the cold water source is not subject to variations in pressure).

110 degrees F. is frequently established as a safe maximum water temperature at the tap. Directors may wish to consult with local health officials concerning appropriate maximum temperatures.

Compliance Demonstration: Director description of techniques in use; visitor feeling water at randomly selected taps.

A-13

Are there sleeping, dining, toilet, bathing and program facilities available to persons with disabilities, or is the camp implementing a plan to come into compliance with the Americans with Disabilities Act?   Yes   No

Interpretation: The intent of the standard is for the camp to address facility accessibility issues as defined by the Americans with Disabilities Act of 1990. The law does not require that all facilities or program areas be accessible, or that all changes be made at once. The ADA law does not require camps to make changes that would fundamentally alter the nature of the camp program. It does require the camp to make "readily achievable" accommodations that do not cause an "undue burden."

It may not be possible to make all areas of camp accessible. However, participation in the normal activities of camp living and activity groups should be fostered and barriers removed or accommodations provided to permit full participation whenever possible. "Available" means that persons have both access and opportunity.

See Appendix C (page 202) for an architectural barriers checklist.

Compliance Demonstration: Director explanation of plans established and/or accommodations provided for persons with disabilities.

A-14

Director's Pre-Visit Evaluation

A. ☐ Yes ☐ No
B. ☐ Yes ☐ No ☐ DNA

Is there a policy in practice that:

A. Prohibits smoking in food preparation and service areas, and in dining facilities during meal periods?   Yes   No

DNA B if no smoking is allowed in camp.

B. Designates smoking areas that are away from children and non-smokers?   Yes   No

Interpretation: Part B of the standard requires that smoking areas away from children and non-smokers be designated. While it is preferable that all such areas be away from children and non-smokers, the designation of some smoking areas meets the minimum requirement of the standard.

Compliance Demonstration: Director/staff explanation of policies and their implementation.

A-15

Director's Pre-Visit Evaluation

☐ Yes   ☐ No   ☐ DNA

DNA if toilet facilities with multiple seats are not located in the main camp or living areas.

In the main camp and living areas, do toilet facilities with more than one seat have at least one toilet with a door or curtain for privacy, available to all?   Yes   No

Interpretation: "Available to all" means that such facilities may be used by all persons (campers and staff). When persons with special needs are served, there should also be toilets affording privacy to them.

Compliance Demonstration: Visitor observation of randomly selected toilet facilities in the main camp and living areas.

A-16

DNA if pit or chemical toilets are not used.

Are pit or chemical toilets screened or vented and provided with toilet lids and self-closing doors? **Yes No**

Director's Pre-Visit Evaluation
☐ Yes   ☐ No   ☐ DNA

Compliance Demonstration: Visitor observation of randomly selected pit or chemical toilets.

> ### DAY CAMP ONLY
> **DNA** A-17 and A-18 if a **RESIDENT** CAMP
> and proceed to A-19

A-17

Are toilets adequate in number based on the following ratios:
1. **One seat for every 30 females,**
2. **One seat for every 50 males and,**
3. **If more than 10 percent of camp population has restricted mobility —**
   a. **One seat for every 20 females,**
   b. **One seat for every 30 males?** **Yes No**

Director's Pre-Visit Evaluation
☐ Yes   ☐ No

Interpretation: Seats to be used in computing toilet ratios are those available to the general camp population and not those in private residences or restricted areas. Up to one third of the seats for males may be substituted with urinals.

Compliance Demonstration: Visitor observation of toilet areas; director explanation of ratios available.

A-18

Are handwashing facilities adjacent to toilets and provided in the ratio of one wash basin or equivalent per 30 persons, with a minimum of two basins for each toilet facility designed to serve more than 5 persons at the same time? **Yes No**

Director's Pre-Visit Evaluation
☐ Yes   ☐ No

Interpretation: A "handwashing facility" is a supply of soap and fresh water, suitable for washing. It does not necessarily imply running water.

When using multiple handwashing units utilizing a spray-type water dispenser, 20 inches of wash basin rim space is equivalent to one wash basin.

Compliance Demonstration: Visitor observation of randomly selected toilet/handwashing areas; director/staff explanation of ratios available.

> **RESIDENT CAMP ONLY**
>
> **DNA A-19 through A-23 if a DAY CAMP**
> and proceed to A-24

A-19

<table>
<tr><td>

Director's Pre-Visit
Evaluation

☐ Yes ☐ No

</td></tr>
</table>

Are toilets adequate in number based on the following ratios:
    1. One seat for every 10 females,
    2. One seat for every 10 males, and
    3. If more than 10% of camp population has restricted mobility —
        a. One seat for every 8 females, and
        b. One seat for every 8 males?   **Yes   No**

Interpretation: Seats to be used in computing toilet ratios are those available to the general camp population and not those in private residences or restricted areas. Up to one third of the seats for males may be substituted with urinals.

Compliance Demonstration: Visitor observation of randomly selected toilet areas; director/staff explanation of ratios available.

A-20

<table>
<tr><td>

Director's Pre-Visit
Evaluation

☐ Yes ☐ No

</td></tr>
</table>

Are handwashing facilities adjacent to toilets and provided in the ratio of one wash basin or equivalent per 10 persons with a minimum of two basins for each toilet facility designed to serve more than 5 persons at the same time?
        Yes   No

Interpretation: A "handwashing facility" is a supply of soap and fresh water, suitable for washing. It does not necessarily imply running water.

When using multiple handwashing units utilizing a spray-type water dispenser, 20 inches of wash basin rim is equivalent to one wash basin.

Compliance Demonstration: Visitor observation of randomly selected toilet/handwashing areas; director/staff explanation of ratios available.

A-21

DNA if a primitive camp.

Are bathing/showering facilities adequate in number based on the following ratios:

    1. All camps — one showerhead or bathtub for each 15 persons in camp, or

    2. Camps specializing in serving persons with restricted mobility — one showerhead or bathtub for each 10 persons in camp?   **Yes No**

Director's Pre-Visit Evaluation
☐ Yes   ☐ No   ☐ DNA

Interpretation: "Primitive camp" refers to those camps whose program is based on a philosophy centered on non-facility, utility-oriented principles. Generally, such camps have few permanent structures or facilities.

Bathing facilities to be used in computing ratios are those available to the general camp population and not those in private residences or restricted areas.

For persons with restricted mobility, aids such as chairs on casters, stools, footrests, non-slip surfaces, and flexible shower heads attached to hoses may provide increased independence. Aids should be provided according to the needs of persons being served.

Compliance Demonstration: Visitor observation of randomly selected showering/bathing areas; director explanation of ratios available.

A-22

DNA if structures are not used for sleeping quarters.

Do permanent sleeping quarters provide the following:

    1. Cross ventilation,

    2. At least six feet between heads of sleepers,

    3. At least 30 inches between sides of beds, and

    4. Adequate space to provide freedom of movement, especially for those using wheelchairs or walkers?   **Yes No**

Director's Pre-Visit Evaluation
☐ Yes   ☐ No   ☐ DNA

Interpretation: "Permanent sleeping quarters" refer to structures, platform tents, covered wagons, etc. that are constructed in a fixed location and are used as primary residences for staff and campers. Temporary shelters such as tents used for overnight camping and backpacking would not fall under this classification.

Beds separated by less than 30 inches but having a fixed partition between them that precludes sneezing or coughing on others is acceptable to meet the standard.

<u>All</u> persons need adequate space, for ease of movement and to facilitate safe exit in an emergency. State regulations range from 30 to 50 square feet of floor space required per person. Such regulations should be considered when designing, constructing, or using buildings.

Persons with restricted mobility need additional space and the arrangement should consider the functional space taken by wheelchairs and other devices themselves.

For persons with restricted mobility, the norm established by ANSI is 50 square feet per person using a walker and 60 square feet per person using a wheelchair.

All persons need adequate space, for ease of movement and to facilitate safe exit in an emergency. State regulations range from 30 to 50 square feet of floor space required per person. Such regulations should be considered when designing, constructing, or using buildings.

Persons with restricted mobility need additional space and the arrangement should consider the functional space taken by wheelchairs and other devices themselves.

For persons with restricted mobility, the norm established by ANSI is 50 square feet per person using a walker and 60 square feet per person using a wheelchair.

Compliance Demonstration: Visitor observation of randomly selected sleeping quarters throughout the camp.

A-23

DNA if no bunk beds are utilized or to bunks only used by persons 16 years or older.

Is there a policy in practice that upper bunks used by children are equipped with guardrails designed to prevent occupants from accidentally rolling out of the bed? **Yes No**

Interpretation: Beds placed against the wall do not require rails on the side facing the wall.

The Consumer Product Safety Commission recommends that the bottom of the rail be no more than 3 ½ inches from the top of the bed frame, and that the top of the rail be at least 5 inches above the top of the mattress.

This standard is not intended to be scored for private residences of year-round staff.

Compliance Demonstration: Visitor observation of randomly selected sleeping areas using bunk beds.

FOOD SERVICE

The food service standards are intended to be applied to the camp's regular food service operation, whether centralized in (a) dining hall(s) or decentralized in living units. They do not need to be applied to occasional cookouts or operations that only serve drinks or snacks.

If someone other than the camp prepares the meals, the food service standards would be scored only if **the camp** is responsible for storage, serving and clean-up of food; or if the camp is the sole user of the on-site services (not restaurants or dorms serving other groups or individuals).

However, camp administrators should consider the requirements of the food service standards, even though those standards may not actually be scored.

If **MEALS** are **NOT** prepared and served in camp,
DNA A-24 through A-29
and proceed to Section B - Administration.

A-24

DNA if no meals are served by the camp.

Is there written evidence that the food service supervisor has training and/or experience in food service management? Yes No

Director's Pre-Visit Evaluation
☐ Yes ☐ No ☐ DNA

Interpretation: The intent of this standard is to assure that the food service staff and operation are supervised by person(s) with training and experience in areas such as sanitary, food protection, and hygiene procedures; personnel supervision; and record keeping. For example, it is the responsibility of the food service supervisor to monitor the obvious health conditions of food service employees to help guard against possible food contamination by persons who are ill.

Compliance Demonstration: Visitor observation of written documentation.

A-25

DNA if camp does not have food preparation and storage facilities.

Are food preparation and storage facilities designed and are procedures being implemented to protect food from rodents and vermin? Yes No

Director's Pre-Visit Evaluation
☐ Yes ☐ No ☐ DNA

Compliance Demonstration: Staff explanation of procedures; visitor observation of food preparation and storage areas.

A-26

DNA if potentially hazardous (perishable) foods are not stored or served in camp, or if no mechanical refrigeration units are used.

To assure storage of potentially hazardous (perishable) foods at 45 degrees F. or below, does the camp maintain:

1. **A** <u>written record of temperatures</u> **noted and initialed daily for each mechanical refrigeration unit storing perishable foods, and**
2. **Evidence that prompt corrective action was taken if temperatures measured above 45 degrees F.?** Yes No

Interpretation: "Potentially hazardous foods" are those foods that consist in whole or in part of milk or milk products, eggs, meat, poultry, fish, shellfish, edible crustacea or other ingredients (including synthetic ingredients) in a form capable of supporting growth of infectious or toxic microorganisms. Such foods should be maintained at temperatures below 45 degrees F. or above 140 degrees F.

This standard applies to mechanical refrigeration units holding potentially hazardous foods in areas such as the camp kitchen, infirmary, staff house, or unit houses. It does NOT apply to year-round staff residences, nor to freezers, ice chests or coolers.

Even though non-mechanical devices such as coolers are not scored in this standard, the camp may establish a procedure that asks families not to send perishable foods (in the case of day camp lunches), or the camp may utilize ice or blue ice in the coolers (in the case of cookouts or temporary storage of food) to maintain the safety of perishable foods.

"Prompt corrective action" means within 24 hours.

See the Appendix (page 203) for a sample temperature chart.

Compliance Demonstration: Visitor observation of written records/charts on mechanical refrigeration units.

A-27

DNA if meals are not prepared or served in camp.

To prevent contamination of foods during preparation and serving, are there procedures in practice that require food handlers to:

A. **Minimize the time that potentially hazardous foods remain in the temperature danger zone of 45 degrees F. to 140 degrees F.?**

Yes No

B. **Use only clean and sanitized utensils and equipment during food preparation?** Yes No

C. **Clean and sanitize food contact surfaces after each use?** Yes No

DNA D if hot food is not served.

D. **Assure cooking and holding of potentially hazardous foods at appropriate temperatures?** Yes No

28

Interpretation: "Food handlers" include food service staff, and any campers or program staff who regularly prepare or serve food in decentralized living units.

"Sanitized utensils" are those which have been cleaned and sanitized according to the guidelines in A-28.

"Food contact surfaces" include anything that contacts raw food during preparation such as counters, cutting boards, knives, etc. Such surfaces should be sanitized with a bleach solution or other commercial sanitizer between times when raw food contacts those surfaces. Local health authorities can give guidance on the strength and frequency of use for such sanitizing agents.

For part D, the intent is that staff be trained to recognize and assure that foods are cooked and held at appropriate temperatures. Most states establish 140 degrees F. as the minimum temperature for holding hot foods, whether in steam tables or on the stove. Camps should have the means and procedures to monitor temperatures periodically. It is not assumed that thermometers need to be in place at all times to measure temperatures.

Compliance Demonstration: Staff explanation of procedures for food storage, holding, and serving; visitor observation of food preparation and serving areas.

A-28

DNA if disposable food service utensils are used exclusively.

To assure proper sanitizing of dishes and food service utensils after each use, are the following procedures in practice:

Director's Pre-Visit Evaluation

☐ DNA
A. ☐ Yes ☐ No
B. ☐ Yes ☐ No

A. **Washing:**

1. **For mechanical dishwashers, there is <u>documentation of daily</u> monitoring to assure:**
   a. **Wash water is at least 100 degrees F.,**
   b. **Rinse water is at least 180 degrees F. or an approved chemical sanitizer is used as specified on its label, and**
   c. **Prompt corrective action was taken when any temperature variance below the minimum was noted; and/or**

2. **For dishes and/or food service utensils washed by hand, there are procedures in practice to assure:**
   a. **Wash and initial rinse temperatures of at least 100 degrees F., and**
   b. **Second rinse process using at least 180 degree F. water or an approved chemical sanitizer?** **Yes No**

B. **Drying:**
   All dishes and food service utensils are air dried? **Yes No**

Interpretation: "Food service utensils" include dishes, silverware and all other utensils used in the preparation or serving of food. Pots and pans which are heated to very high temperatures in the cooking process are exempted from the second rinse requirement, but not from the air-drying requirement.

Directors should be aware of state and local codes concerning acceptable wash water temperatures. Some localities require such water to be 140 degrees F. (minimum).

For dishes washed by hand, camps should have the means and procedures to periodically monitor water temperatures. It is not assumed that thermometers will be in place at all times.

See Appendix (page 203) for a sample temperature documentation chart.

Compliance Demonstration: Visitor observation of chart (where applicable); visitor observation of the washing/drying process in use.

A-29

Director's Pre-Visit
Evaluation

☐ Yes   ☐ No

Are procedures in practice that require all garbage and rubbish containers in kitchen and dining areas be leak-proof or fitted with non-absorbent lining and be covered with a tight-fitting lid or tied securely when not being used in the food preparation or clean-up process?   **Yes   No**

Interpretation: The concern of this standard is the temporary storage of garbage containing food wastes in food service areas prior to removal to permanent storage areas (dumpsters, disposal areas away from site, etc.).

Compliance Demonstration: Visitor observation of garbage storage procedures in food preparation and clean-up areas.

SECTION B — ADMINISTRATION

The Administration standards include those basic administrative practices which relate to creating a positive, protective environment for campers. The standards include policies and procedures related to emergencies, child protection, and other areas of risk management. The Administration standards also call for a review of the camp's business practices.

ALL camps score the Administration standards.

B-1

Within the last three years, has the camp administration completed the *Self-Assessment of Additional Professional Practices***, and are recommendations from that self-assessment currently being implemented?** **Yes No**

Director's Pre-Visit Evaluation
☐ Yes ☐ No

Interpretation: The Self-Assessment can be found on page 177.

Because the scored standards in Camp Accreditation primarily address program quality and health and safety concerns, evaluation of a camp's total operation requires assessing the additional professional practices included in the *Self-Assessment.*

New camp administrators can use the Self-Assessment as a guideline for developing procedures identified as vital to camp operations. Experienced administrators should utilize the self-assessment process to further refine and update existing policies and practices.

Compliance Demonstration: Visitor observation of the completed Self-Assessment; director explanation of recommendations being implemented.

B-2

For the purpose of risk management planning and in addition to the materials required for other Camp Accreditation standards, is there written evidence that the camp administration has taken inventory of its operations to:

A. Identify general health and safety concerns and possible emergency situations unique to the camp and related to:
   1. Natural hazards specific to the site,
   2. Man-made hazards specific to the site,
   3. Operation of facilities and/or equipment,
   4. Disasters such as fire, flood, tornado, hurricane, etc., and
   5. Conduct of campers or staff?   Yes No

B. Specify measures to reduce, control or prevent risks associated with the health and safety concerns and possible emergency situations listed in A including:
   1. Camp safety regulations for those identified areas,
   2. Methods to control access to identified hazards,
   3. Protective devices where appropriate, and/or
   4. Identification of how and when campers and/or staff will be trained to deal with such identified risks?   Yes No

C. Establish emergency procedures to respond appropriately to situations identified in A?   Yes No

Interpretation: The requirements of the Camp Accreditation process address many of the commonly identified risk management concerns. This standard requires the camp to identify and plan for health and safety concerns unique to the camp that are not covered elsewhere. See Appendix (page 204) for planning helps.

In part A, "natural hazards" may include the presence of cliffs, poisonous snakes, wild animals, or other conditions of nature that may pose a risk to humans on the site.

"Man-made hazards" not addressed by other standards may include public roads through camp property, construction activities on the camp site, abandoned wells, or other facilities on the site that may pose a risk.

"Operation of facilities and/or equipment" may include possible loss of power affecting food storage and service or the provision of water, building collapse, explosion, electrocution, etc. Pre-planning to identify resources in case of such situations can save valuable time.

"Conduct of campers and staff" may include allegations of inappropriate staff behavior with campers, incidents due to the use of drugs or alcohol (whether camper or staff), fighting, etc. It may also address regulations for group living areas such as bunks, showers, or other general camp locations.

In part B, the regulations refer to the health and safety concerns identified in part A of this standard and are in addition to those regulations established specifically for activity areas (see the Program standards for activity regulations).

"Protective devices" may include things such as fences, lighting, storm warning systems, and posted warning signs.

In part C, emergency procedures may include plans for fire drills, camp evacuation procedures, specification of designated areas in case of flood, tornado, etc. as appropriate to the camp site, immediate care of the injured, supervision of the uninjured, and notification of appropriate personnel.

Compliance Demonstration: Visitor observation of written materials.

B-3

Has the camp administration:

Director's Pre-Visit Evaluation
A. ☐ Yes ☐ No
B. ☐ Yes ☐ No

A. **Provided staff with written safety regulations and emergency procedures?** Yes No

B. **Implemented a program of training and rehearsal that prepares campers and staff to follow the established regulations and procedures?** Yes No

Interpretation: The intent of this standard is to assure that the safety regulations and emergency procedures developed in standard B-2 are distributed to staff and implemented throughout the camp. (Additional standards in this document, particularly in the program section, will require safety regulations or emergency procedures. Those items are not to be included when scoring this standard. See the Appendix, page 206, for a list of safety regulations and emergency procedures required for Camp Accreditation.)

The camp director should determine appropriate rehearsal intervals for safety regulations and emergency procedures. However, some procedures may require rehearsal with each new camper group.

Compliance Demonstration: Visitor observation of materials distributed to staff; director/staff description of training and rehearsal process.

B-4

To consider needed risk reduction steps, does the camp administration:

Director's Pre-Visit Evaluation
A. ☐ Yes ☐ No
B. ☐ Yes ☐ No

A. **Require staff to complete written reports describing incidents and accidents?** Yes No

B. **Implement a procedure to:**
  1. **Review and analyze, at least annually, when and where incidents, accidents and/or injuries are occurring, and**
  2. **Identify steps to reduce incidents, accidents and injuries?** Yes No

Interpretation: Maintaining accident reports for injuries requiring professional medical treatment is scored in standard E-18.

The intent of part A is to document circumstances, witnesses, and actions in serious situations that result in, or nearly result in, injury or danger to individuals. It is the camp director's responsibility to determine the level of severity or seriousness of incidents to be reported. (See Appendix, page 207.)

Examples may include fires, natural disasters, danger from intruders or trespassers, crises arising out of camper or staff behavior (e.g. fighting, serious emotional outbursts threatening others), or other situations posing serious threat to the safety of others.

It also includes potential serious injury from "near-misses" and other emergencies which may not result in injuries requiring an accident report but which are potentially harmful to campers or staff. Examples may include use of drugs or alcohol by campers or staff, lost campers, or near-drownings.

The intent of part B is to identify patterns of events or actions that may require corrective measures.

Compliance Demonstration: Visitor observation of reports; director/staff description of procedures for review and analysis.

B-5

Does the camp administration have procedures in practice to address possible intrusion of unauthorized persons onto the campsite that include:
  1. Periodic review of security concerns of the site, and
  2. Training for staff, and campers when appropriate, about steps to take in such instances? Yes No

Interpretation: If using public or non-owned sites, "campsite" refers to the living and/or program areas being used by the camp groups(s).

Compliance Demonstration: Staff/director description of training and procedures in use; director description of review process utilized.

B-6

Has the camp administration developed written search and rescue procedures for persons lost, missing, or runaway; and has the staff been trained in their responsibilities to implement those procedures? Yes No

Interpretation: Procedures should include steps, as appropriate, to contact camp authorities, local and state emergency resources, and parents/guardians. In addition, they should specify responsibilities of all staff in carrying out the appropriate procedures.

For instance, staff should be trained to implement a system such as periodic attendance checks and "buddy systems" to help in accounting for campers throughout the day.

Compliance Demonstration: Visitor observation of written procedures; director/staff description of training provided.

B-7

DNA if camp is not operated on property open to the public or does not take campers to public areas.

To specify practices to be used when campers are intermingled with the public, are there written procedures made known to campers and staff that include instructions for:
1. The supervision of campers (location and responsibilities of staff),
2. What to do if separated from the group or approached by a stranger, and
3. Safety in public transportation, walking on public streets, and using public restrooms (as applicable)?   **Yes   No**

Interpretation: This standard applies to <u>all</u> activities where public contact can reasonably be expected including tripping (away from base camp for more than two nights), travel, day or overnight trips, sporting events, and use of public facilities/parks.

When a camp is operating in an area open to the public, procedures for supervision may include some means for identifying/distinguishing campers from the public.

Compliance Demonstration: Visitor observation of written procedures; director/staff description of procedures to instruct campers and staff.

B-8

Is there a written plan for communications in the event of an incident or emergency (including out-of-camp trips) that is reviewed with all staff and specifies:

A.   Lines of communication from persons at the site of the incident to camp administrative and health personnel, and/or community emergency services as appropriate (health, law enforcement, etc.)?   **Yes   No**

B.   Procedures for contacting parents or guardians?   **Yes   No**

C.   Procedures for dealing with the media?   **Yes   No**

Interpretation: This standard applies to all locations, even those which are scored under separate sections, such as aquatics and trip/travel.

It is essential to have procedures for communication carefully and thoroughly developed prior to the pressure of an actual emergency.

Compliance Demonstration: Visitor observation of the written plan; director/staff description of review process with staff.

B-9

Are there written procedures required to be in practice regarding:

    A. **Release of campers who are minors to a parent or to persons other than the legal parent or guardian?**   Yes No

    B. **Verification of absentees or "no-shows?"**   Yes No

Interpretation: Part A includes procedures for releasing campers during or at the end of the camp session. It may also include procedures to identify persons authorized to pick up or visit campers.

For part B, "absentees" are those who are not present when the camp expects to assume responsibility for those individuals. In day camp, this would normally be at the beginning of each day. In resident camp, this would be at the beginning of a session.

Compliance Demonstration: Visitor observation of written procedures; staff explanation of procedures in practice.

B-10

Is there a written policy addressing safety considerations related to camper and staff possession and use of personal sports equipment, vehicles and animals?   Yes No

Interpretation: "Personal sports equipment" may include archery equipment, bats, hockey sticks, or other equipment that should be stored and handled safely for the protection of all. Animals may include pets and animals brought for use in program, such as horses.

Such a policy should address both the acceptability of such personally owned items on the campsite, and the expectations regarding their use and storage.

Compliance Demonstration: Visitor observation of written policy.

B-11

Is there a procedure in practice requiring an annual evaluation by campers, parents, staff, and the camp board or committee of the sponsoring agency (if existing) that:
    1. **Analyzes all areas of camp operation, and**
    2. **Provides feedback to the camp administration on health and safety concerns and program quality?**   Yes No

Interpretation: Evaluation of all phases of the camp operation can provide valuable feedback to address health and safety and program quality issues. Such evaluation may include feedback on the application/enrollment process, the acceptability of camp staff, reactions to camp program, areas where staff training could be increased, the site's maintenance and appearance, and so forth.

Compliance Demonstration: Director explanation of evaluation procedures.

B-12

Is there written evidence that the following insurance coverage is in place:

A. Camper coverage —

    1. Resident campers — Health and accident coverage for each camper?
    2. Day campers — Accident coverage for each camper?   Yes   No

B. Staff coverage —

    1. Resident camp staff:
       a. Workers' compensation for eligible staff, and
       b. Health and accident coverage for each staff member?
    2. Day camp staff:
       a. Workers' compensation for eligible staff, and
       b. Accident coverage for any staff member not covered under workers' compensation?   Yes   No

C. General liability coverage?   Yes   No

DNA D if camp does not own buildings.

D. Fire and extended risk coverage on buildings?   Yes   No

DNA E if vehicles are not used in camp operation.

E. Motor vehicle insurance (as applicable):

    1. Coverage on all owned, hired, or leased vehicles, and/or
    2. Employer's non-ownership liability and/or hired cars insurance on all non-owned vehicles?   Yes   No

DNA F if horseback riding is not offered.

F. Personal accident and injury coverage for participants, and liability coverage for the camp for horseback riding?   Yes   No

Interpretation: Coverage may include self-insurance, which can be verified by evidence of the allocation of particular assets to cover such costs.

Camper and staff coverage may be provided by camp, parents, agency, school, or individual. When the camp does not provide the coverage, written evidence of coverage must be provided, such as the individual's or parent's signature along with the policy number.

While international staff may have insurance provided by the placement organization, administrators need to check contracts to be sure adequate coverage is provided. Workers' compensation is generally required for all employees, including international staff. Directors are advised to check state law for the applicability of workers' compensation insurance to volunteers.

For parts C and F, camp administrators should check on exclusions in liability coverage to be sure all camp programs (tripping, horses, aquatics, ropes course, etc.) are covered.

For part E, motor vehicle insurance, directors are advised to evaluate insurance coverage needed both for vehicles leased for the entire season as well as those hired for a day trip. Vehicles leased for the summer need coverage for liability as well as physical damage (depending on the lease agreement). Many authorities recommend adding such vehicles to the camp's regular auto policy, so that there is coverage just as if the vehicle were owned.

Directors should note the additional transportation standards which are found in standards BT-1 through BT-17 that apply to owned and leased vehicles.

See the insurance checklist in the Appendix (page 209) for further information.

Compliance Demonstration: Visitor observation of policies, binders, or letters of confirmation from agent(s) showing current policies are in place, and evidence of individual coverage or self-insurance (if applicable).

SECTION BT — ADMINISTRATION OF TRANSPORTATION AND VEHICLES

Transportation safety is an important component of the camp's overall risk management planning. The following standards help administrators consider the critical aspects of vehicular safety, driver training, and camper education.

Standards BT-1 and BT-2 apply to all camps. Standards BT-3 through BT-6 apply solely to day camps. Standards BT-7 through BT-17 apply to all camps that provide or arrange for transportation, whether that be to and from camp or as a part of camp program.

DEFINITIONS

Regularly transport means any transportation that can reasonably be anticipated which is provided or arranged by and for the camp. This may include transportation between camp and home, to program locations, and errands or trips with campers or staff - even if only once or twice during the season.

Pick-up and drop-off refers to picking up or returning the camper to his/her home or a central location near home.

Arrival and departure refers to what occurs on camp property as campers come to or leave the camp premises.

ALL CAMPS
score BT-1 and BT-2

BT-1

DNA if trip or travel camp, or if no vehicles are on the camp site.

Is there a plan in practice for control of vehicular traffic on the camp site?
Yes No

Director's Pre-Visit Evaluation
☐ Yes ☐ No ☐ DNA

Interpretation: The concern of this standard is for the protection of pedestrians from vehicular traffic. Attention should be given to concerns such as delivery trucks, camp vans or buses, staff vehicles, camp maintenance vehicles, visitors' vehicles, vehicles utilized in camp program, parking areas, speed limits, traffic restriction areas and controlling pedestrian traffic when necessary.

Some plans may be as simple as designating parking areas and prohibiting traffic in most areas of the campsite. Other campsites which allow motorized traffic may need more elaborate plans.

Camps using public parks or property with public roadways can develop plans for controlling camp pedestrian patterns, especially during heavy traffic periods such as arrival and departure times at day camps.

Compliance Demonstration: Visitor observation of vehicular traffic on the camp site; director description of plan in place.

BT-2

Is there a policy in practice forbidding the transportation of campers and staff in vehicles not designed for passengers? **Yes No**

Interpretation: The intent of this standard is to forbid transportation of campers and staff in the back of pickup trucks or wagons where seats are not attached to the vehicle. The exception to this is for hayrides where wagons are driven at slow speeds (5-10 mph) off public roads, and where protective devices are provided to keep people from falling out or off of the vehicle.

Compliance Demonstration: Director/staff description of policy in place.

```
┌────────────────────────────────────────────────┐
│                 DAY CAMP ONLY                    │
│   If a Resident Camp, DNA BT-3 through BT-6 and  │
│                  proceed to BT-7                 │
└────────────────────────────────────────────────┘
```

BT-3

Director's Pre-Visit Evaluation
A. ☐ Yes ☐ No
B. ☐ Yes ☐ No
C. ☐ Yes ☐ No
D. ☐ Yes ☐ No

Has the camp provided training for campers and staff to implement arrival and departure procedures designed to control traffic and personal safety, including:

    A. Orderly arrival and departure of vehicles carrying campers?

                                                 Yes No

    B. Orderly unloading and loading of cars, vans, and buses? **Yes No**

    C. Clear designation of traffic, parking, and waiting areas? **Yes No**

    D. Staff supervision of arriving and departing campers? **Yes No**

Interpretation: Part A refers to the way in which vehicles are handled on the property. Part B refers to the loading/unloading of campers from those vehicles.

Compliance Demonstration: Visitor observation of arrival and/or departure procedures where possible; director explanation of procedures and training provided.

BT-4

Director's Pre-Visit Evaluation
☐ Yes ☐ No

Are there procedures in practice for parent notification in case of emergency or changes that would affect the child's arrival at home or a pick-up/drop-off time or location? **Yes No**

Interpretation: Examples include cancellation due to unsuitable weather, transportation delay, illness of a child, or an accident requiring professional medical attention.

Compliance Demonstration: Staff description of notification procedures.

BT-5

Are parents/guardians provided written information that includes:
   1. **Pick-up and drop-off times,**
   2. **Pick-up and drop-off safety procedures,**
   3. **Safety rules for van or bus travel if camp provides transportation?**

Yes   No

Interpretation: Safety procedures include safety regulations at the pick-up and drop-off points as well as any camp policies concerning responsibility for the care of children before pick-up and after drop-off.

Compliance Demonstration: Visitor observation of written information provided.

BT-6

DNA if day camp does not provide any transportation or if all travel arranged by the camp is less than one hour each way.

If travel is one hour or more for campers, is it camp policy to provide programming during transit by staff other than the driver?   **Yes   No**

Interpretation: This standard applies to trips and excursions taken by camper groups during the day as well as transportation to and from camp.

Compliance Demonstration: Staff description of policy's implementation.

Accreditation

ALL CAMPS PROVIDING TRANSPORTATION

Standards BT-7 through BT-17 **APPLY** to any transportation provided, planned for, and/or arranged by the camp, whether in owned, leased, private, or commercial land vehicles. They are not intended to be applied to the use of regularly scheduled public transportation (trains, limos, buses, taxis).

This includes, but is not limited to, camp-arranged transportation to and from camp, transportation to activity sites such as pools and lakes, transportation for day trips and field trips, transportation of campers for non-emergency medical trips, and transportation to tripping sites.

These standards are not scored for maintenance vehicles used in the camp operation, unless they are used, in part, for transportation of persons in addition to the driver. However, camp administrators should consider the requirements of these standards in evaluating all vehicle use in camp.

· · · · · · · · · · · · · · · · · · ·

If camp provides **NO TRANSPORTATION**,
(except for emergency transportation)
DNA BT-7 through BT-17
and proceed to Section C — Personnel.

Note: Emergency transportation
is scored in the Health Care section.

BT-7

DNA if vehicle carries only staff.

Is there a policy that requires each vehicle carrying campers to also carry a staff member who has been trained to carry out written accident procedures for:
1. **Providing or securing care for the injured,**
2. **Supervising the uninjured,**
3. **Specifying whom to notify in an emergency, and**
4. **Identifying witnesses and obtaining appropriate accident or emergency information?**   **Yes   No**

Interpretation: The staff member referred to here may be the driver. Camps may also want to specify that the staff member be an adult as defined by governing authorities.

While the standard applies only to vehicles carrying campers, camp administrators should consider these concepts when developing policies and procedures for staff use of vehicles without campers.

Compliance Demonstration: Visitor observation of written accident procedures; director/staff description of policy's implementation.

BT-8

DNA if the camp does not provide transportation for campers in vehicles carrying 16 or more persons (including the driver).

Is there a policy requiring that in each vehicle carrying 16 or more persons there be a staff member in addition to the driver who has been trained in safety responsibilities and group management? **Yes No**

Interpretation: It is intended that this standard be applied to any vehicle larger than a 15-passenger van that is carrying campers. The number in the standard includes the driver.

Examples of safety responsibilities include the management of behavior, accounting for all passengers, use of seat belts, etc.

Compliance Demonstration: Staff description of policy and procedures in use.

BT-9

Are there written safety procedures required to be in practice for all vehicles used to transport campers and staff that include:

A. **Training in safety regulations for traveling in vehicles?** **Yes No**

B. **Loading of vehicles only within the passenger seating capacity limits established by the manufacturer?** **Yes No**

C. **A requirement that participants wear seat belts when they are provided?** **Yes No**

DNA D if vehicles do not travel in convoys.

D. **Convoy travel procedures?** **Yes No**

DNA E if persons are not transported in wheelchairs.

E. **Transporting persons in wheelchairs including:**
   1. **Persons in wheelchairs are seatbelted into the wheelchairs (except when in watercraft), and**
   2. **Wheelchairs are in locked positions and secured to vehicles (except when in watercraft)?** **Yes No**

Interpretation: Safety regulations in part A may include behavior guidelines such as remaining seated, obeying the driver, and orderly loading and unloading of buses or vans.

In part C, participants are required to utilize seat belts in all vehicles which provide them. It is not the intent to mandate seat belts in vehicles such as school buses where seat belts are not required by law. If young children or babies are transported, appropriate child restraint devices should be used.

Compliance Demonstration: Visitor observation of written procedures; director/staff description of implementation.

BT-10

Is there a policy in practice which requires that every vehicle used for transporting campers and staff be equipped with the following:

1. **Stocked first aid kit,**
2. **Reflectors, and**
3. **Fire extinguisher?**   **Yes   No**

Interpretation: "Equipped" means these items are in the vehicle when it is transporting campers or staff. The camp may keep this equipment in a central location, ready to place in vehicles at the appropriate time.

Compliance Demonstration: Visitor observation of randomly selected vehicles and equipment and/or staff description of procedures for equipping vehicles.

BT-11

Are there written policies in practice for campers and staff who are being transported that specify:

A. The availability and location of health information and "Permission to Treat" forms of passengers?   **Yes   No**

B. Adequate supervision to take into account the age, mental ability, and physical condition of all passengers?   **Yes   No**

Interpretation: The intent of part A of this standard is that camps determine <u>when</u> health histories, health exam forms, and/or permission to treat forms be with the group, not to require that they always be carried. For non-medical religious campers, this refers to health histories and non-medical religious waiver forms.

Compliance Demonstration: Visitor observation of written policies; director/staff description of implementation.

BT-12

DNA if private vehicles are not used to transport campers.

Is there written authorization from owners of private vehicles the camp uses to transport campers granting permission to use the vehicle(s) for this purpose?   **Yes   No**

Interpretation: The purpose of this standard is to assure that the owner specifically grants permission for the vehicle to be used for camper transportation. This includes vehicles brought to camp by staff that are owned by parents or others.

This includes all private vehicles used for non-emergency transportation such as that to and from camp when arranged by the camp, transportation for trips, excursions, the doctor or hospital, etc.

Compliance Demonstration: Visitor observation of written authorizations.

BT-13

DNA if no commercial vehicles are leased or rented.

Is there a policy in practice by the camp administration to select provider(s) of commercial vehicles who:
  1. **Implement a system of regular maintenance and safety checks on vehicles, and**
  2. **If any drivers are provided, verify the acceptable driving record and experience of those drivers to transport passengers?   Yes   No**

Interpretation: Information about a leasing company's policies, maintenance procedures, and driver requirements may be found in promotional materials, the leasing contract, or through inquiries concerning such policies.

Compliance Demonstration: Director description of procedures used in selection of vehicle providers.

```
CAMPS PROVIDING DRIVERS

BT-14 through BT-17 are scored for all transportation
when the camp provides drivers, whether the vehicles used
are owned, leased,  rented, or borrowed.

These standards are NOT scored for transportation  in
COMMERCIAL vehicles hired WITH drivers. If ALL
transportation is with hired drivers, DNA BT-14 through
BT-17 and proceed to Section C — Personnel.
```

BT-14

DNA to private vehicles.

Is there written evidence the camp administration requires qualified persons to evaluate the mechanical soundness of all vehicles that regularly transport campers or staff:
  1. **At least quarterly for camps that transport year round, or**
  2. **Within the 3 months prior to seasonal use?   Yes   No**

Interpretation: This standard applies to all vehicles owned or leased by the camp that regularly transport campers. While camps are not required by this standard to obtain maintenance records on private vehicles, owners of such vehicles should recognize that granting specific permission for the vehicle to be used to transport campers implies a responsibility by the owner to prepare the vehicle for that use.

"Qualified persons" includes mechanics or other persons with training and/or experience in vehicle maintenance. For leased vehicles, the evaluation may be done by qualified persons in the leasing company.

"Evaluate mechanical soundness" means checking and making any repair necessary to assure readiness of the vehicles to transport passengers.

See the introduction for the definition of "regularly transport."

Compliance Demonstration: Visitor observation of written documentation such as entries in a vehicle log book, maintenance receipts, etc.; director description of procedures and qualification of persons evaluating.

BT-15

Is there implementation of a written policy on safety checks for all vehicles that regularly transport campers and staff that:

    1. Specifies the frequency of checks, and
    2. Requires checks of:

        a. Lights,
        b. Tires,
        c. Windshield and wiper condition,
        d. Emergency warning systems,
        e. Horn,
        f. Brakes,
        g. Fluid levels?   **Yes   No**

Interpretation: Directors should check local codes for guidance on frequency of safety checks. Some states require many of these items to be checked prior to each use for certain types of vehicles. Written documentation of the check is often required in some states or local jurisdictions.

Compliance Demonstration: Visitor observation of written policy; director/staff description of policy's implementation.

BT-16

Does the camp administration implement procedures to verify that all drivers regularly transporting campers or staff:

    1. Have the appropriate license for vehicles to be driven, and
    2. Have had their driving records reviewed as follows:

        a. For seasonal camps — within 4 months prior to the beginning of the camp season, and/or
        b. For year-round operations — at least annually?   **Yes   No**

Interpretation: Some states and/or insurance policies specify age requirements for drivers who transport children.

Other factors to consider include driving experience, experience driving on the right-hand side of the road, and experience with the type of vehicle to be driven.

"Review" may be conducted through state police records or through evaluation by the camp's insurance agent.

Compliance Demonstration: Director description of procedures utilized.

BT-17:

Is there written evidence that the camp has provided training for drivers who regularly transport campers that includes:

1. **Written procedures for:**
   a. **Backing up,**
   b. **Loading and unloading passengers at the pick-up and/or drop-off points,**
   c. **Dealing with vehicular breakdown or passenger illness,**
   d. **Refueling,**
   e. **Checking the vehicle prior to transportation of campers, and**

2. **Behind-the-wheel training if the vehicle to be driven differs in size or capacity from their regularly-driven vehicle?** **Yes   No**

Interpretation: While the level or amount of training has not been specified by the standard, the intent is to provide camp-specific training which goes beyond that required for a commercial driver's license. It should cover the camp's accepted procedures for such things as loading/unloading, backing up, and vehicle checks. It will vary based on the amount of driving to be done, the driver's familiarity with the vehicle and the driving routes, and so forth.

It may range from behind-the-wheel training on frequently traveled routes to classroom-type training on the camp's procedures. The director is responsible to determine the type and amount of training. The standard defines (see part 2) when behind-the-wheel training <u>must</u> occur.

Compliance Demonstration: Visitor observation of written procedures and training records.

47

SECTION C — PERSONNEL

The key to any camp's success is its personnel. One of the unique features of a camp is the vital and all-encompassing leadership role demanded of its personnel in the camp community. Camp personnel are expected to assume many responsibilities, deliver a wide range of services, and complete numerous tasks in an environment of constant close human interaction, with quality results.

This demanding role requires minimums to be established in screening, hiring, training, and supervising staff. The personnel criteria in this section are the result of experience and the review of research in the area of personnel management.

Maturity and judgment are two critical qualities of a camp staff member. Simple, objective measures for these qualities are not available. In identifying the criteria for staff positions, a number of factors have been listed including education, certification (where available), experience, and age. While it is recognized that age is not equivalent to maturity, it is one referenced and recognized criterion, utilized in conjunction with other factors listed above, to guide the administrator in seeking qualified personnel. It is not intended to be used as the sole criterion for determining acceptability of a staff member.

A chart has been provided in the Appendix to assist directors in documenting compliance with the Personnel standards. The Appendix also contains summary information on staff training content items required throughout the Camp Accreditation standards.

DEFINITIONS

Administrative personnel: Staff with supervisory and administrative responsibilities. Positions may include camp director, assistant director, business manager, food service director, and health supervisor.

Program personnel: Staff directly involved in camp programming and camper supervision. Positions may include unit supervisors, activity specialists, activity coordinators, and counselors.

Counselor-support personnel: Auxiliary staff to aid special-needs campers in daily living tasks. They generally do not have sole camper supervision responsibility and are often called "aides" or "volunteers." They may be paid or unpaid.

Special-needs campers: Campers with physical, medical, or behavioral characteristics that require special consideration in the camp setting. Examples include campers with physical disabilities, emotional disturbances, learning disabilities, mental retardation, or medical conditions such as diabetes, cancer, and asthma.

Primarily serves campers with special needs: More than 50 percent of the campers enrolled for the camp season are special needs campers (see above).

C-1

Does the on-site director have the following qualifications:

A. A bachelor's degree or ACA Camp Director Certification?   Yes No

B. At least two prior seasons of administrative or supervisory experience in an organized camp?   Yes No

DNA C if camp does not primarily serve campers with special needs.

C. If the camp primarily serves campers with special needs, 24 weeks of experience working with that special population?   Yes No

D. Attended a workshop, institute, seminar or course related to camp management, camper or staff development, and/or environmental education within the past three years?   Yes No

E. At least 25 years of age?   Yes No

Compliance Demonstration: Director explanation of qualifications.

Director's Pre-Visit Evaluation

A. ☐ Yes ☐ No
B. ☐ Yes ☐ No
C. ☐ Yes ☐ No ☐ DNA
D. ☐ Yes ☐ No
E. ☐ Yes ☐ No

C-2

DNA if camp does not primarily serve campers with special needs.

Do 20% of the camp administrative personnel and program personnel with staff supervisory responsibilities have a Bachelor's degree in an area relevant to the clientele served, or at least 24 weeks of experience working with the special populations being served?   Yes No

Interpretation: Serving campers with special needs requires skill and experience beyond that required for other camp operations. The intent of this standard is to provide a minimum level of specialized training and experience at the administrative and staff supervisory levels.

The chart in the Appendix (page 211) may be helpful in summarizing the requirements for this standard, as well as for C-4, C-5, and C-6.

Compliance Demonstration: Director explanation of camp's percentage.

Director's Pre-Visit Evaluation

☐ Yes ☐ No ☐ DNA

C-3

Is there a screening and interviewing process in practice that helps determine the suitability of staff to be with campers that includes:
   1. **Verification of previous work (including volunteer) history and/or securing of references, and**
   2. **Interviewing the candidate (either face-to-face or by telephone) by the camp director or a designated representative?**   Yes No

Interpretation: "Verification" means evaluation of work history to determine reasons for any gaps in employment and spot checking to verify that the applicant was employed as claimed.

Director's Pre-Visit Evaluation

☐ Yes ☐ No

Accreditation

References can include reference letters, completed reference forms, or documentation of telephone contact or other discussion.

Standards in other areas such as transportation, aquatics and program also call for specific kinds of background checks and/or documentation of skills which may be checked as part of this screening process. (See standards such as BT-16, D-8, or F-1.)

Interviews of international counselors may be conducted by representatives of a staff placement agency. However, camps are encouraged to make additional personal contact with potential international staff when possible.

Camps need to individually determine the appropriateness of criminal background checks. Some states require such checks by camp directors, some permit them, and some preclude camp directors from obtaining them.

It is not intended that visitors be given access to confidential personnel files.

Compliance Demonstration: Director description of process and visitor observation of documentation (e.g. sample forms, checklists, notes, etc.)

C-4

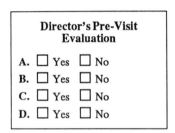

Director's Pre-Visit Evaluation

A. ☐ Yes ☐ No
B. ☐ Yes ☐ No
C. ☐ Yes ☐ No
D. ☐ Yes ☐ No

Are written procedures in practice for the supervision of campers by staff that specify:

A. **Ratios of staff who are on duty with campers in units or living groups and in general camp activities that meet or exceed the following minimums?**

Camper Age	Staff	Resident Campers	Day Campers
4-5 years	1	5	6
6-8 years	1	6	8
9-14 years	1	8	10
15-18 years	1	10	12
19 & over	1	20	20

Yes   No

B. **Exceptions, if any, to the ratios in part A for sessions, or segments of the program day when greater or fewer numbers of staff are required for supervision?**   Yes   No

C. **At least 80% of the staff-camper ratios established in part A are met with staff 18 years of age or older (100% for camps primarily serving persons with special needs)?**   Yes   No

D. **Training that is required for all staff in their supervisory responsibilities when "on duty?"**   Yes   No

Interpretation: For the purpose of this standard, "staff" includes those persons with the responsibility, authority and training to provide direct supervision to camper groups. This may include counselors, general activity leaders, and/or other staff who may provide supervision to campers without assistance. Junior counselors may be included in meeting the ratios in part A only if they are considered staff, and they have received training and supervision to verify their ability to handle camper groups independently.

The ratios above should not include campers in leadership training programs (often called CIT's), or other "counselor support personnel" (see definition), nor should they include staff who have exclusive administrative, office, food service or maintenance duties.

"General camp activities" are those that do not require special technical skills, equipment, or safety regulations other than general ones that apply throughout the camp. Examples include singing, nature studies, religious instruction, crafts, etc. Ratios and qualifications for supervision of specialized program activities are covered in the Program Standards (D Section).

Any exceptions in part B should be in accordance with the type of activity, the area, and the characteristics of the participants as determined by the camp administration. When the camp serves campers with physical, medical or behavioral needs who require additional staff support to participate in camp, the following ratios of staff and counselor-support personnel to campers are suggested:

Camper Description	Staff	Campers
Needing constant and individual assistance or supervision	1	1
Needing close, but not constant assistance or supervision	1	2
Needing occasional assistance	1	4
Needing minimal assistance	1	5

"Segments of the program day" in part B may include times such as free time, rest hour, camper arrival and departure, after lights out, early morning, etc.

The training specified in part D should include supervision practices such as instructions on what to look or listen for; how and where to get additional help; location while "on duty"; and responsibilities specific to the activities, areas, and participants.

There is a chart in the Appendix (page 211) to assist administrators in evaluating compliance with this standard.

Compliance Demonstration: Visitor observation of written procedures; visitor observation of randomly selected camper groups and/or director explanation of ratios available.

C-5

Does the camp's staff recruitment and training process include:

    A. A plan to recruit program and administrative staff whose racial/ethnic diversity reflects that of the camper population served?   Yes No

    B. Training for staff to accept, respect, and be responsive to the multi-cultural diversity of our society?   Yes No

Interpretation: In part A, the intent is for directors to consciously try to provide staff members as role models and resources for minority populations served. A camp whose staff is **more** diverse than its camper population is considered to be in compliance.

Training for staff may include both pre-camp and in-service sessions to help staff recognize and value individual differences within groups, particularly in relation to the camper populations served.

Compliance Demonstration: Director description of recruitment plans and procedures; director/staff description of staff training provided.

C-6

DNA if camper population is over 18 years of age or staff under 18 years are not utilized.

Is there a policy in practice that all program personnel who are under 18 years of age be at least two years older than the camper group with whom they are working?   Yes No

Compliance Demonstration: Director explanation of the policy's implementation; visitor observation of randomly selected camper groups.

C-7

Does the camp provide pre-camp training of the following length for all program personnel:

Day Camp

1. For camps whose season is longer than two weeks — at least 18 hours, 6 or more of which are on the site, or
2. For camps whose season is shorter than two weeks — at least 10 hours, 4 or more of which are on the site?

Resident Camp

1. Long-term staff — at least 5 days in length on the camp site, or
2. Short-term staff — at least 18 hours with 6 or more hours on the camp site?

Trip/Travel Camp

At least 2 days in a residential situation?   Yes   No

Interpretation: See Appendix (page 212) for a list of pre-camp training content topics specified in these standards. They include not only the items in the Personnel section but also routines, procedures, and training specified in other sections of the standards.

The intent is that this training be specific to camp staff responsibilities. While some camp staff may participate in other kinds of training throughout the year, the hours required by this standard must relate directly to camp planning, program, and responsibilities.

"Short term staff" are staff (paid and unpaid) who are contracted for two weeks or less, excluding the training period.

Compliance Demonstration: Director/staff description of training period.

C-8

Is there a system in practice for providing staff with information or training prior to pre-camp to help them:

1. Understand the specific job they will be expected to do,
2. Understand the nature and cultural diversity of the total camp population, and
3. Learn general characteristics of the camp and programs offered?

         Yes   No

Interpretation: The intent of this standard is to help prepare staff for some of the responsibilities they will be assuming.

Information and training resources may include materials such as job descriptions, staff manuals, camp brochures and schedules, articles, slide show, etc.

Compliance Demonstration: Director/staff description of materials and/or training provided.

Accreditation

C-9

Are there procedures in practice for informing all staff of any specific needs of campers for whom they are responsible?   Yes No

Interpretation: The intent is that all appropriate staff be informed of medical, physical, or other needs or restrictions of campers under their supervision, whether in the cabin or in program activities.

This may include information on diet, allergies, medication, rest requirements, and activity restrictions; recognition and care of potential medical problems such as choking, seizures, and hypoglycemia; care and handling of campers with wheelchairs, prosthetic and orthopedic devices; and any other specialized needs or limitations of individual campers.

Compliance Demonstration: Director/staff explanation of procedures and their implementation.

C-10

Is there evidence that training for staff has addressed general practices for effectively relating to campers which include:

   A. **Speaking with and listening to campers in a manner that reflects respect for individuals?**   Yes No

   B. **Focusing attention primarily on campers' needs and interests rather than on other staff and themselves?**   Yes No

Interpretation: Examples of reflecting respect for campers include calling them by name or preferred nickname, using language that is easily understood, providing explanations for actions taken, speaking with campers at eye level, and using techniques that do not intentionally embarrass or ridicule campers or groups of people.

Compliance Demonstration: Director/staff description of training; visitor observation of general camper/staff interactions.

C-11

Is the staff trained to implement written procedures that specify the following:

   A. **Positive behavior management and disciplinary techniques that forbid corporal punishment?**   Yes No

   B. **Appropriate methods and behaviors for relating to campers and other staff?**   Yes No

Interpretation: Part A should include the camp's general philosophy and approach to discipline and any specific progressive steps to be taken when disciplining a camper, as well as identifying inappropriate disciplinary techniques.

Part B includes information and training on establishing positive relationships with campers and should include information on the identification and prevention of child abuse. Procedures should also identify the camp's policies and expectations for staff behavior and/or relationships with each other.

Compliance Demonstration: Visitor observation of written procedures; director/staff description of training provided.

C-12

Are persons who supervise other staff provided:

A. **A list or chart showing whom they are to supervise?**   Yes   No

B. **Guidelines for identifying acceptable performance in the jobs they supervise?**   Yes   No

C. **Training to identify and address inappropriate staff behavior?**
                                                                        Yes   No

D. **Training to carry out their responsibilities in the camp's performance review system?**   Yes   No

Interpretation: Supervision is one of the keys to an effective staff and quality program. The intent of this standard is that camp administrators clearly define and communicate their expectations of supervisors to those with that responsibility.

Effective supervision requires that individuals have a clear picture of who they supervise, or are supervised by, so that two-way communication is enabled. An organizational chart will help to identify this pattern, and help administrators evaluate the amount of supervisory responsibility delegated to any one individual.

Specific training should be provided to staff who have supervisory responsibility for other staff. Training should include how and when to observe staff, what to look for, and how to communicate suggestions for improvement.

To effectively observe and evaluate, supervisors need to be able to identify the acceptable behaviors of the staff positions they supervise. Behaviors may include such things as establishing positive role models for campers, punctuality, treating campers with respect, enforcing safety rules, utilizing appropriate teaching techniques, encouraging positive interactions among campers, problem solving, and so forth.

Supervisors also need to develop skills in identifying and addressing inappropriate staff behavior with campers or with other staff. This may include actions or attitudes resulting from immaturity, inexperience, stress, lack of knowledge, poor judgment, or expectations of the individual that were beyond his/her abilities.

For part D, supervisors need to receive specific training in the content and methods used in evaluating their staff's performance. The performance review system may range from verbal recommendations at the end of a season or session to formal written performance appraisals based on observations and supervisory conferences over the entire summer.

Compliance Demonstration: Director/staff discussion of training and materials provided to supervisors.

C-13

DNA if the entire season is two weeks or less in length.

Is there a system in place for in-service training of all staff who work directly with campers?   **Yes No**

<table>
<tr><td>Director's Pre-Visit Evaluation
☐ Yes ☐ No ☐ DNA</td></tr>
</table>

Interpretation: "In-service" refers to training that occurs during the camp season. It includes methods for providing continuing education and support for staff such as regularly scheduled supervisory conferences, special program activities and skill training sessions, and staff meetings or training sessions relating to human behavior and group dynamics.

Compliance Demonstration: Director/staff description of in-service training opportunities.

C-14

DNA if a day camp.

Does the camp implement a policy that each staff member (including the director) has the following minimum amounts of time free from assigned camp responsibilities:

<table>
<tr><td>Director's Pre-Visit Evaluation
☐ DNA
A. ☐ Yes ☐ No
B. ☐ Yes ☐ No</td></tr>
</table>

    A. Daily — at least two hours?   **Yes No**

    B. During total employment period —

        1. 24 hours or more each two weeks in blocks of not less than 12 consecutive hours, or
        2. If camp primarily serves physically or mentally disabled — 24 consecutive hours off each two weeks?   **Yes No**

Interpretation: "Free from assigned camp responsibilities" means free time during which a staff member is not expected to be at a specific place or performing camp-related responsibilities.

In trip or travel programs, consideration should be given to the staff need for privacy and freedom from camper responsibility.

Compliance Demonstration: Director/staff discussion of procedures to implement the policy.

SECTION D — PROGRAM

Program is the heart of camp. It is here that camp philosophy and objectives are implemented in *a sustained experience which provides a creative, recreational and educational opportunity in group living in the out-of-doors.* Camp programming *utilizes trained leadership and the resources of the natural surroundings to contribute to each camper's mental, physical, social and spiritual growth.*

The Program standards allow the flexibility for each camp to take advantage of its own unique programming strengths and determine its own procedures while still addressing areas requiring planning and thought by camp administrators.

The standards included here are general standards for common camp activities. It is not possible to write specific standards for all potential and unique program activities. However, these standards require the camp administration to address the important considerations in program provision: supervision of the activity, establishment of safety regulations and emergency procedures, definition of activity content, and provision and maintenance of acceptable facilities and equipment. These basic concepts need to be at the core of any activity offered in camp.

This section includes standards broadly applicable to all of camp program (D-1 through D-7), and some standards that are scored only if activities requiring special consideration beyond the general guidelines for camp program and supervision are offered (D-8 through D-43).

DEFINITIONS

Program Activity: An individual event, class, or instructional period occurring under staff leadership or supervision that provides opportunity for recreational or educational participation by campers.

Activity Leader: The staff member providing direct, on-site leadership at any program activity.

D-1

Is there a written statement of goals with specific objectives for camper development that is shared with staff?   **Yes No**

Director's Pre-Visit Evaluation
☐ Yes   ☐ No

Interpretation: Goals express the purpose of the camp's existence and operation. From these broad goals come specific objectives, some of which must identify what the camper will experience as a result of participating in camp program.

Such objectives should be more specific than "the camper will develop socially." They should identify the particular ways campers will develop during their stay at camp. For examples, see the Appendix (page 214).

Goals and objectives of national organizations alone are not sufficient; they should be further refined in terms of the organization's local unit and the specific camp.

Compliance Demonstration: Visitor observation of written goals and objectives; director/staff explanation of dissemination to staff.

D-2

Are there three or more program activities that provide campers the opportunity to experience progression, challenge and success?   **Yes   No**

Interpretation: Such activities should be available for each enrolled age group in camp. The intent is that each camper experience three or more activities, each of which provide the opportunity for progression, challenge, and success.

Compliance Demonstration: Director explanation or visitor observation of program activities.

D-3

To provide balance, does the program provide activities of the following kinds:
    1. Quiet/active, and
    2. Individual/small group/large group?   **Yes   No**

Interpretation: Child development authorities indicate that participation in different kinds of experiences and structures is important in the child development process.

Compliance Demonstration: Director explanation or visitor observation of program activities or program plans.

D-4

To develop environmental awareness and responsibility in campers, does the camp use the outdoors for at least one activity that addresses each of the following:

    A. Appreciation of the natural environment?   **Yes   No**

    B. Ecologically responsible practices?   **Yes   No**

Interpretation: The intent of this standard is that activities be specifically designed to develop awareness and responsibility, rather than simply being activities that happen to occur out-of-doors.

For part A, each age group should have opportunities to learn about the natural world, to develop an understanding of, respect for, and commitment to the preservation of that world.

For part B, activities may range from simple projects such as recycling or wood conservation to more extensive projects in erosion control or composting.

Compliance Demonstration: Director/staff explanation of program activities and/or visitor observation of program activities or plans.

D-5

Are there intentional opportunities for campers to practice decision-making in program activities and in group living activities? **Yes No**

Director's Pre-Visit
Evaluation

☐ Yes   ☐ No

Interpretation: "Intentional opportunities" means there are deliberate occasions where campers may make choices and decisions in how some of their time is spent in scheduled or unscheduled camp activities.

Choices and decisions may be made individually or as part of a group.

Compliance Demonstration: Director/staff explanation of decision-making opportunities.

> D-6 and D-7 **apply** to **all** camp program activities
> **EXCEPT**
> Aquatic and Horseback Riding activities,
> which are scored separately on these concepts.

D-6

Are procedures being implemented which require that each program activity be led by an activity leader who is trained and supervised to:

Director's Pre-Visit
Evaluation

A. ☐ Yes   ☐ No
B. ☐ Yes   ☐ No
C. ☐ Yes   ☐ No
D. ☐ Yes   ☐ No

   A. **Enforce established safety regulations?** **Yes No**

   B. **Work with the types of groups participating in the activity and provide necessary instruction?** **Yes No**

   C. **Identify and manage environmental and other hazards related to the activity?** **Yes No**

   D. **Apply emergency health care procedures related to the activity and the participants?** **Yes No**

Interpretation: The intent is that each program period, session or activity be led by a staff member with the qualifications specified in the standard. While periods of the day such as rest hour, cabin capers, and free time are part of the total camp "program" the camper experiences, their supervision requirements are covered by standard C-4.

It is the director's responsibility to evaluate the skills of activity leaders and provide appropriate supervision and training. This includes a skills evaluation of persons who present certification or other documented experience. This evaluation will generally occur during pre-camp training.

Levels of training and supervision may vary with the type of activity, structure of the camp program, abilities of participants, experience of staff, etc. Activity leaders for specialized activities (D-8 through D-43) may need additional training and supervision that is provided by the certified/trained staff members in charge of those activities.

In part A, "established safety regulations" may include general camp safety regulations developed in standard B-2 and/or those regulations established for a specific activity or areas.

In part B, "types of groups" refers to age, ability levels, or special needs of participants.

In part C, "environmental hazards" may include those related to weather, terrain, or other natural conditions such as animals, poisonous plants, etc.

In part D, it is not assumed that every activity requires a certified first aider. However, activity leaders do need to be oriented to common health concerns associated with that activity such as preventing and treating burns if leading a fire building activity, and so forth.

Compliance Demonstration: Director/staff description of training and supervision practices; visitor observation of randomly selected activities.

D-7

Is staff trained to implement a system to monitor program equipment used by campers and staff that requires it be:

    A. Regularly checked for safety, maintained in good repair, and stored in a manner to safeguard effectiveness?   Yes   No

    B. Appropriate to the size and ability of the user?   Yes   No

Interpretation: Program equipment includes all equipment utilized to carry out program activities such as archery, sports, outdoor living skills, crafts, or other specialized activities.

Compliance Demonstration: Staff/director explanation of training received and procedures used; visitor observation of selected program equipment as stored and used.

SPECIALIZED ACTIVITIES

The remaining standards in the Program section address additional supervision and safety concerns for activities that require some specialized knowledge and/or skills.

They include standards for:

1. Target sports — D-8 through D-12
2. Overnights/all-day hikes/out-of-camp field trips or excursions — D-13 through D-20
3. Adventure/challenge activities — D-21 through D-27
4. Gymnastics — D-28 through D-31
5. Motorized vehicle activities — D-32 through D-37
6. Bicycling — D-38 through D-41
7. Other specialized activities (see criteria, page 76) — D-42 and D-43

Camps may miss no more than one scoreable item in each or any subset to be eligible for accreditation.

DEFINITIONS

Certification: As used in the Program standards, indicates current instructor-level status from a nationally recognized certifying body or organization.

Documented training and experience: Written evidence of competence in a leadership role. This may include records of previous leadership and/or training to instruct the activity, course completion certificates or cards, letters of reference, and/or written evaluation of previous successful leadership work.

See the introduction to each set of activity standards for applicability and/or additional definitions.

TARGET SPORTS

Target sports include archery, riflery,
air riflery, hunting, clout shooting, etc.

If **TARGET SPORTS** are **NOT** offered in camp
DNA D-8 through D-12
and proceed to D-13.

D-8

Is there written evidence that the leader or supervisor of each target sport activity has certification and/or documented training and experience in that type of activity?   Yes   No

Director's Pre-Visit Evaluation
☐ Yes   ☐ No

Interpretation: The intent of this standard is that there be at least one person in camp who is certified/documented/experienced, who is giving supervision to the conduct of each type of target sport activity. This person does not necessarily need to be present at each activity, but does need to provide the training and supervision to enable activity leaders to carry out their responsibilities as listed in standard D-6. Furthermore, this person needs the knowledge and experience to make judgments concerning participants, equipment, safety considerations, supervision and procedures for the activity.

Documentation must be available for each type of target sport activity if more than one is offered (e.g. archery and riflery).

Compliance Demonstration: Visitor observation of written documentation for each type of target sport offered.

D-9

Are written operating procedures developed for each type of target sport activity, based on information from authoritative sources, that are required to be in practice and include at least:
** 1. Eligibility requirements for participation,**
** 2. Camper/staff supervision ratios,**
** 3. Safety regulations, and**
** 4. Emergency procedures?**   **Yes   No**

Interpretation: Camps that offer more than one target sport activity may have a combined set of operating procedures, with exceptions noted for any differences.

Compliance Demonstration: Visitor observation of written operating procedures.

D-10

Are procedures in practice to control access to the target sport activity area(s)?
Yes   No

Interpretation: The intent of this standard is to avoid potentially hazardous situations while the area is in use.

Procedures may include such things as scheduling, education, regulations, or a physical barrier.

Compliance Demonstration: Director/staff explanation of access control procedures; visitor observation of activity area(s).

D-11

Is there a policy in practice that target sports equipment may be used by campers and staff only when a qualified activity leader is present and safety rules are in practice?   **Yes   No**

Interpretation: "Qualified" means the leader at least meets the requirements of standard D-6.

Levels of qualification may vary due to the age of participants and content of the activity session.

Compliance Demonstration: Director/staff explanation of policy's implementation; visitor observation of activities when possible.

D-12

Are participants trained to utilize clear safety signals and/or range commands to control both the activity at the firing line and the retrieval of targets/arrows?

Yes   No

Compliance Demonstration: Visitor observation of activities when possible; staff description of training provided.

Accreditation

OVERNIGHTS, ALL-DAY HIKES, and/or OUT-OF-CAMP FIELD TRIPS or EXCURSIONS

Activities to be scored in this section include those in which participants are away from the primary resources of the main camp for a period of time. They include:

1. Out-of-camp hikes, excursions, field trips, and overnight camping trips of two nights or less (as differentiated from longer trips scored in Section G: Trip/Travel).

2. In-camp overnights or hikes that meet one or more of the following criteria:

   a. potentially hazardous (perishable) foods must be stored by the group;

   b. the camp's permanent toilet facilities are not available for use; and/or

   c. the camp's usual communication system and health care resources are not readily available (within 5-10 minutes).

Note: Activities scored in this section may involve transportation, intermingling of campers with the public, or participation in aquatic or horseback riding activities. Requirements of those standards also apply to these short-term programs and should be considered by directors in planning such activities.

DEFINITIONS

Overnight/short trip activities: a phrase used for brevity to include all activities listed above or that meet the criteria listed above.

. . . .

If **OVERNIGHT/SHORT TRIP** activities
are **NOT** offered in camp program,
DNA D-13 through D-20
and proceed to D-21.

D-13

Director's Pre-Visit Evaluation

☐ Yes ☐ No

Is there written evidence that the leader or supervisor of each type of overnight/short trip activity has documented training and/or experience in that area?   Yes   No

Interpretation: The intent of this standard is that there be at least one person in camp who is trained/experienced, who is giving supervision to the conduct of each type of overnight/short trip activity. This person does not need to be present at each activity, but does need to provide the training and supervision to enable activity leaders to carry out their responsibilities as listed in standard D-6. The amount of training necessary will vary based on the level of the activity (e.g. overnight on camp property vs. overnight off camp property).

Staff members leading field trips should be knowledgeable of group transportation and management procedures, and steps to follow in case emergencies arise.

Compliance Demonstration: Visitor observation of written documentation.

D-14

Are written operating procedures required to be in practice for each type of overnight/short trip activity that include at least:

1. **Eligibility requirements for participation (when appropriate),**
2. **Camper/staff supervision ratios,**
3. **Safety regulations, and**
4. **Emergency procedures?**   **Yes   No**

Director's Pre-Visit Evaluation
☐ Yes   ☐ No

Interpretation: Camps that offer more than one type of overnight/short trip activity may have operating procedures which are combined for similar activities, with exceptions noted for any differences.

Eligibility requirements do not need to be listed if all campers are eligible to participate.

Compliance Demonstration: Visitor observation of written operating procedures.

D-15

Are procedures in practice for each type of overnight/short trip activity that require the following details be planned in advance and made known to a designated person remaining in the main camp:

1. **Roster of participants,**
2. **Departure and return times,**
3. **Inclement weather plans,**

and, for out-of-camp trips and excursions,

4. **Route to be taken, and**
5. **Plans for communications with the designated person in the main camp?**   **Yes   No**

Director's Pre-Visit Evaluation
☐ Yes   ☐ No

Interpretation: "Roster of participants" may be a complete list or a previously identified group (patrol, cabin, unit, etc.), with any exceptions noted.

"Plans for communications" should identify times and/or means of contact that are planned in advance and made known to all parties.

Compliance Demonstration: Director/staff explanation of procedures and implementation.

D-16

Is a procedure in practice that participants receive an orientation prior to each overnight/short trip that includes (as appropriate):

1. **Safety regulations,**
2. **Health and sanitation practices, and**
3. **Practices to protect the environment?**   **Yes   No**

Interpretation: Safety regulations include those developed for D-14, as well as other applicable regulations such as procedures for using public facilities (see standard B-7).

Health and sanitation practices may include those for toileting, handwashing, and general health care.

Practices to protect the environment may include proper trail use, disposal of trash, protection of plants and flowers, etc.

Compliance Demonstration: Director/staff explanation of policy's implementation.

> If **OUT-OF-CAMP** trips or activities
> do **NOT** occur,
> **DNA** D-17 and D-18
> and proceed to D-19.

D-17

Are staff accompanying out-of-camp groups trained in how to get medical help and/or emergency assistance?   **Yes   No**

Interpretation: Training could include communication plans, pre-planned emergency contacts, and methods for obtaining assistance from community services or other agencies or authorities.

Compliance Demonstration: Director/staff description of procedures and training.

D-18

Is there a policy in practice that specifies when the leader of out-of-camp activities must possess emergency information for each member of the group, that includes:

1. **Copy of health history,**
2. **Insurance information, if available, and**
3. **Signed release for emergency treatment or a signed religious waiver exempting the participant from medical treatment?**   **Yes   No**

Interpretation: This standard does not require that the emergency information always be with out-of-camp groups. It does require the camp to have a policy indicating <u>when</u> such records are to be with the group.

Compliance Demonstration: Director/staff description of policy and implementation.

*D-19 Part D MANDATORY

DNA if overnight/short trip activities do not involve food preparation or storage and/or utilize only camp or public water supplies.

Has training been provided to campers and staff in written procedures that require:

DNA A if all drinking water is provided from the camp's approved water supply or by a public water supply.

A. All drinking water be obtained from tested or approved water supplies or be purified by one or more of the following methods: boiling, filtering, and/or chemical treatment?   **Yes No**

DNA B if disposable food utensils are used exclusively or if food utensils are not carried by the group.

B. Food utensils be cleaned and sanitized after each use and protected from contamination between use?   **Yes No**

DNA C if food is not stored or prepared by the group.

C. Food be prepared and stored under safe and sanitary conditions with particular care given to maintaining potentially hazardous foods at proper temperatures?   **Yes No**

DNA D if camp stoves or flammable liquids are not used.

*D. Persons using camp stoves and/or flammable liquids be instructed in their proper use and care and supervised until competency is demonstrated?   **Yes No**

Interpretation: The intent of part A is to address questionable water supplies, not those which have been tested by public authorities for residential or public use. Water from natural bodies of water or springs should be treated if there is no assurance that the supply has been approved for human consumption.

It is the responsibility of the camp to identify the appropriate water purification method based on advice from local officials able to identify possible contaminants for that area or specific water supply.

Food utensils include dishes, cups, eating utensils, and food preparation utensils not heated at least to boiling in the cooking process.

See the Interpretation of A-26 for a definition of potentially hazardous foods.

Compliance Demonstration: Visitor observation of written procedures; director/staff description of implementation.

D-20

DNA if overnights, excursions or trips are not taken to campsites or natural areas.

Are there procedures required to be in practice for conducting each trip with minimal environmental impact including the following, as applicable:

1. **Group size limits — based on the environmental carrying capacity of the site(s) and do not exceed limits set by other jurisdictional authorities?**
2. **Refuse disposal — requiring all refuse to be carried out, be biodegradable, or be disposed of in accordance with regulations governing each area?**
3. **Soap — only biodegradable and non-detergent soap is used at campsites?**
4. **Human waste disposal sites — located a minimum of 100 feet from any water supply, trail, or campsite?**
5. **Human waste — disposed of in a manner which accelerates decomposition, is an environmentally sound practice, and is not offensive to other campers?** **Yes No**

Interpretation: See Appendix (page 227) for a list of recommended, environmentally-sound practices.

Compliance Demonstration: Director/staff explanation of procedures in practice.

ADVENTURE/CHALLENGE ACTIVITIES

Adventure/challenge activities include ropes course activities, spelunking, climbing, rappelling, initiative activities, and similar activities requiring spotting and/or belays.

If **ADVENTURE/CHALLENGE** activities are **NOT** offered,
DNA D-21 through D-27
and proceed to D-28.

D-21

Is there written evidence that the leader or supervisor of each adventure/challenge activity has certification and/or documented training and experience in that type of activity? **Yes No**

Interpretation: The intent of this standard is that there be at least one person in camp who is certified/documented/experienced, who is giving supervision to the conduct of each type of adventure/challenge activity. This person does not necessarily need to be present at each activity, but does need to provide the training and supervision necessary to see to it that each adventure/challenge activity is led by an individual who meets the requirements of standard D-6. Furthermore, the certified/documented person needs the knowledge and experience to make judgments concerning participants, equipment, facilities, safety considerations, supervision and procedures for the activity.

As a general guideline, adventure activity professionals recommend a minimum of 20 hours of instruction and experience in each category of activities included in this section prior to assuming primary leadership. This has not been included as a scored item at this time due to inconsistent availability of professional training across the country.

Even a limited number of low elements or initiative activities requires trained leadership and supervision.

Documentation must be available for each category of adventure/challenge activity, if more than one type is offered (e.g. ropes course and caving).

Compliance Demonstration: Visitor observation of written documentation for each type of adventure/challenge activity offered.

D-22

Are written operating procedures developed for each type of adventure/challenge activity, based on information from authoritative sources, that are required to be in practice and include:

1. **Eligibility requirements for participation,**
2. **Camper/staff supervision ratios,**
3. **Identification of appropriate protective equipment,**
4. **Equipment maintenance procedures,**
5. **Safety regulations, and**
6. **Emergency and/or rescue procedures?**   Yes   No

Director's Pre-Visit Evaluation
☐ Yes   ☐ No

Interpretation: Camps that offer more than one type of adventure/challenge activity may have operating procedures that are combined for similar activities, with exceptions noted for any differences.

"Protective equipment" may include apparel (helmets, gloves, etc.), harnesses, or other safety gear.

Compliance Demonstration: Visitor observation of written operating procedures.

D-23

Are procedures in practice to provide participants a safety orientation before engaging in adventure/challenge activities?   Yes   No

Director's Pre-Visit Evaluation
☐ Yes   ☐ No

Interpretation: The safety orientation should include safety regulations, safety signals to be used as appropriate, and necessary information on the characteristics and boundaries of the area.

Compliance Demonstration: Director/staff description of policy's implementation.

D-24

Are procedures in practice that require all spotters and belayers be:

A. Instructed in proper procedures and directly supervised until competency is demonstrated? Yes No

B. Located in positions from which they can continuously observe (spot) and/or quickly assist any participant? Yes No

Interpretation: All adventure/challenge activities (as defined for these standards) require some level of spotting or belaying. The level of instruction and competency required will vary, depending on the type of activity, the area, and the abilities of participants.

Compliance Demonstration: Visitor observation of activities when possible; director/staff description of procedures.

D-25

DNA if no climbing, rappelling, or spelunking occur.

Is there a policy in practice that requires the use of protective head gear by all participants when climbing, rappelling, or spelunking? Yes No

Compliance Demonstration: Visitor observation of activities when possible; director/staff explanation of policy's implementation.

> If camp does not have a **ropes course, challenge course, climbing wall, rappelling tower, zipline,**
> or other such constructed adventure/challenge area,
> **DNA** D-26 and D-27
> and proceed to D-28.

D-26

Are procedures in practice to control access to activity areas such as ropes courses, rappelling towers, ziplines, etc? Yes No

Interpretation: The intent is to prevent use by unauthorized or unsupervised persons, as well as to avoid potentially hazardous situations when the area is in use.

Procedures may include such things as education, posted regulations, scheduling, dismantling equipment, and/or a physical barrier.

Compliance Demonstration: Visitor observation of activity areas when possible; director/staff description of access control measures.

D-27

Is there written evidence of a maintenance schedule and periodic inspections of all elements utilized in ropes courses or initiative activities?   Yes   No

Interpretation: "Elements" refers to stations or events in ropes courses and challenge courses, and to climbing walls, rappelling towers, zip lines, tarzan swings, etc.

Inspections should be conducted annually, prior to first use, by trained professionals (where available) or by persons with documented experience in constructing and maintaining such elements. In addition, elements should be safety-checked prior to each use.

Compliance Demonstration: Visitor observation of written documentation; director/staff description of procedures.

GYMNASTICS

Gymnastics includes activities utilizing apparatus such as beams, bars, rings, diving training devices, etc. It does not include basic tumbling.

**If GYMNASTICS activities are NOT offered,
DNA D-28 through D-31
and proceed to D-32.**

Director's Pre-Visit Evaluation
☐ Yes   ☐ No

D-28

Is there written evidence that the leader or supervisor of each gymnastics activity has documented training and experience in that activity?   Yes   No

Interpretation: The intent of this standard is that there be at least one person in camp who is trained/experienced, who is giving supervision to the conduct of all gymnastics activities. This person does not necessarily need to be present at all activities, but does need to provide the training and supervision to enable activity leaders to carry out their responsibilities as listed in standard D-6. Furthermore, this person needs the knowledge and experience to make judgments concerning participants, equipment, safety considerations, supervision and procedures for the activity.

Compliance Demonstration: Visitor observation of written documentation.

Director's Pre-Visit Evaluation
☐ Yes   ☐ No

D-29

Are written operating procedures developed for gymnastics activities, based on information from authoritative sources, that are required to be in practice and include:

    1. Eligibility requirements for participation,
    2. Camper/staff supervision ratios,
    3. Identification of appropriate protective equipment,
    4. Equipment maintenance procedures,
    5. Safety regulations, and
    6. Emergency procedures?   **Yes No**

Interpretation: "Protective equipment" may include items such as mats, harnesses, etc.

Compliance Demonstration: Visitor observation of written operating procedures.

D-30

Are procedures in practice to control access to gymnastics equipment?
    Yes No

Interpretation: The intent is to prevent unauthorized or unsupervised use of gymnastics equipment. Procedures may include such things as education, posted regulations, scheduling, or locking equipment or activity areas.

Compliance Demonstration: Visitor observation of activity areas when possible; director/staff description of access control measures.

D-31

Are there procedures in practice requiring that all campers or staff who serve as spotters be:

    A. Instructed in proper procedures and directly supervised until competency is demonstrated?   **Yes No**

    B. Located in positions from which they can continuously observe (spot) and quickly assist any participant?   **Yes No**

Compliance Demonstration: Visitor observation of activities when possible; director/staff description of procedures.

> ## MOTORIZED VEHICLES
>
> These standards should be applied to any activities in which campers operate motorized vehicles such as go-karts, motor bikes, mopeds, etc.
>
> If activities using **MOTORIZED VEHICLES**
> do **NOT** occur in camp
> DNA D-32 through D-37
> and proceed to D-38.

D-32

Is there written evidence that the leader or supervisor of each motorized vehicle activity has documented training and/or experience in leading activities utilizing that type of vehicle?   **Yes   No**

Interpretation: The intent of this standard is that there be at least one person in camp who is documented/experienced, who is giving supervision to the conduct of each type of motorized vehicle activity. This person does not necessarily need to be present at each activity, but does need to provide the training and supervision to enable activity leaders to carry out their responsibilities as listed in standard D-6. Furthermore, this person needs the knowledge and experience to make judgments concerning participants, equipment, supervision, and day-to-day programming for the activity.

The experience of the leader/supervisor should be directly related to the vehicle in use (e.g. go-karts, motor bikes, etc.)

Compliance Demonstration: Visitor observation of written documentation.

Director's Pre-Visit Evaluation
☐ Yes   ☐ No

D-33

Are written operating procedures developed for each type of motorized vehicle activity, based on information from authoritative sources, that are required to be in practice and include:
1. Eligibility requirements for participation,
2. Camper/staff supervision ratios,
3. Safety regulations,
4. Emergency procedures,
5. Equipment maintenance procedures, and
6. Identification of safety concerns related to the use area?   **Yes   No**

Interpretation: "Safety concerns of the use area" refers to maintaining the use area free from observable hazards, the use of impact-absorbing materials in key locations, etc.

Compliance Demonstration: Visitor observation of written operating procedures.

Director's Pre-Visit Evaluation
☐ Yes   ☐ No

D-34

Are procedures in practice to provide participants a safety orientation before engaging in motorized vehicle activities? **Yes No**

Interpretation: The safety orientation should include safety rules and regulations, signals to be used as appropriate, and necessary information on the characteristics and boundaries of the area.

Compliance Demonstration: Director/staff description of policy's implementation.

D-35

Is there a policy in practice that requires the use of protective head gear by all participants (campers and staff)? **Yes No**

Compliance Demonstration: Visitor observation of activities when possible; director/staff description of policy's implementation.

D-36

Is there a designated course or use area which has restricted access? **Yes No**

Interpretation: Access may be restricted through such things as education, posted regulation, scheduling, and/or a physical barrier.

Compliance Demonstration: Visitor observation of course or area when possible; director/staff description of access control measures.

D-37

DNA if go-karts are not used.

Are go-karts equipped with roll bars and restraint devices? **Yes No**

Interpretation: Restraint devices must include seatbelts, harnesses, or restraining bars.

Compliance Demonstration: Visitor observation of go-karts.

```
┌─────────────────────────────────────────────┐
│                  BICYCLING                    │
│        If BICYCLING activities are NOT offered,│
│            DNA D-38 through D-41              │
│             and proceed to D-42.              │
└─────────────────────────────────────────────┘
```

D-38

Is there written evidence that the leader or supervisor of each bicycling activity has documented training and experience in that type of activity?   Yes   No

Interpretation: The intent of this standard is that there be at least one person in camp who is documented/experienced, who is giving supervision to the conduct of all bicycling activities. This person does not necessarily need to be present at all activities, but does need to provide the training and supervision to enable activity leaders to carry out their responsibilities as listed in D-6. Furthermore, this person needs the knowledge and experience to make judgments concerning participants, equipment, supervision, and day-to-day program for this activity.

The experience of the leader/supervisor should be directly related to the level of programming in the activity. For instance, if out-of-camp trips are taken, the individual should have experience leading bike trips.

Compliance Demonstration: Visitor observation of written documentation.

```
┌─────────────────────────┐
│   Director's Pre-Visit   │
│       Evaluation         │
│  ☐ Yes   ☐ No           │
└─────────────────────────┘
```

D-39

Are written operating procedures developed for each type of bicycling activity, based on information from authoritative sources, that are required to be in practice and include:
1. **Eligibility requirements for participation,**
2. **Camper/staff supervision ratios,**
3. **Safety regulations,**
4. **Emergency procedures, and**
5. **Equipment maintenance procedures?   Yes   No**

Interpretation: Safety regulations may include procedures for road usage, night riding, group size, use of hand signals, locations of leaders, etc. "Equipment maintenance procedures" should at least designate persons responsible for maintenance, frequency of checks, and expectations concerning equipment storage.

Compliance Demonstration: Visitor observation of written operating procedures.

```
┌─────────────────────────┐
│   Director's Pre-Visit   │
│       Evaluation         │
│  ☐ Yes   ☐ No           │
└─────────────────────────┘
```

D-40

Is there a policy in practice that requires the use of protective head gear by all participants (campers and staff)? **Yes No**

Compliance Demonstration: Visitor observation of activity when possible; director/staff description of policy's implementation.

D-41

Are procedures in practice to provide participants a safety orientation before engaging in bicycling activities? **Yes No**

Interpretation: The safety orientation should include safety rules and regulations, safety signals and practices as appropriate, and necessary information on the characteristics of the area.

Compliance Demonstration: Director/staff description of policy's implementation.

OTHER SPECIALIZED ACTIVITIES

Score D-42 and D-43 **IF** activities which have not yet been scored (other than aquatics, trip/travel and horseback riding) meet one or more of the following criteria:

1. The activity utilizes equipment, animals, or tools whose use by campers requires supervision by a person skilled in their use (such as power tools, model rocketry, lacrosse).
2. The activity involves camper use of fire or heat-producing equipment or substances (such as woodburning tools or kilns).
3. The activity requires injury protection equipment such as helmets, goggles, or padding (such as wrestling or fencing).

Note: this may include Outdoor Living Skills activities if they were not included in the standards on overnights, D-13 to D-20.

· ·

If no such activities are offered,
DNA D-42 and D-43
and proceed to Health Care.

D-42

Is there written evidence that the leader or supervisor of each activity has certification and/or documented training and experience in that type of activity? **Yes No**

Interpretation: The intent of this standard is that there be at least one person in camp who is certified/documented/experienced, who is giving supervision to the conduct of each identified activity. This person does not necessarily need to be present at each activity, but does need to provides the training and supervision to enable activity leaders to carry out their responsibilities as listed in standard D-6. Furthermore. this person needs the knowledge and experience to make judgements concerning participants, equipment, facilities, safety considerations, supervision and procedures for the activity.

Documentation must be available for each type of activity if more than one is identified.

Compliance Demonstration: Visitor observation of written documentation of training and experience.

D-43

Are written operating procedures developed for each type of specialized activity, based on information from authoritative sources, that are required to be in practice and include at least:
1. Eligibility requirements for participation,
2. Camper/staff supervision ratios,
3. Safety regulations, and
4. Emergency procedures?   Yes   No

Director's Pre-Visit
Evaluation

☐ Yes   ☐ No

Interpretation: The intent of this standard is that for each of the activities identified for these standards, there be ratios, safety regulations and emergency procedures specific to the locations, participants, and program characteristics.

Compliance Demonstration: Visitor observation of written procedures and of randomly selected activities.

SECTION E — HEALTH CARE

While camps vary in their health care needs based on clientele, program, availability of trained health care providers on the camp staff, and distance from professional medical facilities, they do not vary in their need for a well-thought-out health care plan to provide for the needs of campers and staff.

The American Camping Association Standards define minimums in terms of staff, facilities, and procedures for health care, but they also allow for flexibility in determining the focus of the health care plan.

The Health Care standards are applicable to all camps regardless of length of session, clientele or location. Several designated standards are not scored for non-medical religious campers or camps.

These standards are scored for camps that are exclusively trip and/or travel camps.

DEFINITIONS

Health care may include first aid, dispensing of medications, administration of prescribed medical treatment and health procedures as described in the Health Care Plan (E-1) or Health Care Procedures (E-6), and promotion of health and wellness practices in the camp.

E-1

> **Director's Pre-Visit Evaluation**
> ☐ Yes ☐ No

Is there a written Health Care Plan in practice which is reviewed annually and includes general guidelines in the following areas:

1. **Responsibilities and authority of the Camp Health Manager and all other staff providing health care (including first aid),**
2. **General routines for camp health care and sanitation,**
3. **Record keeping,**
4. **Provision of supplies and equipment, and**
5. **Relationships and agreements with medical personnel, hospitals, and providers of emergency care?** **Yes No**

Interpretation: See Appendix (page 215) for a sample outline. The annual review should include the camp administration and the camp's health staff.

"Sanitation" refers to cleanliness, hygiene, and health practices throughout the camp including camper and staff living areas, the dining hall and kitchen, and garbage and waste disposal areas.

Compliance Demonstration: Visitor observation of written plan; director description of review process.

E-2

> **Director's Pre-Visit Evaluation**
> ☐ Yes ☐ No

Is there a procedure in place to have the Health Care Plan reviewed at least once every 3 years by a licensed physician or, if a non-medical religious camp, by a person with health care training approved in writing by the sponsoring program? **Yes No**

Interpretation: The review of the camp's plan may focus on updating recommended procedures, addressing camp health concerns that have arisen since the last review, or revising the plan based on recommendations of current personnel. In situations where the camp's clientele or level of health care staffing has changed considerably, immediate review of the plan is recommended.

Compliance Demonstration: Director description of procedures in place to review the plan; reviewer's name and date of the last review.

E-3

Has the camp designated a Camp Health Care Manager who is on-site when campers are present and who has the day-to-day responsibility to supervise health care in camp? **Yes No**

Director's Pre-Visit
Evaluation

☐ Yes ☐ No

Interpretation: The concern of this standard is that a designated individual have as his/her primary responsibility the on-going duty to monitor health care, maintain records, and implement the health care plan. This individual or his/her designate should be on-site at all times when campers are present.

For exclusively trip/travel camps, "on-site" means with the trip or travel group.

Compliance Demonstration: Organizational chart and/or job description identifying individual with these responsibilities, or director description of individual fulfilling this capacity.

E-4

DNA for exclusively trip and/or travel camps.

Director's Pre-Visit
Evaluation

☐ Yes ☐ No ☐ DNA

Is there written evidence that the Camp Health Manager is qualified as follows:

DAY CAMPS:
1. **Is a licensed physician or registered nurse, or has access by phone to a licensed physician or registered nurse with whom prior arrangements have been made in writing to provide consultation and/or other medical support to the camp; or**
2. **If the camp primarily serves persons with special medical needs — Is a licensed physician or registered nurse; or**
3. **If a non-medical religious camp — Is an individual meeting qualifications specified in writing by the religious program?**

RESIDENT CAMPS:
1. **Is a licensed physician or registered nurse, or is in consultation with a licensed physician or registered nurse who is on the campsite daily, or**
2. **If camp primarily serves persons with special medical needs — Is a licensed physician or registered nurse who is on duty at all times, or**
3. **If a non-medical religious camp — Is an individual meeting qualifications specified in writing by the religious program?**

Yes No

79

Interpretation: <u>For Day Camps:</u> In part 1, access by phone should be to a specific doctor, nurse, or clinic who is familiar with the camp's health care needs. Access to a 911 emergency phone system does not qualify as access to specific medical personnel who are providing on-going consultation to oversee camp health.

<u>For Resident Camps:</u> In part 1, the daily consultation may include such things as checking current health concerns or recent treatments and reviewing the medical log and/or accident reports.

"On the campsite daily" means there is time each day when a person so licensed is on the property to consult with the health care staff, review actions taken, and provide further guidance in implementing the camp's Health Care Plan.

Nurses and doctors who are not licensed to practice in the camp's locale are qualified to meet this standard **only if** they are temporarily licensed or recognized by the state in which the camp is located. Camp directors are advised to check the applicability of malpractice insurance to non-U.S. trained or licensed personnel.

For camps primarily serving persons with special medical needs, provision must be made for similarly qualified substitutes when the physician or RN must be away from camp for more than 12 hours in a resident camp or more than 1 day in a day camp. For periods less than this, a licensed practical nurse or a graduate nurse may be used.

Compliance Demonstration: Visitor observation of appropriate licenses, authorizations, or written arrangements where appropriate; director description of arrangements/scheduling.

*E-5 PART A MANDATORY

Director's Pre-Visit Evaluation
A. ☐ Yes ☐ No
B. ☐ Yes ☐ No

To provide first aid, does the camp require that staff with the following qualifications be on duty in camp at all times when campers are present:

   *A. Licensed physician, or registered nurse, or emergency medical technician, or paramedic, or a staff member currently certified in American Red Cross Standard First Aid (minimum requirement), Medic First Aid, or the equivalent? Yes No

   B. Staff member(s) currently certified for the age level of persons served in cardiopulmonary resuscitation (CPR) from the American Red Cross, the American Heart Association, or the equivalent? Yes No

Interpretation: The intent of this standard is that camps have a person on duty at all times who is at least certified in first aid. Licensed practical nurses, licensed vocational nurses, and physician's assistants have not been listed here since those licenses do not universally require training in first aid. When such emergency training can be documented, it can be considered equivalent.

CPR certification is available for infants (0-1 year old), children (1-8 years), and adults (8 years and older).

State requirements for certified persons on site may vary from this minimum standard. Directors are advised to check state regulations.

In non-medical religious camps, there must be a person on duty who is designated to handle health and accident situations who meets the qualifications specified in writing by the religious body.

Compliance Demonstration: Staff/director description of process in place to assure coverage; visitor observation of licenses, certification cards.

E-6

DNA if a non-medical religious camp or if all health care is provided by licensed physicians.

Are standing orders annually approved in writing by a licensed physician or is there evidence that written health care procedures are reviewed annually by a licensed physician, and do such orders/procedures include at least the following:
1. **Procedures for dealing with common illnesses or injuries, and**
2. **Procedures for health screening (except in day camps)?** **Yes   No**

Director's Pre-Visit Evaluation
☐ Yes   ☐ No   ☐ DNA

Interpretation: "Standing orders" generally refer to specific treatments authorized by a licensed physician that are implemented by other licensed personnel.

"Health care procedures" are less specific than standing orders and may include commonly accepted treatments for minor illnesses or injuries, general first aid guidelines, procedures for initial health screening, and identification of points at which professional medical treatment or advice should be sought. Such procedures should be developed, revised, or reviewed by a licensed physician.

While it is preferable to secure signed standing orders, an informal review of written procedures may be necessary if the camp is unable to obtain the signed orders. It is suggested that the camp's health care manager be present to review the orders/procedures with the camp's physician when possible.

See the Appendix (page 217) for a general outline of standing orders/health care procedures.

Compliance Demonstration: Visitor observation of signed standing orders, or of health care procedures with date and identification of reviewer noted.

E-7

Does the camp have a written policy that specifies activities or locations where first aid and/or CPR certified personnel are required to be present at the site or the activity? **Yes   No**

Director's Pre-Visit Evaluation
☐ Yes   ☐ No

Interpretation: The intent is that camps evaluate where, in addition to locations specified in the standards, they may need certified persons, based on characteristics of participants, location of the activity, type of activity, etc.

In non-medical religious camps, the policy should specify where persons qualified to meet the requirements of *E-5 should be located (see interpretation to *E-5).

Compliance Demonstration: Visitor observation of the written policy and certification cards of staff members.

*E-8 MANDATORY

Has the camp administration implemented a policy requiring signed health histories that ask for all of the following to be on-site for <u>all campers</u> and <u>all staff:</u>

    1. Description of any current health conditions requiring medication, treatment, or special restrictions or considerations while at camp,

And, except for non-medical religious camps,

    2. Record of past medical treatment,
    3. Record of immunizations including date of last tetanus shot, and
    4. Record of allergies?   **Yes   No**

Interpretation: This standard applies to all staff, including maintenance, food service, administrative and program staff, as well as to campers. Particular attention should be paid to obtaining complete current information on international campers and staff.

A "health history" is an annually updated record of one's past and present health status that is completed by the individual or by the parent/guardian if a minor.

The required signature serves as evidence that the individual, parent, or guardian has supplied the information and that, to the best of their knowledge, it is up to date and accurate. If the individual is a minor, the form is to be signed by the parent or guardian.

See Appendix (page 218) for a sample health history and health examination record form.

Compliance Demonstration: Visitor observation of randomly selected camper and staff health histories.

E-9

Have health histories been completed or updated within the six months prior to camp attendance?   **Yes   No**

Compliance Demonstration: Visitor observation of randomly selected health histories.

E-10

For all campers and staff who are minors, does the camp require signed permission to seek emergency medical treatment, or in the event of a non-medical religious camper or staff member, a signed religious waiver?
     Yes   No

Interpretation: There may be instances when parents or guardians may refuse to sign such a release. In that event, to be in compliance with this standard, the camp should have written record of such a refusal.

See the Appendix (page 221) for a sample religious waiver form, and a sample health form containing emergency treatment permission (page 219).

Compliance Demonstration: Visitor observation of selected permission forms or waivers.

RESIDENT CAMP ONLY

If a DAY CAMP or a NON-MEDICAL RELIGIOUS CAMP,
DNA E-11 and 12 and proceed to E-13.

E-11

In resident camp, is a policy being implemented to conduct health screening for all campers within 24 hours of arrival at camp and for all staff prior to camper arrival, by persons with the following qualifications:

> 1. **For resident camps not otherwise specified below — licensed physician, registered nurse, or adult following specific written instructions of a licensed physician, or**
> 2. **For camps primarily serving persons with special medical needs — licensed physician, registered nurse, or a graduate nurse or licensed practical nurse under the immediate supervision of a licensed physician or registered nurse?** **Yes No**

Director's Pre-Visit Evaluation
☐ Yes   ☐ No

Interpretation: This standard applies to all staff including maintenance, food service, administrative and program staff, as well as to all campers.

For campers, screening may be conducted at bus pick-up points or group departure points just prior to leaving for camp, or as close as possible to the time of arrival in camp, but no longer than 24 hours after arrival.

The purpose of screening is to:

> 1. Identify observable evidence of illness, injury or communicable disease;
> 2. Review and update the health history; and
> 3. Identify any current medical treatment (including medications).

Particular attention should be paid to allergies and dietetic restrictions.

Compliance Demonstration: Visitor observation of documentation of qualifications of person screening (if licensed) or written instructions from physician (if required); director/staff description of screening process.

E-12

For each camper and staff member in resident camp, does the camp administration require a health examination by licensed medical personnel within the 24 months prior to camp attendance, as evidenced by a signed health examination form or a signed examination record that indicates:

1. Any physical condition requiring restriction(s) on participation in the camp program,
2. Date of the health examination,
3. Any current or on-going treatment and/or medications, and
4. Date the form was signed?   Yes   No

Interpretation: "Licensed medical personnel" includes licensed physicians, certified or certification-eligible nurse practitioners, or other medical personnel licensed by the state to conduct health examinations.

A "health examination record" is a form that includes the items listed in the standard.

Note that an individual may submit either a health exam form or a health exam record, as long as the information required by this standard is included.

When exemption from a physical examination is requested for religious reasons by individual campers or staff, the camp should request a signed statement attesting that there is no physical impairment which interferes with camp activity and that the individual is also free from communicable or contagious disease. The statement should release the camp from responsibility for any impairment of health resulting because of this exemption. This exemption is only applicable to members in good standing of religious bodies adhering to faith practices rather than reliance upon medical treatment. See the Appendix, page 221, for a sample of such a release/waiver.

When campers or staff are examined upon arrival at camp by licensed medical personnel, there is compliance with the intent of this standard.

Compliance Demonstration: Visitor observation of randomly selected camper and staff health records.

ALL CAMPS SCORE E-13 through E-21

---

*E-13 MANDATORY

DNA to trip camps and to non-medical religious camps.

Is there evidence that emergency transportation is available at all times for medical emergencies, provided by either:

1. The camp, or
2. Community emergency services with whom prior arrangements have been made in writing?   Yes   No

Interpretation: "Available" means that designated emergency transportation is in operational order and has enough fuel to reach primary emergency locations.

"Arrangements... in writing" may include notification letters to municipal providers of emergency transportation services when the camp is within the geographic service district of the provider. Notification should identify the dates and precise location of the camp area being utilized.

Compliance Demonstration: Visitor observation of vehicle(s) available to use in a medical emergency, or written notification to or verification from community emergency services.

E-14

Does the camp provide training for camp staff on written procedures that:
1. **Identify their role and responsibilities in camp health care,**
2. **Prepare them to use supplies and equipment with which they may be furnished,**
3. **Identify those situations which should be attended to only by certified health personnel, and**
4. **Mandate the use of universal precautions and identify procedures to be followed when dealing with body fluids and medical waste?**

Yes   No

Interpretation: All staff require some training to identify the limits and expectations of their participation in the delivery of health care, including first aid and the supervision of camper health and hygiene in camp.

Typical camp instruction may include handling choking and seizures, first aid procedures, bedwetting, homesickness, persons in wheelchairs or those who use prosthetic or orthopedic devices, and so forth. Attention should be given both to recognition of these situations and to proper staff handling of them.

Instruction should be provided on the contents, use, availability, and re-supply of first aid kits. In addition, training should identify proper use of any other equipment or supplies to be used by staff.

"Universal precautions" are those work practices and housekeeping procedures which assume that all human blood and specified human body fluids are infectious for HIV, HBV, and other bloodborne pathogens. The use of barriers (masks, gloves, etc.), handwashing, sanitizing procedures and appropriate waste disposal are mandated by federal regulations. State departments of health can give guidance on appropriate handling and disposal procedures. "Medical waste" includes such things as syringes, needles, or dressings wet with body fluids or blood.

Compliance Demonstration: Visitor observation of written procedures; staff description of training received.

E-15

DNA if there are never hikes, trips, or activity locations where the Camp Health Manager is not immediately available.

For activity locations or situations where the Camp Health Manager is not present or nearby, is there a policy being implemented that requires a staff member be immediately available who is oriented to:

1. **Provide for routine health care needs of the participants, and**
2. **Handle life threatening medical emergencies related to the health conditions of the participants and the environmental hazards associated with the area?**   **Yes   No**

Interpretation: This standard applies to overnights, out-of-camp trips, or activity locations some distance from help in case of an emergency, as well as to times when the Camp Health Manager is on a day off or out of camp.

"Life-threatening medical emergencies" refers to known or reasonably expected potential emergencies related to known health conditions of the participants of this particular activity. If a child has epilepsy, for instance, a staff member should be trained in how to handle seizures. Or if a child is known to be allergic to bee stings, a staff member should be specifically oriented to deal with that need.

Orientation may include instructions concerning medications for group participants, any restrictions for group members, and/or general health instructions particular to the activity (e.g.sunburn precautions, dehydration, altitude sickness, hypothermia, etc.).

Compliance Demonstration: Staff description of the policy's implementation.

E-16

DNA if camp does not primarily serve persons with special medical needs.

To meet the special medical needs of participants, are the following available:

A. **Sufficient medical staff to meet the needs of participants equivalent to minimums established in the Appendix; or if ratios are not addressed in the Appendix, health care staff as approved in writing by a licensed physician?**   **Yes   No**

B. **A system for evaluating the camp's ability to meet participants' special medical needs prior to enrollment?**   **Yes   No**

C. **Information about the camp's philosophy and health management practices that is shared with parents/participants prior to enrollment so they can identify the camp's approach to medical concerns?**

Yes   No

Interpretation: "Special medical needs" include all disabling conditions which require special medical or health attention or care while the participant is in camp including chronic conditions such as insulin-dependent diabetes, or epilepsy; illnesses such as cancer; or physically disabling conditions such as spina bifida; etc.

See Appendix (page 222) for the medical staffing requirements recommended by organization sponsors of camps for persons with special medical needs.

Compliance Demonstration: Director/staff description of medical staff, systems, and practices in place; visitor observation of written approval of licensed physician (if required).

E-17

Is the camp implementing procedures to maintain the following information on-site for each camper and staff member:

1. Full name,
2. Age,
3. Home address and telephone number,
4. Name, address, and telephone number including business phone(s) of adult(s) responsible for each minor,
5. Telephone number(s) of persons to contact in case of emergency during the individual's stay at camp, and
6. Name and telephone number of individual's physician or health care facility (if available)? **Yes   No**

Director's Pre-Visit Evaluation
☐ Yes   ☐ No

Interpretation: The intent of this standard is to have appropriate information immediately available in case of an emergency. "If available" in #6 means that if the individual has a regular family physician or clinic, the information should be requested.

Compliance Demonstration: Visitor observation of randomly selected records.

E-18

Is the camp implementing procedures to maintain the following records for use during camp, and to keep them at least for the period of statutory limits:

A. A daily health log in which the following information is recorded in ink:

1. Date, time, and name of person injured or ill,
2. General description of injury or illness,
3. Description of treatment (if administered), including any treatment administered away from the health care facility,
4. Administration of any routine medications, and
5. Initials of person evaluating and treating? **Yes   No**

B. Accident reports completed for all accidents resulting in injury requiring professional medical treatment? **Yes   No**

C. Health histories, permission to treat forms, and health examination forms/records (except for day camps)? **Yes   No**

Director's Pre-Visit Evaluation		
A. ☐ Yes	☐ No	
B. ☐ Yes	☐ No	
C. ☐ Yes	☐ No	

Interpretation: A bound book with pre-printed page numbers and lined pages is frequently used to meet part A of this standard because of its acceptability in a court of law. Such a system is particularly helpful when multiple persons keep health records, or they are kept by persons without extensive medical training. Any system used should be reviewed by medical and legal counsel.

The administration of drugs on a daily, routine schedule to a number of campers may be recorded in one entry at the end of the session by appending daily medication records to the log.

"Professional medical treatment" includes all medical attention by or consultation with a licensed physician following an accident.

Computerized records are not acceptable under this standard because there is not a method of ascertaining when records have been altered.

Information in the log is usually not as specific as that required for accident or incident reports. However, detailed accident information should be readily available if needed.

The ACA Publications Department sells a "Camp Health Log" which can be used to meet the requirements of part A of this standard. "Accident/Incident Report Forms" are also available.

Compliance Demonstration: Visitor observation of logs, reports, and other forms; director description of the process of maintaining records.

E-19

<table>
<tr><td>

Director's Pre-Visit Evaluation

☐ Yes ☐ No ☐ DNA

</td></tr>
</table>

DNA if no drugs are kept in camp, or to insulin if the camp primarily serves campers with diabetes and the written camp philosophy of diabetes management requires self-administration of insulin.

To prevent the unauthorized use of drugs, does the camp require that all drugs be stored under lock (including those needing refrigeration), except when in the controlled possession of the person responsible for administering them, and:

1. **For prescription drugs — dispensed only under the specific directions of a licensed physician, and**
2. **For non-prescription drugs — dispensed only under the written health care procedures (see E-6), or under the signed instruction of the parent/guardian or the individual's physician?   Yes   No**

Interpretation: The intent of this standard is that all camper and staff medications be stored under the control of the Camp Health Manager. Exceptions would be for a limited amount of medication for life-threatening conditions <u>carried</u> by a camper or staff person (e.g. bee sting medication, inhaler), or limited medications approved for use in first aid kits.

When staff reside in quarters where camper access is restricted or prohibited, it is suggested that any medications in that area be locked, though it is not required by this standard.

"Drugs" include all prescription medications, as well as all over-the-counter drugs which are potentially hazardous if misused (e.g., aspirin, cold tablets, etc.)

"Controlled possession" means under the immediate and direct supervision or control of a staff member, to prevent access by unauthorized persons.

The Camp Health Manager should be aware of all medications in the possession of persons on the camp property, whether or not they are kept in the health care facility.

"Specific directions of a licensed physician" includes directions on an original prescription bottle, a note on the signed health examination record, or something in writing from a licensed physician.

It is most desirable to have medications locked in a cabinet at all times, particularly if narcotics are involved. However, in cases where there is full-time medical staff and the infirmary or first aid area is in a permanent building, it is acceptable to have the entire building or room where medication is kept locked when not under direct supervision of the health care staff. Those drugs needing refrigeration may be stored in a locked refrigerator, or in a locked container within the refrigerator.

The DNA for insulin applies ONLY to camps primarily serving campers with diabetes (more than 50% of enrolled campers are diabetic) where the camp educational philosophy of diabetes management specifies that camper control of insulin is part of the training program.

Compliance Demonstration: Visitor observation of drug storage; staff description of the procedures in use.

E-20

Is there an infirmary or health care shelter available to handle first aid and emergency cases which provides:

> **1. Protection from the elements,**
> **2. First aid and dispensary area,**
> **3. Available toilet(s),**
> **4. Available water for drinking and cleaning?**

And, except for day, trip or travel camps,

> **5. One bed per 50 campers and staff, and**
> **6. Isolation, quiet and privacy?**   **Yes No**

Director's Pre-Visit Evaluation
☐ Yes   ☐ No

Interpretation: "Available" toilets and water means they should be located in or next to the infirmary area so that ill or injured persons have easy access. Sufficient amounts of water for drinking and cleansing should be on hand.

Trip and travel camps may meet this standard by designating a specific area for use.

Compliance Demonstration: Visitor observation of the facility in use.

E-21

Has the camp administration implemented a procedure that requires continual supervision of campers in the infirmary or health care shelter?　　Yes　No

Interpretation: "Continual supervision" means that at least one staff member is always present when campers are in the infirmary for health or medical reasons. It may be the health care manager or a staff member who is following the directions of the manager.

Compliance Demonstration: Staff description of procedures in place.

90

SECTION F — AQUATICS

The Aquatic standards are to be applied to all aquatic program activities including, but not limited to, swimming, recreational boating, waterskiing, sailboarding, scuba diving, rafting, water park activities, inner tubing, and synchronized swimming.

When activities are conducted <u>near</u> bodies of water, lifeguarding precautions are often required. If it is possible that a person could be in the water (intentionally or unintentionally), and if rescue would require the skills of someone trained in more than elementary, non-swimming forms of rescue, the Aquatic standards apply.

Exceptions: 1) Aquatic activities occurring as part of a trip or travel program (see definitions) shall be scored by those standards (G section). 2) Use of commercial vessels operated by licensed personnel, such as ferries and fishing boats for hire, need not be scored under the aquatic standards.

These standards have been developed primarily for facilities and programs occurring on camp property or under camp staff supervision. **However,** standards F-21 through F-24 are scored for facilities and programs occurring off the camp property that are guarded, conducted and/or instructed by persons other than camp staff members. When camp administrators select such "public facilities" for use in camp program, the requirements established in standards F-1 through F-20 should be considered even if those standards are not scored.

DEFINITIONS

Aquatic activity: Any activity, whether recreational or instructional, occurring in, on, or near water.

Aquatic area: The physical site of a specific aquatic activity. The aquatic area for swimming may be a pool, a lake, the ocean front, or other body of water. On a lake, there may be several aquatic areas, such as one for swimming, another for boating, and another for waterskiing.

Certification as used in these standards denotes that the individual holds the appropriate level of certification, and that such certification is current (it has not expired).

Equivalent certification allows for certifications from other countries and/or other nationally recognized organizations. A chart of certifications from other countries is included in the Appendix (page 224). If the certification is not listed on that chart, directors should contact the Standards Department at the national office of ACA or the placement organization that secured the individual, for further information.

Lifeguard or **guard:** A staff member with the required certification to provide lifesaving and rescue skills.

Lookout: Sometimes called "watcher" or "observer," may be any non-certified staff member assigned by and under the direct supervision of certified aquatic personnel, used in addition to those certified persons.

Staffed public facility: A facility not on the campsite, such as a public pool or water park; or a service providing equipment and access to an aquatic site, such as a whitewater guiding company on the river. Persons other than camp staff are responsible for the site and for supervision of the activity.

> Score standards F-1 to F-20 for
> all aquatic activities **EXCEPT**
> those occurring at <u>staffed</u> public facilities.
>
> Camps that **ONLY** use staffed public facilities
> should DNA F-1 through F-20 and
> proceed to standards F-21 through 24.

F-1

Is the aquatic facility, staff, and program operation of each aquatic area supervised by a staff member who meets the following qualifications:

    A. Certification — Holds or has evidence of having held one of the following certifications:
        1. Lifeguard Training or Water Safety Instructor from the American Red Cross, or
        2. Aquatic Instructor, BSA, or
        3. YMCA Progressive Swimming Instructor, or
        4. Equivalent certification?   **Yes No**

    B. Experience — **Has at least six weeks previous experience in a management or supervisory position at a similar aquatic area?**
                                                Yes No

    C. Age — **Is at least 21 years old?**   **Yes No**

Interpretation: While it is desirable that a person have current certification, it is more important that a qualified, experienced individual be designated to oversee and administer aquatics programs. Certification alone does not indicate that an individual has administrative experience in the broader aspects of aquatic management.

Separate aquatic activities in camp such as swimming and boating may have separate staff persons serving in this function, or one person may be supervising all aquatic areas.

Compliance Demonstration: Visitor observation of certification card(s); director/staff description of qualifications.

*F-2 Part A MANDATORY

DNA if no swimming activities occur. (<u>Does</u> apply to activities such as diving, surfing, snorkeling, skin diving, and water slides, as well as swimming.)

Is there a policy in practice that each <u>swimming activity</u> be guarded by a staff member who is:

*A. Certified — Holds one of the following:
1. **American Red Cross Lifeguard Training or Advanced Lifesaving, or**
2. **YMCA Lifeguard, or**
3. **Lifeguard BSA, or**
4. **Royal Lifesaving Bronze Medallion, or**
5. **Equivalent certification?**   Yes   No

B. Skilled — Has demonstrated skill in rescue and emergency procedures specific to the aquatic area and activities guarded?   Yes   No

C. Trained and supervised to:
1. **Enforce established safety regulations,**
2. **Provide necessary instruction, and**
3. **Identify and manage environmental and other hazards related to the activity?**   Yes   No

Interpretation: This standard applies to all scheduled activities, whether instructional or recreational. Staff use of aquatic facilities during their free time is covered in standard F-11. Scuba activities are scored in standard F-15.

In part A, American Red Cross Basic Lifeguarding is an acceptable certification for guarding in pools or other contained swimming areas not affected by tides, currents, waves, and the like.

"Demonstrated skill" in part B refers to the ability to execute the skills represented by certification, in the location (pool, ocean, river, etc.) and specific to the aquatic activity guarded. These skills must be verified by the camp aquatics supervisor.

In part C-3, other hazards may include equipment hazards such as chlorine leaks, and hazards associated with the physical condition of participants (endurance, tiredness and cold, etc.). "Management" of hazards may include involving other staff (as in repairs to equipment).

Compliance Demonstration: Visitor observation of certification cards; director/staff description of training and supervision; visitor observation of randomly selected swimming activities.

*F-3 Part A MANDATORY

DNA if no aquatic activities other than swimming occur. (Does apply to activities such as canoeing, sailing, rowing, waterskiing, rafting, tubing, boardsailing, etc.)

At each aquatic activity <u>other than swimming</u> is there a policy in practice that a staff member be on duty who is:

> ***A. Certified — Holds one of the following:**
> > **1. American Red Cross Lifeguard Training, Advanced Lifesaving, or Emergency Water Safety, or**
> > **2. YMCA Lifeguard, or**
> > **3. Lifeguard BSA, or**
> > **4. Royal Lifesaving Bronze Medallion, or**
> > **5. Instructor rating in the appropriate craft, or**
> > **6. Equivalent certification?** Yes No
>
> **B. Skilled — Has demonstrated skill in rescue and emergency procedures specific to the aquatic area and activities?** Yes No
>
> **C. Trained and supervised to:**
> > **1. Enforce established safety regulations,**
> > **2. Provide necessary instruction, and**
> > **3. Identify and manage environmental and other hazards related to the activity?** Yes No

Interpretation: This standard applies to all scheduled activities. Staff use of aquatic facilities during their free time is covered in standard F-11.

"On duty" means physically present, continuously observing the activity and ready to quickly assist and perform rescues appropriate to training received.

See interpretation to F-2 for explanations of demonstrated skill and managing hazards.

Compliance Demonstration: Visitor observation of certification cards; director/staff description of training and supervision; visitor observation of randomly selected aquatic activities other than swimming.

Director's Pre-Visit Evaluation

☐ DNA
A. ☐ Yes ☐ No
B. ☐ Yes ☐ No
C. ☐ Yes ☐ No

F-4

Are there procedures in practice for both swimming and non-swimming activities which require that:

> **A. All lifeguards and lookouts be attentive to their responsibilities at all times and be located in positions from which they can observe and readily assist participants?** Yes No
>
> **B. The number of lifeguards and lookouts on duty for participants meets or exceeds ratios that have been established in writing?** Yes No

Interpretation: Lifeguards and/or lookouts (see definition) need to be readily available: in guard chairs, on docks, or beaches, or in boats, depending on the activity and the area.

Director's Pre-Visit Evaluation

A. ☐ Yes ☐ No
B. ☐ Yes ☐ No

Ratios for each activity should be established in accordance with the type of activity, the area, and the characteristics of the participants. See the Appendix (page 225) for factors to consider.

Compliance Demonstration: Visitor observation of written ratios and of randomly selected aquatic activities.

*F-5 Part B MANDATORY

Is there a policy in practice requiring that a staff member be present and accessible at each separate aquatic location or facility (pool, lake, river, etc.) who holds the following current certification(s):

    A. American Red Cross Standard First Aid or the equivalent?   Yes No

    *B. Cardiopulmonary Resuscitation for the age level served from the American Red Cross, the American Heart Association, or the equivalent?   Yes No

Interpretation: The intent is to have certified staff members available at locations for camper aquatic activities. Certification requirements for staff use of aquatics facilities are included in the policies required for F-11.

In part B, CPR certification is available for infants (0-1 yr), children (1-8 yrs), and adults (8 yrs and over). If young children are served, Child CPR is the appropriate certification level.

Even though some first aid and lifeguarding certifications require CPR as a prerequisite, all certification dates must be verified for currency. CPR must be renewed every year.

For non-medical religious camps, a person meeting the qualifications specified in writing by the religious program to meet emergency situations must be present and accessible.

Compliance Demonstration: Visitor observation of certification cards.

F-6

Are safety regulations established in writing for all aquatic activities and are procedures in practice to orient aquatics participants to those safety regulations?   Yes No

Interpretation: Regulations should be specific to the aquatic area and activity. This includes such things as pool rules, boating regulations, navigation rules, diving restrictions, safety signals or commands, behavior rules, required PFD use, non-swimmer restrictions, etc.

Compliance Demonstration: Visitor observation of written safety regulations; director/staff description of orientation.

F-7

Are written emergency and accident procedures that deal specifically with near-drownings and other aquatic accidents established for all aquatic areas in camp and rehearsed periodically by lifeguards, aquatic instructors and lookouts? Yes No

Interpretation: Procedures and rehearsals should be specific to each aquatic area in camp.

Compliance Demonstration: Visitor observation of written procedures; director/staff description of rehearsals and procedures.

F-8

DNA if lookouts are not used.

Are procedures being implemented that require each lookout to demonstrate elementary forms of non-swimming rescue and be oriented to their responsibilities? Yes No

Interpretation: See Aquatics Introduction for definition of lookout.

Orientation for lookouts should include procedures for enforcement of safety regulations, their role and responsibility in assisting with accident and emergency procedures, and expectations for routine aquatics supervision.

Compliance Demonstration: Staff/director description of procedures used.

F-9

Is there a policy in practice which requires that all persons, prior to participating in swimming and non-swimming aquatic activities, be:
  1. **Evaluated and classified as to swimming ability, and**
  2. **Assigned to areas, equipment, facilities, and activities commensurate with their abilities?** Yes No

This standard applies to campers and staff in both instructional and recreational activities in swimming, boating, etc.

A swim test is not necessarily implied for all activities. Campers may be interviewed and placed in appropriate activities and/or areas until actual skills are demonstrated.

Even if assignment to the activity presumes beginner or non-skilled level for everyone, individuals should still be evaluated to identify any fears or conditions that could affect their safety.

Compliance Demonstration: Staff description of evaluation and assignment procedures.

F-10

Are there safety systems utilized by campers and staff at all aquatic activities that enable lifeguards and lookouts to quickly account for all participants?

Yes   No

Interpretation: The "buddy system" is a common example of a safety system for swimmers. It is not the only safe system, and others may be employed to meet this standard. Tag boards and equipment check out systems may be more appropriate for boating or other aquatic activities.

Compliance Demonstration: Visitor observation of randomly selected aquatic activities; staff description of the system(s) in use.

*F-11 Parts A and B MANDATORY

Is there a written policy in practice which establishes procedures for <u>staff</u> use of aquatic facilities that specifies:

DNA A if no swimming facility available.

*A. <u>For swimming</u> — Certified guards (as in F-2) are present at all times, and procedures specify when guards or lookouts must be out of the water?

Yes   No

DNA B if no facilities available for aquatic activities other than swimming.

*B. <u>For activities other than swimming</u> — Qualifications for use, safety regulations, and times when facilities and equipment may be used by staff; and if certified personnel are not present, a checkout system is utilized?

Yes   No

Interpretation: This standard applies to all aquatic area use by staff such as swimming, boating, skiing, etc. Camp policy may state <u>no</u> staff use during times when regular aquatic activities and guards are not scheduled.

Factors such as age, type of area or facility, size of group, time of day, and regular aquatic schedule should be considered.

This standard applies <u>only</u> to staff members and the requirements of part B are <u>in addition</u> to the standard requiring the wearing of PFDs by all persons in small craft.

The purpose of the checkout system in part B is to assure that someone in camp is aware that staff are utilizing watercraft.

Compliance Demonstration: Visitor observation of written policy; staff description of procedures.

F-12

DNA if natural bodies of water are not used for aquatic activities in camp.

If a natural body of water is used for aquatic activities, are there procedures in practice that require:

A. The following conditions be met:

1. Methods for controlling camper access are in practice,

2. Known hazards are eliminated or activities near them are controlled,

3. Facility equipment is regularly checked and maintained, and

4. Separate areas are designated for aquatic activities? **Yes No**

B. Rescue equipment be readily available and in good repair? **Yes No**

Interpretation: Controlling camper access does not necessarily imply physical barriers, but may also include methods such as education, posting regulations, etc.

Hazards such as drop-offs, currents, and submerged objects should be eliminated when possible or clearly designated with warnings.

Facility equipment includes things such as docks, ladders, secured rafts, diving boards, etc. A system for safety checks and regular maintenance should be in place.

Areas for separate activities (boardsailing, swimming, waterskiing, canoeing, fishing, etc.) may be designated by physical markers or by education, regulations, and/or scheduling.

Swimming areas should have a clearly defined shallow area for non-swimmers and defined diving area(s). Swimming areas for non-swimmers may be defined by ropes, buoys, booms, or deck markings; diving areas may be marked or posted, or designated in regulations.

In part B, "rescue equipment" should include items such as backboards, ring buoys, reaching devices, or designated rescue boats, as appropriate to the activity.

Compliance Demonstration: Visitor observation of aquatic areas; staff description of procedures in use.

F-13

DNA if persons in wheelchairs are not near bodies of water (natural or constructed).

Is there a procedure in practice requiring that seatbelts or ties be removed from persons who are in wheelchairs while in watercraft or near bodies of water?

Yes No

Interpretation: "Near bodies of water" includes all locations from which there is a possibility of the chair rolling into the water.

Compliance Demonstration: Visitor observation of activities when possible; staff description of procedure utilized with persons in wheelchairs.

> If **NO SWIMMING** activities occur,
> **DNA** F-14 through F-16
> and proceed to F-17

F-14

DNA if <u>instructional</u> activities are not conducted in swimming.

Are procedures being implemented that require the following conditions be met at all <u>instructional</u> activities in <u>swimming</u>:

A. **A staff person with current WSI from the American Red Cross, YMCA Progressive Swimming Instructor, Aquatic Instructor BSA, or equivalent certification is present?** **Yes No**

B. **If the certified instructor is in the water with participants, a lookout is out of the water continuously watching over the activity?** **Yes No**

DNA C if non-certified instructional assistants are not used.

C. **If non-certified instructional assistants are used, they function under the direct on-site supervision of a certified instructor, follow the specific directions of that instructor, and possess rescue skills appropriate to the activity?** **Yes No**

Interpretation: A WSI-certified person does not necessarily have Lifeguard certification. If not, an additional certified lifeguard is necessary to maintain compliance with mandatory standard *F-2.

"Non-certified instructional assistants" are teaching assistants without current certification who are under the immediate supervision and direction of the certified instructor.

Compliance Demonstration: Visitor observation of certification cards; staff description of procedures; visitor observation of swimming lessons when possible.

Director's Pre-Visit Evaluation
☐ DNA
A. ☐ Yes ☐ No
B. ☐ Yes ☐ No
C. ☐ Yes ☐ No ☐ DNA

*F-15 MANDATORY

DNA if scuba diving does not occur.

Do procedures require that a staff person with current Scuba Instructor rating from the Professional Association of Diving Instructors (PADI), National Association of Underwater Instructors (NAUI), Scuba Schools International (SSI), YMCA, or equivalent certification be present whenever scuba diving occurs? **Yes No**

Compliance Demonstration: Visitor observation of certification card(s).

Director's Pre-Visit Evaluation
☐ Yes ☐ No ☐ DNA

F-16

DNA if a swimming pool is not used.

If a swimming pool is used, are there procedures in practice that require:

  A. The following conditions be met:

    1. Access is controlled by a fence or other physical barrier,

    2. Water depths are clearly marked,

    3. Routine maintenance procedures appear to be in practice to address sanitation and safety concerns, and

    4. Pool rules are posted in a visible location?   **Yes No**

  B. Rescue equipment be readily available and in good repair?   **Yes No**

Interpretation: "Sanitation and safety concerns" include such things as chemical storage, covered drains, non-skid deck, ladders and diving boards in good repair, clear water, and absence of dirt, debris and algae.

Pool rules may include items such as no glass in pool area, no running, no diving in shallow end, etc.

In part B, "rescue equipment" should include at least reaching devices and a backboard.

Compliance Demonstration: Visitor observation of pool area and equipment; staff description of maintenance and sanitation procedures.

```
┌─────────────────────────────────────────────────┐
│              WATERCRAFT ACTIVITIES                │
│   Watercraft activities include all use of small craft │
│   (canoeing, sailing, rowing, kayaking, rafting,  │
│   motorboating, etc.) as well as boardsailing, tubing, water │
│   skiing, etc.                                    │
│                                                   │
│            If NO watercraft activities occur,     │
│               DNA F-17 through F-20 and           │
│                   proceed to F-21                 │
└─────────────────────────────────────────────────┘
```

DEFINITIONS

Small craft: Recreational boats up to 26 feet in length, such as canoes, kayaks, sailboats, rowboats, ski boats, rafts, etc.

Boardsailing: Also called sailboarding, windsurfing; operating a non-motorized, one-person sailing craft.

F-17

Is the camp implementing procedures which require that a staff person with the following qualifications be on duty at these activities:

DNA A if small craft activities do not occur.

A. **Small craft activities (canoeing, sailing, rowing, rafting, etc.) — Current boating instructor rating in the appropriate craft from the American Red Cross or other equivalent certification; or documented experience indicating knowledge and skill in teaching and/or supervision specific to the boating activities conducted?** Yes No

DNA B if aquatic activities other than swimming, scuba diving and small craft activities do not occur.

B. **Other aquatics activities such as waterskiing, boardsailing, etc. — Current instructor rating from nationally recognized certifying body; or documented experience indicating specific knowledge and skill in teaching the activity?** Yes No

```
┌──────────────────────────┐
│   Director's Pre-Visit   │
│        Evaluation        │
│  A. ☐ Yes  ☐ No  ☐ DNA   │
│  B. ☐ Yes  ☐ No  ☐ DNA   │
└──────────────────────────┘
```

Interpretation: The intent of this standard is to provide appropriate instructor-level supervision of these activities. If this person is not also qualified to guard the activity, camps may need a second individual to maintain compliance with mandatory standard *F-3.

This standard applies to both instructional and recreational activities. The level of skill and experience required will vary with the aquatic area and type of activity. Supervising rowing on a shallow pond does not require the same level of expertise as instructing waterskiing on a large lake.

Compliance Demonstration: Visitor observation of certification cards or other documentation of training and experience.

F-18

Are there procedures being implemented that require all campers and staff in watercraft to wear personal flotation devices (PFDs) that are safe for use?

Yes   No

Interpretation: Appropriate PFDs are to be worn by all campers and staff in all types of small craft such as canoes, rowboats, sailboats, and on sailboards, water skis, and so forth.

"Safe for use" means PFDs are:
1. U.S. Coast Guard approved,
2. Proper type, size and fit for each user,
3. Buoyant, as tested annually, sufficient to support designated weight, and
4. Safety checked immediately prior to use.

Every PFD used must be in serviceable condition (clasps, zippers, etc. working) and appropriate for the type of water and the activity. See Appendix (page 226) for a description of PFD types and uses.

PFDs must be worn on all craft under 26 feet in length. For boats over 26 feet in length, regulations that are applicable to the craft as determined by regulating organizations governing the body of water in use should be followed.

Compliance Demonstration: Visitor observation of PFD use in randomly selected watercraft activities; director/staff description of procedures and implementation.

F-19

Do procedures require that all persons using watercraft be provided the following training prior to use:
1. **Boarding and debarking, trimming, and movement on the craft,**
2. **The use of PFDs, and**
3. **Self-rescue in case of capsize or swamping?**   **Yes   No**

Interpretation: The use of PFDs may include floating in PFDs to test fit and acquaint participants with buoyancy supplied, if participants' physical condition and/or water conditions permit.

Training in self-rescue may include an actual "tip test" for appropriate craft, where conditions permit.

Compliance Demonstration: Visitor observation of randomly selected watercraft activities when possible; director/staff description of training procedures.

F-20

Are there procedures in practice for safety checks and regular maintenance for each of the following as applicable:
1. **Motorized watercraft, and**
2. **Non-motorized craft such as sailboards, canoes, rafts, etc?**

Yes   No

Interpretation: Items used in the operation of the craft such as paddles, motors, tow-ropes, sails, etc. are to be included in the procedures for safety checks and maintenance.

Compliance Demonstration: Visitor observation of watercraft; director/staff description of procedures.

STAFFED PUBLIC FACILITIES

Score standards F-21 through F-24 on
ANY staffed public facilities used by the camp.

Score standards F-21 through F-24 on
ANY staffed public facilities used by the camp.

If **ONLY** F-21 through F-24 are scored,
a camp may miss **no more than one** scoreable
(non-mandatory) item.

If **NO** staffed public facilities or services
are used for swimming or non-swimming
aquatics activities,
DNA F-21 through F-24 and
proceed to Section G — Trip/Travel.

*F-21 Parts A, B, and C MANDATORY

Is there a written policy in practice requiring that persons with the following qualifications be on duty at all aquatic activities as specified:

DNA A if no swimming activities occur.

* **A. Swimming activities — Holds one of the following:**
    1. **American Red Cross Lifeguard Training or Advanced Lifesaving, or**
    2. **YMCA Lifeguard, or**
    3. **Lifeguard BSA, or**
    4. **Royal Lifesaving Bronze Medallion, or**
    5. **Equivalent certification?**   Yes   No

DNA B if no other-than-swimming activities occur.

* **B. Other than swimming activities — Holds any one of the certifications listed in Part A, or American Red Cross Emergency Water Safety, or Instructor rating in the appropriate craft?**   Yes   No

* **C. Cardiopulmonary Resuscitation (CPR) certification?**   Yes   No

Interpretation: This standard applies to all swimming and boating activities, whether instructional or recreational.

If persons other than camp staff are on duty at the activity, the camp administrator must have assurances that the qualifications required by this standard are met. Such assurances may be in a letter from the facility manager, advertised personnel requirements for guard or guide positions, or local laws or regulations.

Compliance Demonstration: Visitor observation of written policy; director verification of guard/supervisor qualifications.

F-22

Is there a policy in practice requiring that all persons, prior to participating in swimming and non-swimming aquatic activities, be:
  1. **Evaluated and classified as to swimming ability, and**
  2. **Assigned to areas, equipment, facilities, and activities commensurate with their abilities?**   **Yes   No**

Interpretation: Applies to both instructional and recreational activities in swimming and boating.

A swim test is not necessarily implied for all activities. Campers may be interviewed and placed in appropriate activities and/or areas until actual skills are demonstrated.

Even if assignment to the activity presumes beginner or non-skilled level for everyone, individuals should still be evaluated to identify any fears or conditions that could affect their safety.

Compliance Demonstration: Staff description of evaluation and assignment procedures.

F-23

Is there a procedure being implemented which requires that participants in all aquatic activities be oriented to safety regulations and emergency procedures?   **Yes   No**

Interpretation: Regulations and procedures should be specific to the aquatic area and activity and may be a combination of rules and procedures from the public facility and those of the camp.

Compliance Demonstration: Director/staff description of orientation provided.

F-24

Are there procedures being implemented which require that personal flotation devices (PFDs) that are safe for use be worn by all persons in watercraft activities? **Yes No**

Interpretation: PFDs are to be worn by all campers and staff in all types of small craft such as canoes, rowboats, and sailboats, and on sailboards, water skis, etc.

"Safe for use" means that PFDs are:

1. Coast Guard approved,
2. Of proper type, size and fit for each user,
3. Sufficiently buoyant to support designated weight,
4. And in serviceable condition (clasps, zippers, etc. working).

PFDs must be appropriate for the type of water and the activity. See Appendix (page 226) for a description of PFD types and uses.

PFDs must be worn on all craft under 26 feet in length. For boats over 26 feet in length, regulations that are applicable to the craft as determined by regulating organizations governing the body of water in use should be followed.

Compliance Demonstration: Director/staff description of procedures for PFD usage.

Accreditation

SECTION G — TRIP and TRAVEL

The Trip & Travel standards apply to any activity sponsored by the camp that meets one or more of the following definitions:

TRIPPING or TRIP CAMPING: A program in which a group of individuals move under their own power or by individually guided vehicle or animal (e.g. bicycle, horse, boat) and travel from one campsite to another for three nights or more (as differentiated from overnight camping).

TRIP CAMP: A camp whose area of program specialization is tripping.

TRAVEL CAMPING: A program in which a group uses motorized transportation to move from one site to another for three nights or more, for experiences in different environments. Motorized transportation is normally a van, bus, or car, though it may also be a plane, boat, train, or a combination of those vehicles.

TRAVEL CAMP: A camp whose singular specialty is travel camping. While many different activities occur in travel camps, the entire program is without a base location, and program activities are based upon environments encountered as the group moves from location to location.

Activities not meeting any of the above definitions such as field trips out of camp or overnights of two nights or less (whether on or off camp property) are scored in the Program standards (Section D, see page 64).

Standards covering aquatic activities have been included in this section; therefore, the aquatic standards (Section F, page 91) need not be applied to tripping or travel camping programs. (They are, of course, applicable to other parts of camp program that do not meet the Trip or Travel Camping definitions.)

If, while tripping or traveling, camps are also participating in other activities such as horseback riding or bicycling, those appropriate sections of the standards would also be scored.

Activities scored in this section may also involve transportation or intermingling of campers with the public. Requirements of those standards apply to the activities scored in this section and should be considered by directors when planning such activities.

G-1

<table>
<tr><td>Director's Pre-Visit
Evaluation</td></tr>
<tr><td>A. ☐ Yes ☐ No</td></tr>
<tr><td>B. ☐ Yes ☐ No</td></tr>
</table>

Is there a policy in practice that there be a staff leader with each trip and/or travel group who:

A. **Possesses documented:**

1. **Skills relevant to the trip or travel activities,**
2. **Endorsements or observations of good judgment and ability to assume leadership independently,**
3. **Experience in appropriately handling camper behavior, and**
4. **Experience on trips of similar size, duration, locale, mode of travel, and program focus?**   Yes   No

B. **Is at least 21 years of age?**   Yes   No

Interpretation: The intent is that one designated leader on each trip possess all of the listed qualifications.

"Documented" evidence of qualifications may include evaluations of the staff member from previous trips, letters of reference referring to the requirements of the standard, evaluations from those who trained the staff member, or staff performance reviews from previous summers.

Compliance Demonstration: Director explanation of leader qualifications; visitor observation of documentation.

G-2

Is there a policy in practice that, accompanying each trip, there is:

1. **At least one staff member in addition to the leader, OR**
   If a group has a total of 6 or fewer participants who are all at least 14 years of age and have been selected and prepared to share leadership responsibilities and meet emergency situations — a minimum of one qualified trip/travel leader, and
2. **Sufficient staff to meet or exceed camper/staff ratios that have been established in writing?**　　　　　　　　　　　**Yes　No**

Director's Pre-Visit Evaluation
☐ Yes ☐ No

Interpretation: A "qualified" trip/travel leader is one who meets the qualifications of G-1.

Camper/staff ratios should be no less than the minimums identified in C-4, and should be based on the activity, the area, and the characteristics and skills of the participants.

Compliance Demonstration: Director/staff description of policy's implementation; visitor observation of written ratios.

G-3

Are trip and travel staff members trained to assess safety concerns, enforce safety regulations, and handle emergency situations related to:

1. **Type of activities,**
2. **Characteristics of participants, and**
3. **Geography and climate?**　　　　　　　　　　**Yes　No**

Director's Pre-Visit Evaluation
☐ Yes ☐ No

Interpretation: "Training" may come from experience in leading similar programs, sessions conducted during staff orientation, or leadership development programs designed to train or certify trip or travel leaders.

Compliance Demonstration: Director/staff description of training provided.

*G-4 MANDATORY

Is there a policy in practice that at least one staff person with each trip or travel group is currently certified in American Red Cross Standard First Aid or the equivalent? Yes No

Interpretation: American Red Cross Standard First Aid includes CPR training. If "equivalent" first aid certification is used to meet this standard, documentation of CPR training must also be included to be in compliance with the intent of the standard.

Non-medical religious camps meet this standard by providing a person who meets the qualifications established in writing by the religious organization to meet emergency situations.

Compliance Demonstration: Visitor observation of first aid certification cards; director/staff explanation of the policy's implementation.

G-5

For each type of trip/travel program, do written procedures specify:

A. **Eligibility requirements for participation?** Yes No

B. **A process to inform campers and their parents of the nature of the activity, the degree of difficulty or physical challenge required by that activity, and the camper's responsibility for maintaining a level of fitness necessary to participate in the activity?** Yes No

C. **Procedures to follow if a participant cannot continue with the trip or travel program?** Yes No

Interpretation: Eligibility requirements should take into account age, experience, and type of participants as well as length of trip, location and skill level required.

The concern of part B is that camps fully explain the activities so that campers and parents know the nature and demands of the activity and understand the expectation that campers cannot put themselves purposely at risk by not following safety rules, avoiding food or sleep, taking drugs that are not prescribed for them, etc.

In part C, procedures for one who "cannot continue" may include situations such as illness, injury, family emergency, or behavioral problems.

Compliance Demonstration: Visitor observation of written procedures; director explanation of process used to inform campers/parents.

*G-6 Part B MANDATORY

Are all campers and staff required to participate in pre-trip orientation that includes at least:

    A. General information on:
        1. Written safety regulations and emergency procedures,
        2. First aid procedures,
        3. Health and sanitation practices, and
        4. Practices to protect the environment?   **Yes No**

    *B. Information and training on how and where to obtain medical and/or emergency assistance on the trip?   **Yes No**

Director's Pre-Visit Evaluation
A. ☐ Yes ☐ No
B. ☐ Yes ☐ No

Interpretation: The training for part B could include communication plans, pre-planned contact points, identification of types of emergency assistance available in the trip area, and methods for obtaining assistance. The exact locations of assistance may be carried in various forms including maps which are marked with locations, addresses, and/or phone numbers of known emergency medical facilities, and locations where phone access is possible.

Compliance verification: Visitor observation of written regulations and procedures; staff description of orientation, information and training provided.

G-7

DNA for non-medical religious camps.

In order to identify observable evidence of illness, injury or communicable disease, does the camp require screening of each camper and staff member within 18 hours of departure and return of each trip or travel experience?
    Yes No

Director's Pre-Visit Evaluation
☐ Yes   ☐ No   ☐ DNA

Interpretation: The purpose of screening is to:
    a. Identify any observable evidence of illness or communicable disease,
    b. Identify any personal medications that must be included in the trip health supplies, and/or
    c. Review the handling of current health concerns.

Compliance Demonstration: Director/staff description of process/procedure.

G-8

Do procedures require that the trip and/or travel leader possess the following emergency information for each member of the group:
    1. Copies of health histories, and
    2. Signed permission from parents or guardians of each minor to seek medical treatment or a signed religious waiver?   **Yes No**

Director's Pre-Visit Evaluation
☐ Yes   ☐ No

Interpretation: See the Appendix (page 221) for a sample religious waiver.

Compliance Demonstration: Director/staff description of procedures.

G-9

Do procedures require that the trip or travel group carry documents that fully identify the group, its leadership, insurance coverage, and home base or contact?   Yes No

Compliance Demonstration: Director/staff description of procedures.

G-10

Do procedures require that a written itinerary be filed with the base camp, or in the absence of a base camp, with a responsible individual; and with jurisdictional authorities (when required)?   Yes No

Compliance Demonstration: Director/staff description of procedures.

*G-11 Part D MANDATORY

Are staff and campers trained in written procedures that require:

DNA A if all drinking water is obtained from a public water supply.

A. **All drinking water be obtained from tested or approved water supplies and/or purified by one or more of the following methods: boiling, filtering, and/or chemical treatment?**   Yes No

DNA B if disposable utensils are used exclusively or if food utensils are not carried by the group.

B. **Food utensils be cleaned and sanitized after each use and protected from contamination between use?**   Yes No

DNA C if food is not stored or prepared by the group.

C. **Food be prepared and stored under safe and sanitary conditions with particular care given to maintaining potentially hazardous foods at proper temperature?**   Yes No

DNA D if stoves or flammable liquids are not used.

*D. **All persons using camp stoves or flammable liquids be instructed in their proper use and care, and be supervised until competency is demonstrated?**   Yes No

Interpretation: It is the intent of part A that water be safe for drinking. The primary concern is for questionable water supplies, not those which have been tested by public authorities for residential or public use such as those from national park faucets or pumps. Water from natural bodies of water or springs should be treated if there is no assurance that the supply has been approved for human consumption.

It is the responsibility of the camp to identify the appropriate purification method based on advice from local officials able to identify possible contaminants for that area.

Food utensils include dishes, cups, eating utensils, and food preparation utensils not heated at least to boiling in the cooking process.

See the interpretation of standard A-26 for a definition of "potentially hazardous foods."

Compliance Demonstration: Visitor observation of written procedures; camper/staff description of procedures.

G-12

DNA if liquids not fit for human consumption are not carried on the trip.

Are procedures in practice which require that water bottles be clearly distinguishable by shape, color, or style from bottles containing liquids not fit for human consumption, and that each container of non-consumable liquids be clearly marked as to its contents? **Yes No**

Director's Pre-Visit Evaluation
☐ Yes   ☐ No   ☐ DNA

Interpretation: The intent of this standard is to prevent accidental consumption of liquids in bottles containing fuel, soaps, disinfectants, etc.

Compliance Demonstration: Staff/camper description of procedures in use.

G-13

Is there a written procedure in practice specifying safety checks and regular maintenance of equipment utilized on trips? **Yes No**

Director's Pre-Visit Evaluation
☐ Yes   ☐ No

Interpretation: Equipment includes items such as boats, paddles, axes, tents, stoves, backpacks, saddles, PFD's, etc. Equipment should be checked prior to and during the trip.

Compliance Demonstration: Visitor observation of written procedures; staff description of safety checks and equipment maintenance.

G-14

Are there procedures in practice for conducting each trip with minimal environmental impact that include the following as applicable:

1. **Group size limits — based upon the environmental carrying capacity of the site(s) and do not exceed limits set by other jurisdictional authorities?**
2. **Refuse disposal — requiring all refuse be carried out, be biodegradable or be disposed of in accordance with regulations governing each area?**
3. **Soap — only biodegradable and non-detergent soap is used at campsites?**
4. **Human waste disposal sites — located a minimum of 100 feet from any water supply, trail, or campsite?**
5. **Human waste — disposed of in a manner which accelerates decomposition, is an environmentally sound practice, and is not offensive to other campers?** **Yes   No**

Interpretation: See Appendix (page 227) for a list of recommended, environmentally-sound practices.

Compliance Demonstration: Staff description of procedures and implementation.

IF **no AQUATIC ACTIVITIES** occur on the trip
DNA G-15 through G-19
and proceed to G-20.

*G-15 MANDATORY

Is there a policy in practice requiring that all aquatic activities be guarded/supervised by:

1. **For aquatic trips, where the primary activity or mode of travel is in/on the water, a staff member who:**
   a. **Is certified in American Red Cross Lifeguard Training, Advanced Lifesaving, Emergency Water Safety, Instructor rating in the appropriate craft, or the equivalent, and/or**
   b. **Has documented skills and training in water rescue and emergency procedures specific to the location and the activity; and/or**
2. **For travel or backpacking trips, where aquatic activity is incidental, a staff member who is certified in American Red Cross Lifeguard Training, Advanced Lifesaving, Emergency Water Safety, or the equivalent?** **Yes   No**

Interpretation: "Staff member," for the purpose of this standard, refers to a camp staff member or a staff person of the outfitter or aquatic organization/facility providing the instruction and/or supervision of the activity.

The intent of this standard is to require an appropriate level of supervision and skill, depending on the activity. In part #1, documented skills must specifically address water rescue skills appropriate for the activity, the craft, and the type of aquatic area in use (e.g. white-water rafting, deep-lake canoeing, open-water sailing, etc.).

In part #2, because the primary skills required of non-aquatic trip staff members are not specific to aquatic safety and rescue, certification, as listed, is required as a minimum to supervise activities such as occasional swimming or boating.

If the aquatic activity is staffed by persons other than camp staff, the director or trip/travel leader must have assurances that the qualifications required by this standard are met.

Compliance Demonstration: Visitor observation of certification card(s) or other written documentation; director/staff description of policy's implementation.

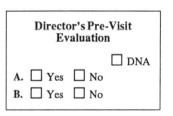

G-16

Do procedures require that each aquatic activity be conducted in accordance with written procedures and guard/participant ratios that have been developed according to the type of activity, the area, and the characteristics of the participants? **Yes No**

Director's Pre-Visit Evaluation
☐ Yes   ☐ No

Interpretation: "Procedures" may include suggested locations of guards/staff, required use of PFD's, safety regulations specific to the type of activity, and emergency procedures.

"Characteristics of the participants" includes not only skill level and experience in the specific aquatic activity but also the age and maturity of participants.

Compliance Demonstration: Visitor observation of written procedures and ratios; staff description of procedures being followed.

G-17

DNA if natural bodies of water are not used for aquatic activities.

Do procedures require that whenever a natural body of water is used for aquatic activities, the following conditions are met:

A. Rescue equipment in working condition is readily available?

Yes No

Director's Pre-Visit Evaluation
☐ DNA
A. ☐ Yes   ☐ No
B. ☐ Yes   ☐ No

B. Staff and campers are trained to identify hazardous water conditions and to implement appropriate actions? **Yes No**

Interpretation: Rescue equipment such as reaching or throwing devices should be appropriate to the activity, even on trips not oriented to water activities.

Hazardous water conditions may include such things as rapids, high waves, submerged objects, rip tides, or strong currents.

Compliance Demonstration: Staff description of procedures and training.

G-18

Director's Pre-Visit Evaluation
☐ Yes ☐ No ☐ DNA

DNA if watercraft activities do not occur.

Do procedures require that personal flotation devices (PFD's) that are safe for use be worn by all persons in watercraft activities? **Yes No**

Interpretation: When contracted services are responsible to provide all equipment, the camp should assure that PFD's are provided for campers and staff and used in accordance with the requirements of this standard.

"Safe for use" means PFD's are:

1. U.S. Coast Guard approved,
2. Of proper type, size and fit for each user,
3. Sufficiently buoyant to support designated weight, and
4. Safety checked immediately prior to use.

See the Appendix (page 226) for a description of Coast Guard approved PFDs.

PFDs must be worn on all craft under 26 feet in length. For boats over 26 feet in length, regulations that are applicable to the craft as determined by regulating organizations governing the body of water in use should be followed.

Compliance Demonstration: Staff description of procedures in use.

G-19

Director's Pre-Visit Evaluation
☐ DNA
A. ☐ Yes ☐ No
B. ☐ Yes ☐ No

DNA if small craft are not used.

Do procedures require that all persons using small craft be provided the following training in the appropriate craft prior to use:

A. Handling, trimming, loading, and movement on the craft? **Yes No**

B. Self-rescue in case of capsize or swamping situations? **Yes No**

Interpretation: Part B may include an actual "tip test" when conditions permit.

Compliance Demonstration: Staff description of procedures and training.

```
┌─────────────────────────────────────────┐
│              TRAVEL ONLY                  │
│         DNA G-20 and G-21 if              │
│         **Trip Camp or Tripping**         │
└─────────────────────────────────────────┘
```

G-20

DNA if commercial transportation is used.

Do procedures require that there be a minimum of one relief driver for each two vehicles?　　　　　　　　　　　　　　　　　　**Yes　No**

Compliance Demonstration: Staff description of procedures.

Director's Pre-Visit Evaluation		
☐ Yes	☐ No	☐ DNA

G-21

DNA if trips are 5 days or less in length.

Do the operating procedures require that there be at least one full intervening non-travel day between each four consecutive travel days?　　　　**Yes　No**

Compliance Demonstration: Staff description of procedures.

Director's Pre-Visit Evaluation		
☐ Yes	☐ No	☐ DNA

Accreditation

SECTION H — HORSEBACK RIDING

The Horseback Riding standards apply to all horseback riding activities including, but not limited to, English riding, western riding, trail riding, bareback riding, ring work, vaulting, and pony rides.

While the standards have been developed primarily for facilities and programs occurring on camp property and under camp staff supervision, there are some standards (H-14 through H-17) that are scored for "staffed public facilities" — facilities not on the campsite that are open to the public. Camp staff may accompany a group, but the staff of the facility is responsible for the site and for riding supervision and/or instruction. When such "public facilities" are used for camp program, administrators should consider the requirements established in standards H-1 through H-13 even if those standards are not scored.

> Score standards H-1 through H-13
> on **ALL** riding activities **EXCEPT** those
> occurring at staffed public facilities.
>
> This includes all riding activities occurring on
> camp property, or off camp property but under
> camp staff supervision.
>
> Camps that **ONLY** use staffed public facilities
> should DNA H-1 through H-13 and
> proceed to standards H-14 through 17.

H-1

Director's Pre-Visit Evaluation

☐ DNA

A. ☐ Yes ☐ No
B. ☐ Yes ☐ No
C. ☐ Yes ☐ No

DNA to pony rides.

Is there a staff member who oversees all horseback riding facilities, staff and program operations and who meets the following qualifications:

    A. **Certification — holds one of the following:**

        1. **Certification from an organization or riding school with instructor training, or**
        2. **Documented endorsements of previous successful experience in formal horseback riding instruction?**   **Yes No**

    B. **Experience — has at least six weeks previous experience in a management or supervisory position at a horseback riding facility?**

                                                 Yes No

    C. **Age — is at least 21 years of age?**   **Yes No**

Interpretation: "Pony rides" (see DNA) are activities in which the animal is led or controlled by a mechanical device or a trained individual other than the rider.

In part A, "instructor training" refers to courses that require skills and competency in riding and which focus on riding instruction techniques as well as stable management. See the Appendix (page 231) for a list of organizations that offer such training.

Documented experience may include letters of reference from former employers, students, or co-workers as well as brochures or advertisements announcing programs and listing the individual as instructor.

"Formal instruction" requires that the program for which the individual served as instructor was conducted as an established program in which students enrolled, followed a systematic course of training, and required demonstration of prescribed levels of knowledge and competency.

In part B, experience should include background in supervising a total operation in areas including instruction, stable management, care and feeding of horses, scheduling, staff supervision, and equipment care.

Compliance Demonstration: Visitor observation of certification card or other documented evidence; director/staff explanation of qualifications.

H-2

Are procedures being implemented which require that each riding activity be led by a staff member who is trained and supervised to:

	Director's Pre-Visit Evaluation

A. **Enforce established safety regulations?**   Yes No

B. **Work with types of groups participating in the activity and provide necessary instruction?**   Yes No

C. **Identify and manage environmental and other hazards related to the activity and the participants?**   Yes No

D. **Apply emergency procedures related to the activity and the participants?**   Yes No

Director's Pre-Visit Evaluation
- A. ☐ Yes ☐ No
- B. ☐ Yes ☐ No
- C. ☐ Yes ☐ No
- D. ☐ Yes ☐ No

Interpretation: This standard applies to all camper and staff activities, whether instructional or recreational.

"Types of groups" refers to age, size, ability levels or special needs of participants.

Hazards in part C may include such things as trail conditions, temperament of horses, and behavior of participants (fear, excitement, endurance, etc.)

Compliance Demonstration: Director/staff description of training and supervision practices; visitor observation of randomly selected riding activities.

H-3

Are procedures in practice that require a staff member currently certified in American Red Cross Standard First Aid or the equivalent be on duty at each horseback riding activity?   Yes No

Director's Pre-Visit Evaluation
☐ Yes ☐ No

Interpretation: "On duty" means readily available to render needed assistance.

Non-medical religious camps meet this standard by providing a person meeting the qualifications specified in writing by the religious program to meet emergency situations.

Compliance Demonstration: Visitor observation of certification card(s); director/staff explanation of procedure's implementation.

H-4

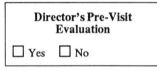

Are minimum ratios of horseback riding staff to campers established in writing and required to be in practice at each activity? Yes No

Interpretation: Ratios should be established in accordance with those recommended by authoritative sources and with the type of riding activity, the characteristics of participants, and the riding area.

The certified/experienced staff member who oversees the horseback riding program is in the best position to determine appropriate ratios for each type of activity.

Compliance Demonstration: Visitor observation of written ratios; director/staff explanation of implementation.

H-5

Director's Pre-Visit Evaluation
☐ Yes ☐ No

Are safety regulations established in writing and are procedures being implemented that require all persons be oriented to those regulations prior to participation? Yes No

Interpretation: Safety regulations may include such things as requirements for helmets and boots, procedures for approaching horses, facility access and use limits, trail procedures, etc.

Compliance Demonstration: Visitor observation of written safety regulations; staff description of orientation procedures used.

H-6

Director's Pre-Visit Evaluation
☐ Yes ☐ No

Are there written accident and emergency procedures that are specific to the horseback riding activities offered? Yes No

Interpretation: Procedures should be identified for accidents such as a fall from a horse or injury from a kick. They should also include steps for responding to emergencies such as a runaway horse or situations occurring on trails away from the central camp area where transportation of victims must be considered.

Compliance Demonstration: Visitor observation of written procedures.

H-7

Is there a system in practice to:
1. **Evaluate and classify participants' riding ability, and,**
2. **Assign them to horses, equipment, and activities commensurate with their ability?** Yes No

Interpretation: This standard applies to instructional and recreational riding activities for both campers and staff.

Evaluation does not necessarily imply a riding test. Participants may be interviewed and assigned to appropriate horses or activities until actual skill is demonstrated.

Even if assignments presume beginner or non-skilled level for everyone, individuals should still be evaluated to identify experience with the activity, comfort level, or fears that could affect their safety.

Compliance Demonstration: Staff description of procedures utilized.

H-8

Is there a policy in practice that requires the following safety apparel be worn by campers and camp staff:

DNA A for vaulting activities.

A. **Shoes or boots which provide protection from:**
   1. **Injury from being stepped on by horses, and,**
   2. **If stirrups are used, feet becoming wedged into the stirrup (when stirrups are not specifically designed to prevent this occurrence)?** Yes No

B. **Long trousers?** Yes No

C. **Protective head gear, constructed to minimize head injury in a fall, that fits the rider comfortably, does not obscure vision, and is secured by a strong chin strap?** Yes No

Interpretation: Shoes or boots that have firm, hard coverings offer protection far beyond tennis shoes or other soft-bodied shoes. A heel that prevents the shoe or boot from sliding too deeply into the stirrup can prevent the foot from becoming dangerously wedged.

This standard does not require the camp to use a particular kind of helmet. In consultation with authoritative sources, the camp administrator should determine the appropriate type of helmet based on the type and level of activity. Most horsemanship organizations (see Appendix, page 231) can supply lists of protective head gear that have undergone safety tests and have met minimum criteria for protection.

Compliance Demonstration: Visitor observation of horseback riding activity when possible; staff description of policy and procedures in practice.

H-9

Is staff trained to implement a daily safety check of riding equipment, and is equipment that is not in good repair removed from service?   **Yes   No**

Compliance Demonstration: Visitor observation of equipment in use at riding activities; staff description of training received and procedures in use.

H-10

Does the camp implement procedures that require horseback riding instructors to work with horses and classify them as to their suitability for various levels of riding skill before campers and staff use them?   **Yes   No**

Interpretation: Evaluating horses is especially important early in the season when they have not been ridden much. Horse disposition can change from year to year, or with the addition of new horses.

Compliance Demonstration: Staff description of classification procedures.

H-11

Is the staff trained to check daily the physical soundness of each horse, and remove unsound horses from the riding program?   **Yes   No**

Interpretation: A check for "physical soundness" includes checking for problems that may affect the performance or disposition of the horse, such as saddle sores, lameness, or a sore mouth.

Compliance Demonstration: Staff description of procedures and training.

H-12

Are procedures in practice to limit the maximum work day for a horse to:
1. **In the riding ring — no longer than 6 total hours made up of working sessions that are no longer than 3 continuous hours, and**
2. **On the trail — no longer than 8 total hours in working sessions that are no longer than 4 continuous hours?**   **Yes   No**

Interpretation: A "working session" is a period of continuous use without any lengthy break. In most circumstances, morning and afternoon riding periods would constitute separate working sessions.

Compliance Demonstration: Staff description of scheduling procedures.

H-13

Are stables, corrals, paddocks, and riding rings:

A. **Located away from living areas, with procedures in practice to control access?** Yes No

B. **Clean, free from accumulation of manure, and provided with a safe, clean, plentiful supply of water?** Yes No

Interpretation: "Away from" means that living areas (other than those for persons caring for horses) are located far enough from livestock to avoid increased flies, insects, undue odor, increased dust and dirt, etc.

Access may be controlled by such things as scheduling, education, or regulations, as well as with posted "off limits" signs and physical barriers.

In part B, water should be readily available, but should not create a safety hazard such as could be caused by having tubs of water inside the riding ring.

Compliance Demonstration: Visitor observation of stable and corral areas; staff description of procedures to maintain cleanliness and control access.

STAFFED PUBLIC FACILITIES)

Score H-14 through H-17 if ANY
staffed public riding facilities,
not under the control of the camp, are utilized.

If **ONLY** H-14 through H-17 are scored,
a camp may miss **no more than one** scoreable item.

If staffed public facilities are **NOT** used,
DNA H-14 through H-17.

H-14

Is there a policy in practice by the camp administrator to select provider(s) of horseback riding activities that:

1. **Verify acceptable qualifications of riding leaders,**
2. **Provide horses suitable for the skill levels of participants, and**
3. **Utilize equipment that is appropriate in size and type and is in good repair?** Yes No

Interpretation: Information about the facility's riding instructor qualifications, equipment, and operating procedures may be found in promotional materials, specified in the leasing/use agreement, or verified by personal observation and inquiry of a camp representative.

Compliance Demonstration: Director description of procedures used in selection.

H-15

Are procedures in practice requiring that participants in all horseback riding activities be oriented, prior to their participation, to established safety regulations and emergency procedures? **Yes No**

Interpretation: Rules and procedures may be a combination of those established by the riding facility and those specified by the camp for their participants.

Compliance Demonstration: Director/staff description of orientation provided.

H-16

Is there a system in practice to:
1. **Evaluate and classify participants' riding ability, and**
2. **Assign them to horses, equipment, and activities commensurate with their ability?** **Yes No**

Interpretation: Evaluation does not necessarily imply a riding test. Participants may be interviewed and assigned to appropriate horses or activities until actual skill is demonstrated.

Even if assignments presume beginner or non-skilled level for everyone, individuals should still be evaluated to identify experience with the activity, comfort level, or fears that could affect their safety.

Compliance Demonstration: Staff description of system utilized.

H-17

Is there a policy in practice that requires the following safety apparel be used by campers and camp staff:

DNA A for vaulting activities.

A. **Shoes or boots which provide protection from:**
1. **Injury from being stepped on by horses, and,**
2. **If stirrups are used, feet becoming wedged into the stirrup (when stirrups are not specifically designed to prevent this occurrence)?** **Yes No**

B. **Long trousers?** **Yes No**

C. **Protective head gear constructed to minimize head injury in a fall, that fits the rider comfortably, does not obscure vision, and is secured by a strong chin strap?** **Yes No**

Interpretation: See interpretation of H-8.

Compliance Demonstration: Staff description of policy's implementation; visitor observation of riding activities if possible.

Part 3

Standards for Site Approval

Standards for Site Approval

INTRODUCTION

American Camping Association Approved Site describes the facilities and services offered to another camp director or program operator. This designation is appropriate for sites that provide camp-style facilities and basic services to school systems, short-term camp operators, other community agencies, or other rental groups who retain the primary responsibility for their own program.

The Site Approval standards include:

Core Standards that are applied to all sites seeking Site Approval:
SA — Site and Facilities
SB — Administration, Personnel, Transportation and Health Care

Activity Standards that are applicable only if these activities or facilities are offered to user groups:
SF — Aquatics
SH — Horseback Riding

SECTION SA — SITE and FACILITIES

The physical setting of the site operation is an integral part of the total experience for groups utilizing the site. While administration and services are important to providing a healthy atmosphere for groups, site and facilities contribute to the success of the overall experience.

SA-1

Is there a written Comprehensive Plan that has been reviewed in the past three years which assesses current conditions and projects future needs in the areas of:

A. Site and facility development and/or management?	Yes	No
B. Programs and services offered to user groups?	Yes	No
C. Market?	Yes	No
D. Finance and administration?	Yes	No
E. Environmental protection and preservation?	Yes	No

Director's Pre-Visit Evaluation
A. ☐ Yes ☐ No
B. ☐ Yes ☐ No
C. ☐ Yes ☐ No
D. ☐ Yes ☐ No
E. ☐ Yes ☐ No

Interpretation: The plan is a management tool which provides information for ongoing operation as well as direction for future development.

A master site plan (part A) typically includes a description of the physical site when all goals in terms of landscape, buildings, and facilities are reached. If the primary goals for development have been achieved, the master site plan then centers upon long-term maintenance, replacement, and improvement of buildings, facilities, and landscape.

"Market" in part C refers to the population the site is reaching and wishes to reach with its program/facilities.

In part E, long-term planning for environmental protection and preservation is necessary to protect the site investment and to preserve a quality environment.

See the Appendix (page 228) for an outline of a sample Comprehensive Plan.

Compliance Demonstration: Visitor observation of plan; director description of review process.

SA-2

Director's Pre-Visit Evaluation
☐ Yes   ☐ No

Does the site or accessible area provide natural resources to enrich an outdoor living experience? **Yes No**

Interpretation: "Accessible" refers to areas available on a regular basis, located either on the site or in close proximity to the site.

Compliance Demonstration: Visitor observation of natural resources; director description of availability.

SA-3

Director's Pre-Visit Evaluation
☐ Yes   ☐ No

To provide for the protection of the site, has contact been made in writing with local fire and law enforcement officials? **Yes No**

Interpretation: Contact should be made just prior to opening in a seasonal operation, and annually in a year-round operation.

In situations where the site is automatically covered by municipal fire and police service, the site should still notify those officials of site operation dates and potential number of persons on the site.

Compliance Demonstration: Visitor observation of letter(s) to or from local officials.

SA-4

Does the site administrator implement a system to have annual examination(s) conducted by qualified person(s) of the following fire equipment and areas:

1. Smoke detectors and other detection devices — availability and location,
2. Fire extinguishers — type, location and readiness,
3. Fireplaces and chimneys,
4. Storage and use areas for flammable materials and fuel,
5. Open fire areas, and
6. Cooking areas? **Yes No**

Interpretation: "Qualified persons" include fire-fighting professionals, insurance underwriters, fire-fighting equipment distributors, and other forest/fire officials who have recognized expertise in fire safety inspections. Site personnel with training and experience also may be qualified.

Compliance Demonstration: Director or Site administrator's description of system to conduct annual evaluation.

SA-5

DNA if on a community (public) water supply.

Is there written confirmation that all water sources used for drinking or food preparation purposes meet state guidelines for approval and have been tested:

1. If a seasonal water supply, within 30 days preceding the first use by user groups or staff, or
2. If a continuously used water supply, within the past three months (quarterly); and
3. If initial test results do not meet state guidelines, there is evidence that specific recommendations of local health officials are being implemented to correct the problem? **Yes No**

Interpretation: This standard applies to water which comes from the site's own wells or reservoir system, not to water provided by a municipal or other water authority responsible for its own testing.

The Environmental Protection Agency periodically updates rules affecting water testing requirements. The rules vary based on the source of water (ground, surface, or both) and are also subject to modification by state authorities. Testing frequency requirements range from weekly to annually. Directors are advised to contact local health authorities to confirm local test requirements.

"Continuously used" means the water supply is used throughout the calendar year. "Seasonal water supply" means the water supply is in use for only a portion of the year.

In a situation where the state or local authorities require testing after occupancy or in some other time period not in conformity with the 30-day requirement of the standard, the site must have a test completed by another qualified laboratory within the timeframe specified by the standard to be in compliance with the standard.

Compliance Demonstration: Visitor observation of dated test results; director verification of recommended corrective steps (if applicable).

SA-6

DNA if no utilities on site.

For the purpose of safety in an emergency, are blueprints, charts, or physical descriptions indicating the location of all electrical lines and cutoff points, gas lines and valves, and water cutoff points:

    1. Available on site, or

    2. Is the telephone number of the person or agency with that information prominently posted?   **Yes No**

Compliance Demonstration: Visitor observation of copies of charts, blueprints or descriptions, or of the posted phone number.

SA-7

DNA if no electrical service on site.

Does the site administration require that an electrical evaluation be conducted annually by (a) qualified person(s)?   **Yes No**

Interpretation: Evaluations should be conducted in all facilities with electrical service including the swimming pool, water pumps, living areas, program buildings or areas, food service and storage areas, maintenance areas, and dining halls.

The evaluation should include at least a visual observation of areas and facilities to check for such things as damaged or loose wires or fixtures, electrical equipment needing repair or replacement, face plates and panel fronts in place, correct-sized fuses and circuit breakers, and appropriately grounded receptacles.

Particular attention should be paid to facilities which have little or no use during some seasons, where damage from rodents or weather may have occurred.

"Qualified persons" could include site staff, maintenance personnel, persons identified as qualified by local statute/regulation, or other persons with training and/or experience in basic electrical evaluation, as well as electricians or other licensed persons.

Compliance Demonstration: Director description of procedures and personnel used to conduct the annual evaluation.

SA-8

Is the site free from observable evidence of a sewage disposal problem, or is there evidence that specific recommendations of local health officials are being implemented to correct the problem?   **Yes No**

Compliance Demonstration: Visitor observation of septic system areas; demonstrated implementation of health department recommendations where applicable.

SA-9

Is there evidence that the site administrator has a system to implement regular safety checks of equipment, facilities, and program areas used by groups?

Yes   No

Interpretation: "Regular" safety checks will vary based on frequency of use, availability of representatives of the site administrator on site, and type of equipment or facilities being used. Periodic checks should be made of play equipment; activity areas such as ropes courses, aquatic areas, fields, etc; living areas, or other buildings used by groups. Administrators should be able to describe the system in use, or show job descriptions listing this responsibility and maintenance procedures addressing this need.

Compliance Demonstration: Visitor observation of selected program areas and equipment; director/staff description of system and procedures.

SA-10

Is there evidence that a systematic maintenance routine is in effect throughout the site that results in:

A.   **Buildings (including toilets), paths, and activity locations maintained in good repair?**

Yes   No

B.   **Clean and sanitary conditions?**

Yes   No

Interpretation: Part A includes all buildings and program areas in camp. Railings, porches, floorboards, screens, and doors are examples of items that should show signs of regular maintenance and repair.

Part B includes garbage and rubbish disposal areas, kitchen garbage disposal systems and area, toilet areas, program areas and buildings. In addition to being "in repair" (part A), there should be signs of regular cleaning, garbage/trash collection, and regular activity to keep the area free of accumulated dirt, grease, mildew, and trash.

Compliance Demonstration: Visitor observation of site areas; director description of maintenance routines.

SA-11

Is there evidence that permanent disposal of garbage is scheduled to prevent build up beyond the capacity of closed containers?

Yes   No

Compliance Demonstration: Visitor observation of garbage storage; director/staff description of schedule.

Site Approval

SA-12

To protect site supplies and equipment from damage, deterioration, and unauthorized use, are storage facilities available and in use during site operation?   **Yes No**

Compliance Demonstration: Visitor observation of randomly selected storage facilities; director/staff description of storage procedures.

*SA-13 MANDATORY

DNA if firearms or ammunition are not stored on site.

Are firearms and ammunition owned by site owner/operator or site staff stored under lock?   **Yes No**

Interpretation: This standard is not intended to be applied to homes or buildings or apartments on camp property that are used solely as private residences of staff, designed for the exclusive use of the individual staff and/or families who live there, and not accessible to user groups. Guns stored in the back of trucks, however, that are accessible to user groups must be locked to meet the requirement of this standard.

Compliance Demonstration: Visitor observation of firearm and ammunition storage.

*SA-14 MANDATORY

Is there implementation of policies requiring that gas and liquid flammables, explosives, and poisonous materials be:
   1. **Stored in covered, safe containers that are plainly labeled as to contents,**
   2. **Handled only by persons trained or experienced in their safe use,**
   3. **Stored in locations separate from food?**   **Yes No**

Interpretation: Liquid flammables include gasoline, kerosene and other liquid fuels. Poisonous materials include bleach, many cleaning agents, insecticides, weed killers, or other substances labeled as poisonous.

Directors may want to check with local officials for other recommendations concerning storage and handling of flammable or poisonous substances.

Participants who are under the direct supervision of trained personnel while learning to use materials are in compliance with the standard.

Compliance Demonstration: Visitor observation of storage and handling of listed substances; director description of handling procedures.

SA-15

DNA if power tools are not used by site staff.

Does the site administration have a policy in practice that requires power tools:
1. **Be provided with necessary safety devices,**
2. **Be in good repair, and**
3. **Be operated only by those persons trained and experienced in their use?**   **Yes   No**

Interpretation: This standard applies to tools utilized in program activities as well as in maintenance.

Compliance Demonstration: Visitor observation of power tools and their use, where possible; director/staff description of policy and practices.

*SA-16 Parts A and C MANDATORY

DNA if user groups or site staff never stay overnight in buildings.

Are all buildings used by site staff or user groups for sleeping constructed or equipped with the following safety features:

*A. At least one emergency exit in addition to the main door or entrance?
                                                                Yes   No

DNA B if 30% or more of the wall area is screened or open.

B. Smoke detection equipment in working order?   **Yes   No**

DNA C if all sleeping quarters are at ground level.

*C. A direct means of emergency exit to the outside from each sleeping floor that does not have a ground level entrance?   **Yes   No**

Interpretation: The concern of this standard is the protection of human life. The entire standard applies ONLY to sleeping quarters located in buildings. "Buildings," for the purposes of this standard, are permanent, enclosed structures that remain intact regardless of season. Tents and adirondack shelters are not considered buildings for the purposes of this standard.

In part A, emergency exits should be located opposite from entrances so that they could be used if the main entrance is blocked. "Emergency exit" does not imply a particular structure or evacuation device, but means a quick, safe, accessible alternative exit. Approval of state or local fire officials or insurance underwriters provides guidance to acceptable escape plans. Windows with screening could be considered emergency exits if occupants are informed of procedures for exit and could easily and safely escape through them.

Ground level entrances should be accessible without the use of lifts or elevators to facilitate easy access and quick evacuation for all persons. In split level buildings that have ground level access on only one side, emergency exits from upper level sleeping quarters must facilitate quick, safe evacuation of all persons in case the ground level exit is blocked.

In part B, it is not suggested or implied that fire detection and alarm devices are inappropriate in all structures not included in this definition of buildings. However, due to the wide diversity of such shelters, these devices are not required universally.

In part C, "... to the outside" means that either the escape is on the outside of the building or an enclosed stairway exits directly to the outside when it reaches ground level.

While camp owners should be concerned about the provision of safety in all sleeping quarters on the property, it is <u>not</u> the intent of this standard to require observation by visitors of private, permanent residences of year-round staff.

Compliance Demonstration: Visitor observation of randomly selected sleeping areas, particularly those facilities with sleeping floors that do not have ground level entrances.

SA-17

DNA if site has no permanent sleeping quarters.

Do permanent sleeping quarters provide the following:
1. **Cross ventilation,**
2. **At least six feet between heads of sleepers,**
3. **At least 30 inches between sides of beds, and**
4. **Adequate space to provide freedom of movement, especially for those using wheelchairs or walkers?**   **Yes   No**

Interpretation: "Permanent sleeping quarters" refer to structures, platform tents, covered wagons, etc. that are constructed in a fixed location and are used as primary residences for staff and/or user groups. Temporary shelters such as tents used for overnight camping and backpacking would not fall under this classification.

Beds separated by less than 30 inches but having a fixed partition between them that precludes sneezing or coughing on others is acceptable to meet the standard.

All persons need "adequate space" for ease of movement and to facilitate safe exit in an emergency. State regulations range from 30 to 50 square feet of floor space required per person. Such regulations should be considered when designing, constructing or using buildings.

Persons with restricted mobility need additional space and the arrangement should consider the functional space taken by wheelchairs and other devices.

For persons with restricted mobility, the norm established by ANSI is 50 square feet per person using a walker and 60 square feet per person using a wheelchair.

Compliance Demonstration: Visitor observation of randomly selected sleeping quarters throughout the site.

SA-18

DNA if no bunk beds are used or to bunks only used by persons 16 and older.

Is there a policy in practice that upper bunks used by children are equipped with guardrails designed to prevent occupants from accidentally rolling out of the bed?   **Yes   No**

Interpretation: Beds placed against the wall do not require rails on the side facing the wall.

The Consumer Product Safety Commission recommends that the bottom of the rail be no more than 3 ½ inches from the top of the bed frame, and that the top of the rail be at least 5 inches above the top of the mattress.

This standard is not intended to be applied to private residences of year-round staff.

Compliance Demonstration: Visitor observation of randomly selected sleeping areas using bunk beds.

SA-19

DNA if day use only or a primitive site.

Are bathing/showering facilities adequate in number based on the following ratios:
1. **All camps — one showerhead or bathtub for each 15 persons on site, or**
2. **Camps specializing in serving persons with restricted mobility — one showerhead or bathtub for each 10 persons on site?**   **Yes   No**

Interpretation: "Primitive site" refers to those sites whose program is based on a philosophy centered on non-facility, utility-oriented principles. Generally, such sites have few permanent structures or facilities.

Bathing facilities to be used in computing ratios are those available to the general site population and not those in private residences or restricted areas.

For persons with restricted mobility, aids such as chairs on casters, stools, footrests, non-slip surfaces, and flexible shower heads attached to hoses may provide increased independence. Aids should be provided according to the needs of persons being served.

Compliance Demonstration: Visitor observation of showering/bathing areas; director explanation of ratios.

Site Approval

SA-20

DNA if no hot water available on site.

To prevent scalding, is there a system in practice for regulating the hot water temperature other than by individual adjustment at the taps of bathing, showering and handwashing facilities? **Yes　No**

Interpretation: Temperatures may be regulated by:

    a. thermostatically controlled temperature regulating valves,
    b. water heater thermostats, or
    c. properly adjusted mixing valves (provided the cold water source is not subject to variations in pressure).

110 degrees F. is frequently established as a safe maximum water temperature at the tap. Directors may wish to consult with local health officials concerning appropriate maximum temperatures.

Compliance Demonstration: Director description of techniques in use; visitor feeling water at randomly selected taps.

SA-21

Are there sleeping, dining, toilet, bathing and program facilities available to persons with disabilities, or is the camp implementing a plan to come into compliance with the Americans with Disabilities Act? **Yes　No**

Interpretation: The intent of the standard is for the camp to address facility accessibility issues as defined by the Americans with Disabilities Act of 1990. The law does not require that all facilities or program areas be accessible, or that all changes be made at once. The ADA law does not require camps to make changes that would fundamentally alter the nature of the camp program. It does require the camp to make "readily achievable" accommodations that do not cause an "undue burden."

It may not be possible to make all areas of camp accessible. However, participation in the normal activities of camp living and activity groups should be fostered and barriers removed or accommodations provided to permit full participation whenever possible. "Available" means that persons have both access and opportunity.

See Appendix C (page 202) for an architectural barriers checklist.

Compliance Demonstration: Director explanation of plans established and/or accommodations provided for persons with disabilities.

SA-22

Is there a policy made known to user groups and site staff that:

    A. Prohibits smoking in food service and preparation areas? **Yes　No**

    B. Designates areas on the site where smoking is and/or is not permitted? **Yes　No**

Compliance Demonstration: Director/staff description of policy and method of dissemination; director explanation of implementation.

SA-23

Is shelter from inclement weather available for all persons on site?   Yes   No

Interpretation: Shelter from inclement weather is an important concern on day use sites as well as resident sites. Shelter may consist of temporary tarps and rain flies, as well as permanent structures.

Compliance Demonstration: Visitor observation of available shelter(s).

SA-24

Are toilets adequate in number based on the following ratios:
1. **Resident site —**
   a. **One seat for every 10 females, and**
   b. **One seat for every 10 males, or**
   c. **If more than 10 percent of user group population has restricted mobility — one seat for every 8 females, and one seat for every 8 males?**
2. **Day use only site —**
   a. **One seat for every 30 females, and**
   b. **One seat for every 50 males, or**
   c. **If more than 10 percent of user group population has restricted mobility — one seat for every 20 females, and one seat for every 30 males?**   **Yes   No**

Interpretation: Seats to be used in computing ratios are those available to the general site population and not those in private residences or restricted areas. Up to one third of the seats for males may be substituted with urinals.

Compliance Demonstration: Visitor observation of toilet areas; director explanation of ratios available.

SA-25

Are handwashing facilities adjacent to toilets and provided in the following ratios:
1. **Resident site — one wash basin or equivalent per 10 persons, with a minimum of two basins for each toilet facility designed to serve more than 5 persons at the same time?**
2. **Day use only — one wash basin or equivalent per 30 persons, with a minimum of two basins for each toilet facility designed to serve more than 5 persons at the same time?**   **Yes   No**

Interpretation: When using multiple handwashing units utilizing a spray-type water dispenser, 20 inches of wash basin rim space is equivalent to one wash basin.

Compliance Demonstration: Visitor observation of randomly selected toilet/handwashing areas; director explanation of ratios available.

Site Approval

SA-26

DNA if toilet facilities with multiple seats are not located in the main camp or living areas.

In the main camp and living areas, do toilet facilities with more than one seat have at least one toilet with a door or curtain for privacy, available to all?

Yes   No

Interpretation: "Available to all" means that such facilities may be used by all persons (user groups and staff). When persons with special needs are served, there should also be toilets affording privacy to them.

This standard does not apply to every toilet facility on site, but to those most likely to be used frequently, such as those near the dining hall and in resident units.

Compliance Demonstration: Visitor observation of randomly selected toilet facilities in the main camp and living areas.

SA-27

DNA if pit or chemical toilets are not used.

Are pit or chemical toilets screened or vented and provided with toilet lids and self-closing doors?

Yes   No

Compliance Demonstration: Visitor observation of randomly selected pit or chemical toilets.

FOOD SERVICE

The Food Service standards are to be scored **IF** food service **AND/OR** food service facilities are provided for user groups by site owner/operator.

If **NO** food services or food service facilities are provided for user groups, **DNA** SA-28 through SA-35 and proceed to Section SB — Administration.

SA-28

Does the camp administration implement procedures to protect food preparation and storage areas from rodents and vermin?   **Yes No**

Compliance Demonstration: Visitor observation of food preparation and storage areas; staff description of procedures used.

Director's Pre-Visit Evaluation
☐ Yes   ☐ No

SA-29

To assure storage of potentially hazardous foods at a temperature of 45 degrees F. or less in mechanical refrigeration devices, is there evidence that the site administrator provides:

1. **Thermometers for all mechanical refrigeration units,**
2. **Instructions to food service staff and/or user groups to regularly monitor temperature, and**
3. **A system to report and immediately correct temperatures above 45 degrees F.?**   **Yes No**

Director's Pre-Visit Evaluation
☐ Yes   ☐ No

Interpretation: "Potentially hazardous foods" are those foods that consist in whole or in part of milk or milk products, eggs, meat, poultry, fish, shellfish, edible crustacea or other ingredients (including synthetic ingredients) in a form capable of supporting growth of infectious or toxic microorganisms. Such foods should be maintained at temperatures below 45 degrees F. or above 140 degrees F.

This standard applies to mechanical refrigeration units in areas such as the kitchen, infirmary, staff house or unit houses. It does NOT apply to year-round staff residences.

User groups and/or site staff should know to whom and how to report temperature problems in refrigerators. Temperature charts for mechanical devices are not required by this standard, but may assist administrators in establishing a monitoring and reporting system. See the Appendix (page 203) for a sample chart.

"Immediately correct" means within 24 hours.

Compliance Demonstration: Visitor observation of thermometers in refrigeration units; staff explanation of procedures and system for reporting/correction.

SA-30

DNA if disposable food service utensils are used exclusively.

To assure proper sanitizing and storage of dishes and food service utensils after each use, does the site administrator require that the following written procedures be implemented:

   A. Washing:

      1. For mechanical dishwashers —

         a. Wash water is at least 100 degrees F. and

         b. Rinse water is at least 180 degrees F. or an approved chemical sanitizer is used as specified on its label; and/or

      2. For dishes and food service utensils washed by hand —

         a. Wash and initial rinse temperatures of at least 100 degrees F., and

         b. Second rinse process using at least 180 degree F. water or an approved chemical sanitizer?   Yes No

   B. Drying:

      All dishes and food service utensils are air dried?   Yes No

   C. Storage:

      Food service utensils used for eating and serving are protected from dust and contamination between use?   Yes No

Interpretation: "Food service utensils" include dishes, silverware and all other utensils used in the preparation or serving of food. Pots and pans used in cooking and baking which are heated to very high temperatures in the cooking process are exempted from the second rinse requirement, but not from the air-drying requirement.

Directors should be aware of state and local codes concerning acceptable water temperature for washing. Some localities require wash water of 140 degrees F. (minimum).

Although documentation of regular monitoring of temperatures is not required by the standard, sites should have the means and procedures to periodically monitor water temperatures and immediately correct inadequate temperatures. Temperature charts may assist administrators in establishing a monitoring and reporting system. See the Appendix (page 203) for a sample chart.

Compliance Demonstration: Visitor observation of written procedures, dishwasher temperatures, dishwashing process, and food service utensil storage.

SA-31

DNA if dining facilities are not provided.

Do dining facilities provide:

   A. Adequate space at tables and between tables?   Yes No

   B. Protection from problem insects?   Yes No

Interpretation: This standard applies only to permanent, enclosed structures used for dining.

"Adequate space" means enough space for freedom of movement about the dining hall during meal times and to facilitate safe exit in an emergency.

Problem insects could include either types or quantities of insects that constitute a health problem.

Compliance Demonstration: Visitor observation of dining facilities.

```
IF owner/operator is NOT providing
the food service,
DNA SA-32 through SA-35
and proceed to Section SB — Administration.
```

SA-32

To prevent contamination of foods during preparation, holding, and serving, are there procedures in practice that require food service staff to:

A. Minimize the time that potentially hazardous foods remain in the temperature danger zone of 45 degrees F. to 140 degrees F?

Yes   No

B. Use only clean and sanitized utensils and equipment during food preparation?   Yes   No

C. Clean and sanitize food contact surfaces after each use?   Yes   No

DNA D if hot food is not served.

D. Assure cooking and holding of potentially hazardous foods at appropriate temperatures?   Yes   No

E. Implement appropriate personal hygiene procedures?   Yes   No

Director's Pre-Visit Evaluation		
A. ☐ Yes ☐ No		
B. ☐ Yes ☐ No		
C. ☐ Yes ☐ No		
D. ☐ Yes ☐ No ☐ DNA		
E. ☐ Yes ☐ No		

Interpretation: See Interpretation of SA-29 for definition of "potentially hazardous foods."

"Sanitized utensils" are those which have been cleaned and sanitized according to the guidelines in SA-30.

Food contact surfaces include anything that contacts raw food during preparation such as counters, cutting boards, knives, etc. Such surfaces should be sanitized with a bleach solution or other commercial sanitizer between times when raw food contacts those surfaces. Local health authorities can give guidance on the strength and frequency of use for such sanitizing agents.

For part D, the intent is that staff be trained to recognize and assure that foods are cooked and held at appropriate temperatures. Most states establish 140 degrees F. as the minimum temperature for holding hot foods, whether in steam tables or on the stove. Sites should have the means and procedures to monitor temperatures periodically. It is not assumed that thermometers need to be in place at all times to measure temperatures.

139

"Personal hygiene procedures" include things such as handwashing, general cleanliness, procedures and precautions with a cold, etc.

Compliance Demonstration: Visitor observation of selected food preparation and/or clean-up processes; staff explanation of procedures.

SA-33

Does the site administration require that all garbage and rubbish containers in kitchen and dining areas be leak proof or fitted with non-absorbent lining and covered with a tight-fitting lid or tied securely when not being used in the food preparation or clean-up process? **Yes No**

Interpretation: The concern of this standard is the temporary storage of garbage containing food wastes in food service areas prior to removal to permanent storage areas (dumpsters, disposal areas away from site, etc.).

Compliance Demonstration: Visitor observation of randomly selected kitchen and dining areas; director description of implementation.

SA-34

Is there written evidence that the following food records are maintained:
   1. **Menus,**
   2. **Records and inventories of food supplies purchased, or**
   3. **If food services are contracted — records of menus and number of meals served?** **Yes No**

Compliance Demonstration: Visitor observation of randomly selected food records.

SA-35

Is there a procedure being implemented to have menus planned and/or approved by a nutritionist, dietician, or other person qualified to evaluate the nutrition and balance of the meals served? **Yes No**

Interpretation: The intent of this standard is to assure that meals are well-balanced and nutritionally sound.

A nutritionist is a home economist with a food nutrition major. A dietician is a person who has received a baccalaureate degree with major studies in food and nutrition, and who has completed a supervised food service experience.

The person approving menus does not need to be part of the on-site staff.

Compliance Demonstration: Director/staff explanation of procedure and qualifications of person approving menus.

SECTION SB — ADMINISTRATION

The Administration standards include those basic administrative practices that relate to creating a positive, protective environment for participants. The standards include policies and procedures related to emergencies, the establishment of good business practices, transportation, personnel, health care, and other areas of risk management.

ACA Approved Sites range from sites where no representative of the camp operation is physically present while the user group is on the property to sites that provide a full staff and various program facilities which may or may not be staffed.

Therefore, administrative practices will vary widely depending on the need. These standards provide for the development of procedures in important areas for each site such as risk management and transportation without dictating the content of those procedures.

Many of the policies and procedures required by these standards may be provided to a user group with a copy of their contract/agreement.

SB-1

For the purpose of risk management planning and <u>in addition to</u> the materials required for other Site Approval standards, is there written evidence that the site administration has taken inventory of its operations to:

Director's Pre-Visit Evaluation
A. ☐ Yes ☐ No
B. ☐ Yes ☐ No
C. ☐ Yes ☐ No

A. **Identify general <u>health and safety concerns</u> and possible <u>emergency situations</u> unique to the site and related to:**
   1. **Natural hazards specific to the site,**
   2. **Man-made hazards specific to the site,**
   3. **Operation of facilities and/or equipment,**
   4. **Conduct of people?**   **Yes   No**

B. **Specify <u>measures to reduce, control or prevent risks</u> associated with the health and safety concerns and possible emergency situations listed in A including:**
   1. **Site safety regulations for those identified areas,**
   2. **Methods to control access to identified hazards,**
   3. **Protective devices where appropriate, and/or**
   4. **Identification of how and when user groups and/or staff will be trained to deal with such identified risks?**   **Yes   No**

C. **Establish <u>emergency procedures</u> to respond appropriately to situations identified in A?**   **Yes   No**

Interpretation: The requirements of the Site Approval standards address many of the commonly identified risk management concerns. This standard requires the site administration to identify and plan for health and safety concerns, <u>unique to the site</u>, that are not covered elsewhere.

In part A, "natural hazards" may include the presence of cliffs, bodies of water, poisonous snakes, wild animals, or other conditions of nature that may pose a risk to humans on the site.

"Man-made hazards" not addressed by other standards may include public roads through the property, construction activities on the site, abandoned wells, activity areas such as ropes courses or climbing walls, or other facilities on the site that may pose a risk.

"Operation of facilities and/or equipment" may include possible loss of power affecting food storage and service or the provision of water, building collapse, explosion, electrocution, etc. Pre-planning to identify resources in case of such situations can save valuable time.

"Conduct of people" includes actions of staff, participants, guests or trespassers. It might include areas such as allegations of child abuse, incidents due to the use of drugs or alcohol, vandalism, theft, or behavior of trespassers. It may also address regulations for group living areas including but not limited to bunks, showers, or other general camp locations.

For part B, 4, the site administration should consider a variety of methods to orient and inform user groups, especially those staying on site for limited amounts of time, or those on sites with no staff in residence. Posted regulations and procedures, staff orientation of all members of user groups, and written procedures provided to the group leader prior to arrival on site are examples of training methods.

"Protective devices" may include things such as fences, lighting, storm warning systems, and warning signs.

In part C, emergency procedures may include plans for fire drills, site evacuation procedures, specification of designated areas in case of flood or tornado, etc. as appropriate to the site, immediate care of the injured, supervision of the uninjured, and notification of appropriate personnel. The complexity of plans will vary based on site use and the availability of staff when user groups are present.

Note that the requirements of this standard do not result in the completion of a full Risk Management Plan. Thorough planning requires the consideration of operational financial risks as well as health and safety concerns. Advice from legal and insurance counsel or other risk management specialists should be sought to develop a comprehensive risk management planning strategy.

See the Appendix (page 204) for helps in fulfilling the requirements of this standard.

Compliance Demonstration: Visitor observation of written materials.

SB-2

<table>
<tr><td>

Director's Pre-Visit Evaluation

☐ Yes   ☐ No

</td><td>

Is there a procedure in practice to provide user groups with a written copy of safety regulations and emergency procedures?   **Yes   No**

</td></tr>
</table>

Interpretation: The intent of this standard is to assure that the safety regulations are distributed to user groups. This information is often provided with the contract. It should include all safety regulations, not just those identified in standard SB-1.

Compliance Demonstration: Visitor observation of written rules and regulations; director/staff description of dissemination procedures.

SB-3

Is there a system in practice to provide user groups with written procedures for:

A. Search and rescue of persons lost, missing, or runaway?   Yes No

B. Obtaining emergency assistance including law enforcement, and fire officials?   Yes No

C. Contacting site owners or their representatives?   Yes No

D. Steps to follow in case of disasters on the site?   Yes No

Interpretation: It is essential to have procedures for communication developed prior to the pressure of an actual emergency. "Lost, missing, or runaway" procedures should identify appropriate law enforcement or safety officials the user group could contact if site owners/operators are not available on the property. Written procedures for parts B and C may include information posted by telephones as well as distributed information.

Part D may include procedures to follow in the event of any weather-related emergency as well as more serious events such as fire, flood, earthquake, tornado, hurricane, etc.

Compliance Demonstration: Visitor observation of written procedures; staff description of dissemination procedures.

SB-4

Does the site owner provide to the person responsible for each user group a written agreement that includes the following information:

    1. Terms of use (cost, dates, times, insurance, etc.),
    2. Refund policy,
    3. Services provided, and
    4. Equipment available for use and additional cost for same (if any)?   Yes No

Interpretation: This information is often part of an information packet supplied as part of the contract or lease agreement. For part #1, the site owner should identify the insurance coverage provided by the site and any requirements for coverage that is to be provided by the user group.

Compliance Demonstration: Visitor observation of information and/or forms utilized.

SB-5

DNA if site owner/operator provides health services. (Note: Standards SB-23 through 28 must be scored if this standard is scored DNA.)

Is there written evidence that the site administrator informs user groups of the following:

    1. That a person currently certified at least in Standard First Aid or equivalent be on site when participants are present, and

    2. The phone number and location of emergency medical treatment services including ambulance (if available), and the nearest doctor or hospital?   **Yes No**

Interpretation: The intent of part 1 of this standard is that there always be a person available on site who is certified at a minimum in Standard First Aid.

For part 2, phone numbers and directions should be posted by telephones for easy access.

Compliance Demonstration: Visitor observation of written information provided user groups.

*SB-6 MANDATORY

Is there evidence that transportation is available at all times for any medical emergencies of user groups provided by either:

    1. The site, or

    2. Community emergency services with whom prior arrangements have been made in writing, or

    3. The user group, as evidenced by a written policy requiring the group to provide their own emergency transportation?   **Yes No**

Interpretation: "Available" means that designated emergency transportation vehicles are in operational order and have enough fuel to reach primary emergency locations.

When the primary emergency vehicle is off the site, there must be a specific plan for the availability of other transportation. Emergency transportation may include air, water, and snow vehicles as well as automobiles, vans, etc.

Compliance Demonstration: Staff description of procedures; visitor observation of written arrangements, policy or vehicles.

SB-7

Does the site administration have a written policy that is made known to user groups regarding use and storage of the following:

    1. Firearms and ammunition,

    2. Gasoline, flammable liquids, explosives, and poisonous substances, and

    3. Hand and power tools?   **Yes No**

Interpretation: The intent of this standard is that the site owner provide any groups bringing firearms, flammables, or power tools with the minimum site regulations concerning acceptable locations for their use, and any conditions governing their use and storage. Even if the policy of the site is that no firearms are to be brought or used, that policy should be made known to groups.

See the interpretation to Camp Accreditation standards A-8, A-9, and A-10 for further information on correct storage of these items.

Compliance Demonstration: Visitor observation of written policies; staff description of dissemination to user groups.

SB-8

Is there evidence that the site administration has a policy which is made known to user groups that forbids the transportation of participants in vehicles not designed for passengers? **Yes No**

Director's Pre-Visit Evaluation
☐ Yes   ☐ No

Interpretation: The intent of this standard is to forbid transportation of persons in the back of pickup trucks or wagons where seats are not attached to the vehicle. The exception to this is for hayrides where wagons are driven at slow speeds (5-10 mph) off public roads, and where protective devices are provided to keep people from falling out or off of the vehicle.

Compliance Demonstration: Staff description of policy and method of dissemination to user groups.

SB-9

Is there written evidence that the camp administrator provides user groups with safety regulations concerning the use of vehicles on the camp site? **Yes No**

Director's Pre-Visit Evaluation
☐ Yes   ☐ No

Interpretation: Regulations should identify parking areas, areas of the camp site where vehicles are permitted, and regulations to be followed when utilizing vehicles for transportation of participants.

Compliance Demonstration: Visitor observation of written regulations; staff description of method of dissemination to user groups.

SB-10

Is there written evidence that the site has the following insurance coverage:

A. General liability coverage, including specific coverage for program services that are offered to user groups?   Yes   No

DNA B if site does not have buildings.

B. Fire and extended risk coverage on buildings?   Yes   No

DNA C if staff are not employed.

C. Health and accident and/or workers' compensation coverage for each employee?   Yes   No

DNA D if vehicles are not used in site operation.

D. Motor vehicle insurance (as applicable):
1. **Coverage on all owned, hired, or leased vehicles, and,**
2. **Employer's non-ownership liability and/or hired car insurance on all non-owned vehicles?**   Yes   No

Interpretation: Coverage may include self-insurance, which can be verified by evidence of the allocation of particular assets to cover such costs.

Part A includes coverage for program areas that are available to user groups such as horseback riding and ropes courses that are often excluded from general liability coverage.

Staff coverage may be provided by the site or the individual. When the camp does not provide the coverage, written evidence may be the individual's or parent's signature along with the policy number.

While not specifically required by this standard, contract liability is a type of insurance that site owners should evaluate with their agent as to its necessity in the site operation.

For part D, motor vehicle insurance, directors are advised to evaluate insurance coverage needed both for vehicles leased for an extended period as well as those hired for a day trip. Vehicles leased for a season need coverage for liability as well as physical damage (depending on the lease agreement). Many authorities recommend adding such vehicles to the regular auto policy, so that there is coverage just as if the vehicle were owned.

See the insurance checklist in the Appendix (page 209) for further information.

Compliance Demonstration: Visitor observation of policies, binders, or letters of confirmation from agent(s) showing current policies in place, and evidence of self-insurance or individual coverage (if applicable).

SB-11

Does the site administration utilize a system of fiscal management that includes:
1. **A budget for planning,**
2. **A bookkeeping system for tracking income and expenses, and**
3. **A year-end audit?**   **Yes   No**

Interpretation: The important consideration in this standard is verification of a fiscal management system which facilitates accountability, evaluation and planning. Therefore, specific fiscal figures need not be shown.

An "audit" is a regular examination and verification of accounts and may be conducted either internally or externally. This standard does not mandate that a certified audit be completed.

It does require an auditing/review procedure. Directors should check with legal and/or tax counsel to determine the appropriate type of review procedure for the business operation.

Compliance Demonstration: Director description of fiscal management system in use.

SB-12

Have arrangements been made for access to legal counsel as needed?
                                                                        Yes   No

Interpretation: "Access" means the site administrator has made some prior arrangements (formal or informal) with legal counsel to be available for advice as problems or questions arise.

Compliance Demonstration: Director explanation of arrangements.

Site Approval

147

DEFINITIONS

Program personnel refers to persons directly involved with site users in programming and may include such positions as counselors, unit supervisors, activity coordinators and specialists.

Director's Pre-Visit Evaluation			
A. ☐ Yes	☐ No		
B. ☐ Yes	☐ No		
C. ☐ Yes	☐ No	☐ DNA	
D. ☐ Yes	☐ No	☐ DNA	

SB-13

Has the site administration provided written job descriptions for staff in the following positions:

    A. Administrative personnel?   Yes   No

    B. Program personnel?   Yes   No

DNA C if health personnel are not provided.

    C. Health personnel?   Yes   No

DNA D if support personnel are not provided.

    D. Support personnel?   Yes   No

Interpretation: Job descriptions may be included in the written terms of agreement, separate documents, or in form letters to the individuals whose jobs are described.

Staff may be full or part time, paid or unpaid.

"Administrative personnel" refers to persons with supervisory responsibility and may include positions such as director, assistant director, maintenance supervisor, and food service director.

"Health personnel" are persons employed to perform health-related functions and duties and may include the health manager, doctors, nurses, first aiders, and other persons charged primarily with health and/or first aid responsibilities.

"Support personnel" are those who provide services to the site other than activity programming and may include positions such as office work, maintenance, food service, aides or volunteers, and drivers.

Compliance Demonstration: Visitor observation of job descriptions; director/staff description of distribution.

SB-14

Is there a policy in practice to provide each employee with a written employment agreement which includes the following:

    1. Salary or wages, if applicable,
    2. Term of employment,
    3. Benefits, and
    4. Reference to job description and personnel policies, if existing?

                                                Yes No

Interpretation: This standard applies to all personnel, both paid and unpaid.

The written agreement may include contracts, offer and acceptance letters, or confirming letters.

Compliance Demonstration: Visitor observation of sample agreement; director description of policy's implementation.

Director's Pre-Visit Evaluation
☐ Yes   ☐ No

SB-15

Has the site administration provided staff with written personnel policies that address all of the following:

    1. Remuneration,
    2. Time off,
    3. Absence from work,
    4. Insurance,
    5. Conditions of severance,
    6. Performance evaluation,
    7. Personal conduct, and
    8. Any special conditions of service?   Yes No

Compliance Demonstration: Visitor observation of written policies; director/staff description of distribution.

Director's Pre-Visit Evaluation
☐ Yes   ☐ No

SB-16

Are staff members provided with or do they have access to a staff organization chart?   Yes No

Interpretation: A staff organization chart provides an overview of the entire staffing pattern and shows lines of responsibility among staff.

Compliance Demonstration: Visitor observation of chart; director/staff description of distribution or access.

Director's Pre-Visit Evaluation
☐ Yes   ☐ No

Site Approval

```
┌─────────────────────────────────────────────────────┐
│                   TRANSPORTATION                      │
│  These standards are intended to be applied to        │
│  transportation for user groups in vehicles           │
│  arranged for or provided by the site owner/operator. │
│                                                       │
│  They are not scored for maintenance vehicles used    │
│  in the site operation, unless those vehicles are     │
│  used, in part, for transportation. However, site     │
│  administrators should consider the requirements of   │
│  these standards in evaluating all vehicle use on     │
│  site.                                                │
│  · · · · · · · · · · · · · · · · · · · · · · · · · ·  │
│         SCORE SB-17 through SB-22 ONLY IF             │
│          site operator provides transportation        │
│                for user groups, whether in            │
│            owned, leased or commercial vehicles.      │
│                                                       │
│      If site owner does NOT provide transportation,   │
│             DNA SB-17 through SB-22 and               │
│                 proceed to SB-23.                     │
└─────────────────────────────────────────────────────┘
```

DEFINITIONS

Regularly transport means transportation planned and arranged by the site, such as field trips and transportation to and from program sites, or transportation to the site from centralized pick-up points (bus stations, airports, etc.).

SB-17

Is there written evidence that the camp administration requires qualified persons to evaluate the mechanical soundness of all site vehicles that regularly transport user groups:

1. At least quarterly for sites that transport year-round, or
2. Within the 3 months prior to seasonal use?   Yes   No

Interpretation: This standard applies to all vehicles owned or leased by the site owner that regularly transport user groups. While site owners are not required by this standard to obtain maintenance records on private vehicles, owners of such vehicles should recognize that granting specific permission for the vehicle to be used to transport user groups implies a responsibility by the vehicle owner to prepare it for that use.

"Qualified persons" includes certified mechanics or other persons with training and/or experience in vehicle maintenance.

"Evaluate mechanical soundness" means checking and making any repair necessary to assure readiness of the vehicles to transport passengers.

Compliance Demonstration: Visitor observation of documentation which may include such things as entries in a vehicle log, or receipts from garages for services performed; director description of procedures and qualifications of persons evaluating.

SB-18

Is there implementation of a written policy on safety checks for all vehicles that regularly transport user groups that:

    1. Specifies frequency of checks, and
    2. Requires checks of:
        a. Lights,
        b. Tires,
        c. Windshield visibility, including wipers,
        d. Emergency warning systems,
        e. Horn,
        f. Brakes,
        g. Fluid levels?   **Yes No**

> Director's Pre-Visit Evaluation
> ☐ Yes ☐ No

Interpretation: Directors should check local codes for guidance on frequency of safety checks. Some states require many of these items to be checked prior to each use for certain types of vehicles. Written documentation of the check may be required is some states or local jurisdictions.

Compliance Demonstration: Visitor observation of written policy and director description of policy's implementation.

SB-19

Is there evidence that the site administration requires every site vehicle that is used for transporting user groups or site staff be equipped with a first aid kit and emergency accessories?   **Yes No**

> Director's Pre-Visit Evaluation
> ☐ Yes ☐ No

Interpretation: "Emergency accessories" include reflectors, fire extinguishers, or other supplies necessitated by weather conditions such as shovels and blankets.

Compliance Demonstration: Visitor observation of randomly selected vehicles and equipment and/or staff description of procedures for equipping vehicles.

SB-20

DNA if site does not provide drivers.

> Director's Pre-Visit Evaluation
> ☐ Yes ☐ No ☐ DNA

Does the site administration implement procedures to verify that all drivers provided by the site who regularly transport user groups:

    1. Have the appropriate license for vehicles to be driven, and
    2. Have had their driving records reviewed at the time of hire and at least annually thereafter?   **Yes No**

Interpretation: Some states and/or insurance policies specify age requirements for drivers who transport children.

Other factors to consider include driving experience, type of vehicle experience, and experience driving on the right-hand side of the road.

"Review" may be conducted through state police records or through evaluation by the site's insurance agent.

Compliance Demonstration: Staff description of procedures utilized.

SB-21

<table>
<tr><td colspan="2">Director's Pre-Visit Evaluation</td></tr>
<tr><td>A.</td><td>☐ Yes ☐ No</td></tr>
<tr><td>B.</td><td>☐ Yes ☐ No</td></tr>
<tr><td>C.</td><td>☐ Yes ☐ No</td></tr>
<tr><td>D.</td><td>☐ Yes ☐ No ☐ DNA</td></tr>
<tr><td>E.</td><td>☐ Yes ☐ No ☐ DNA</td></tr>
</table>

Are there written safety procedures required to be in practice for all vehicles used to transport campers and staff that include:

A. Training in safety regulations for traveling in vehicles? Yes No

B. Loading of vehicles only within the passenger seating capacity limits established by the manufacturer? Yes No

C. A requirement that participants wear seat belts when they are provided? Yes No

DNA D if vehicles do not travel in convoys.

D. Convoy travel procedures? Yes No

DNA E if persons are not transported in wheelchairs.

E. Transporting persons in wheelchairs including:
    1. Persons in wheelchairs are seatbelted into the wheelchairs (except when in watercraft), and
    2. Wheelchairs are in locked positions and secured to vehicles (except when in watercraft)? Yes No

Interpretation: Safety regulations in part A may include behavior guidelines such as remaining seated, obeying the driver, and orderly loading and unloading of buses or vans.

In part C, participants are required to utilize seat belts in all vehicles which provide them. It is not the intent to mandate seat belts in vehicles such as school buses where seat belts are not required by law. If young children or babies are transported, appropriate child restraint devices should be used.

Compliance Demonstration: Visitor observation of written regulations; staff description of other procedures.

SB-22

<table>
<tr><td colspan="2">Director's Pre-Visit Evaluation</td></tr>
<tr><td>☐ Yes</td><td>☐ No</td></tr>
</table>

Is there a written policy that requires passengers be oriented to safety regulations and emergency procedures? Yes No

Interpretation: This orientation may include, but is not limited to, policies concerning seatbelt use, appropriate behavior while the vehicle is in motion, loading and unloading vehicles, and what to do in case of vehicular breakdown, etc.

Compliance Demonstration: Visitor observation of written policy; staff description of orientation given.

*SB-23 Part A — MANDATORY

To provide first aid, does the site administration require staff with the following qualifications to be on duty at all times when user groups are present:

*A. Licensed physician, or registered nurse, or emergency medical technician, or paramedic, or an adult currently certified in American Red Cross Standard First Aid (minimum requirement), Medic First Aid, or the equivalent?   Yes   No

B. An adult currently certified in age appropriate cardiopulmonary resuscitation (CPR) from the American Red Cross, American Heart Association, or the equivalent?   Yes   No

Director's Pre-Visit Evaluation
A. ☐ Yes ☐ No
B. ☐ Yes ☐ No

Interpretation: The intent of this standard is that sites have a person on duty who is at least certified in first aid. Licensed practical nurses, licensed vocational nurses and physician's assistants have not been listed here since those licenses do not universally require training in first aid. When such emergency training can be documented, it would be considered equivalent.

CPR certification is available for infants (0-1 year), children (1-8 years), and adults (8 years and older).

In non-medical religious sites, there must be a person on duty who is designated to handle health and accident situations who meets the qualifications specified in writing by the religious body.

Compliance Demonstration: Director/staff description of process in place to assure coverage; visitor observation of licenses or certifications.

SB-24

Are site staff who are responsible for providing health care given training based on written procedures that:

1. Identify their role and responsibilities in site health care,
2. Prepare them to use supplies and equipment with which they may be furnished,
3. Identify those situations which should be attended to only by certified medical personnel, and
4. Mandate the use of universal precautions and identify procedures to be followed when dealing with body fluids and medical waste?
                                                    Yes   No

Director's Pre-Visit Evaluation
☐ Yes ☐ No

Site Approval

153

Interpretation: All site staff require some training to identify the limits and expectations of their participation in the delivery of health care, including first aid.

Typical instruction may include handling choking, seizures, severe allergic reactions, and first aid procedures.

Instruction should be provided on the content, use, availability, and re-supply of first aid kits. In addition, training should identify proper use of any other equipment or supplies to be used by staff.

"Universal precautions" are those work practices and housekeeping procedures which assume that all human blood and specified human body fluids are infectious for HIV, HBV, and other bloodborne pathogens. The use of barriers (masks, gloves, etc.), handwashing, sanitizing procedures and appropriate waste disposal are mandated by federal regulations. State departments of health can give guidance on appropriate handling and disposal procedures. "Medical waste includes such things as syringes, needles, or dressings wet with body fluids or blood.

Compliance Demonstration: Visitor observation of written procedures; staff description of training and procedures.

SB-25

Director's Pre-Visit Evaluation
☐ Yes ☐ No ☐ DNA

DNA if a non-medical religious site.

Are standing orders annually approved in writing by a licensed physician or is there evidence that written health care procedures are reviewed annually by a licensed physician?   **Yes   No**

Interpretation: "Standing orders" generally refer to specific treatments authorized by a licensed physician that are implemented by other licensed personnel such as nurses.

"Health care procedures" are less specific than standing orders and may include commonly accepted treatments for minor illnesses or injuries, general first aid guidelines, and identification of points at which professional medical treatment or advice should be sought. Such procedures should be developed, revised, or reviewed by a licensed physician.

See the Appendix (page 217) for a general outline of standing orders/health care procedures.

Compliance Demonstration: Visitor observation of signed standing orders, or of health care procedures with date and identification of reviewer noted.

SB-26

Does the site administration implement procedures to maintain the following records for use during site operation, and to keep them at least for a period of statutory limits:

Director's Pre-Visit
Evaluation

A. ☐ Yes ☐ No
B. ☐ Yes ☐ No

A. A health log in which the following information is recorded in ink:

   1. Date, time, and name of person injured or ill,

   2. General description of injury or illness,

   3. Description of treatment (if administered), including any treatment administered away from the health care facility,

   4. Administration of any routine medications, and

   5. Initials of person evaluating and treating?   Yes No

B. Accident reports completed for all accidents resulting in injury requiring professional medical treatment?   Yes No

Interpretation: A bound book with pre-printed page numbers and lined pages is frequently used to meet part A of this standard because of its acceptability in a court of law. Such a system is particularly helpful when multiple persons keep health records, or they are kept by persons without extensive medical training. Any system used should be reviewed by medical and legal counsel.

The administration of drugs on a daily, routine schedule to a number of participants may be recorded in one entry at the end of the session by appending daily medication records to the log.

"Requiring professional medical treatment" means all medical attention by or in consultation with a licensed physician following an accident (see part B).

Computerized records are not acceptable under this standard because there is not a method of ascertaining when records have been altered. Information in the log is usually not a specific as that required for accident or incident reports. However, detailed accident information should be readily available if needed.

The ACA Publications Department sells a "Camp Health Record Log Book" which can be used to meet the requirements of part A of this standard. "Accident/Incident Report Forms" are also available.

Compliance Demonstration: Visitor observation of logs, reports and other forms; site administrator description of process to maintain records.

SB-27

To prevent the unauthorized use of drugs, does the site administration require that all drugs dispensed by site health staff be:

Director's Pre-Visit
Evaluation

☐ Yes ☐ No

   1. Stored under lock (including those needing refrigeration), and

   2. Dispensed as follows:

     a. For prescription drugs — dispensed only under the specific direction of a licensed physician, and

     b. For non-prescription drugs — dispensed only under the site's written health care procedures, or under the signed instruction of the parent/guardian or the individual's physician?   Yes No

Site Approval

Interpretation: This standard applies to those medications and drugs kept to provide first aid on site, as well as any prescription medications collected and/or dispensed by site staff.

"Drugs" include all prescription medications as well as all over-the-counter drugs which are potentially hazardous if misused (e.g., aspirin, cold tablets). The intent of this standard is to prevent accidental and unauthorized use.

Exceptions would be for a limited amount of medication for life-threatening conditions <u>carried</u> by a participant or staff person (e.g. bee sting medication, inhaler), or limited medications approved for use in first aid kits.

Compliance Demonstration: Visitor observation of storage of drugs; staff description of procedures in use.

SB-28

Is there an infirmary or health care shelter available to handle first aid and emergency cases which provides:

     1. Protection from the elements,
     2. First aid and dispensary area,
     3. Available toilet(s),
     4. Available water for drinking and cleaning?

And, except for day use,

     5. One bed per 50 participants and staff, and
     6. Isolation, quiet and privacy?   **Yes   No**

Interpretation: "Available" toilets and water means they should be located in or next to the infirmary area so that ill or injured persons have easy access. Sufficient amounts of water for drinking and cleansing should be on hand.

Compliance Demonstration: Visitor observation of facility available for use.

SECTION SF — AQUATICS

> Score Aquatic section **ONLY IF** site makes
> **AQUATIC FACILITIES** available to user groups,
> whether or not staff is provided.

DEFINITIONS

Aquatic activity: Any activity, whether recreational or instructional, occurring in, on, or near water.

Aquatic area: The physical site of a specific aquatic activity. The aquatic area for swimming may be a pool, a lake, the ocean front, or other body of water. On a lake, there may be several aquatic areas: one for swimming, another for boating, and another for waterskiing.

Certification as used in these standards denotes that the individual holds the appropriate level of certification, and that such certification is current (it has not expired).

Equivalent certification allows for certifications from other countries and/or other nationally recognized organizations. A chart of certifictions from other countries is included in the Appendix (page 224). If the certification is not listed on that chart, directors should contact the Standards Department at the national office of ACA or the placement organization that secured the individual, for further information.

Lifeguard or **guard:** A person with the required certification to provide lifesaving and rescue skills.

*SF-1 MANDATORY

*DNA if swimming activities do not occur. (**Does** apply to activities such as diving, surfing, snorkeling, skin diving, and water slides, as well as swimming.)*

Is a policy in practice that either the site administration provides, or there is written evidence that each user group is required to provide, persons who hold one of the following current certifications to guard each <u>swimming</u> activity:

> **1. American Red Cross Lifeguard Training or Advanced Lifesaving,**
> **2. YMCA Lifeguard,**
> **3. Lifeguard BSA,**
> **4. Royal Lifesaving Bronze Medallion, or**
> **5. Equivalent certification?**   **Yes   No**

Director's Pre-Visit Evaluation		
☐ Yes	☐ No	☐ DNA

Interpretation: This standard applies to all swimming activities, whether recreational or instructional.

The policy may also specify recommended ratios of lifeguards to participants. See the Appendix (page 225) for factors to consider in establishing guarding ratios.

Compliance Demonstration: Director/staff explanation of policy's implementation; visitor observation of site staff certification cards and/or written policy for user groups.

*SF-2 MANDATORY

DNA if aquatic activities other than swimming do not occur. (Does apply to canoeing, rowing, sailing, waterskiing, boardsailing, etc.)

Is a written policy in practice that requires <u>each aquatic activity other than swimming</u> be supervised as follows:

DNA A if no youth groups are served.

*A. For youth groups — The site administration provides or there is written evidence that the youth group is required to provide a person who has:

1. American Red Cross Lifeguard Training, Advanced Lifesaving, or Emergency Water Safety,
2. YMCA Lifeguard,
3. Lifeguard BSA,
4. Royal Lifesaving Bronze Medallion,
5. Instructor rating in the appropriate craft, or
6. Equivalent certification?   Yes No

DNA B if no all-adult or family groups are served.

*B. For all-adult groups or for families with the parent(s) present and supervising —

1. Same as in part A, <u>or</u>
2. All-adult groups or families are oriented to written procedures requiring that:
a) PFDs be worn by all persons at all times,
b) Safety regulations be followed, and
c) A designated checkout system be utilized?   Yes No

Interpretation: In part B, "family group" means the parent/guardian is supervising his/her own children. When other people's children are involved, part A of the standard must be met.

"All-adult group" means every member of the group participating in the activity is an adult.

The purpose of the checkout system is to assure that someone in camp is aware that adults or families are utilizing watercraft. This system may identify the persons involved, the equipment in use, the approximate area of use and time of return.

Compliance Demonstration: Visitor observation of written policy; visitor observation of site staff certification cards and/or written policy and procedures for user groups; director/staff explanation of implementation.

Director's Pre-Visit Evaluation

☐ DNA
A. ☐ Yes ☐ No ☐ DNA
B. ☐ Yes ☐ No ☐ DNA

SF-3

Is there a policy that the site administration provides, or is there written evidence that each user group is required to provide, at least one person at each separate aquatic location or facility (pool, lake, river, etc.) holding certification in the following:

A. Standard First Aid (minimally) from the American Red Cross or the equivalent?   Yes No

B. Cardiopulmonary resuscitation for the appropriate age level from the American Red Cross, the American Heart Association, or the equivalent?   Yes No

Interpretation: CPR certification is available for infants (0-1 yr), children (1-8 yrs), and adults (8 yrs and over). If young children are served, Child CPR certification is appropriate.

Even though some first aid and lifeguarding certifications require CPR as a prerequisite, all certification dates must be verified for currency. CPR must be renewed every year.

For non-medical religious organizations, a person having the qualifications specified in writing by the religious program to handle emergency situations meets the intent of the standard.

Compliance Demonstration: Visitor observation of site staff certification cards and/or written user group policy.

SF-4

Are safety regulations established in writing for all aquatic activities and is there a system in practice to orient participants to those regulations?
                                                                 Yes No

Interpretation: Regulations should be specific to the aquatic area and activity. This includes such things as pool rules, boating regulations, navigation rules, appropriate and/or restricted areas of use, diving restrictions, safety signals or commands, behavior rules, required PFD use, non-swimmer restrictions, etc.

Orientation for user groups may be provided in writing if site staff are not supervising the activity.

Compliance Demonstration: Visitor observation of written safety regulations; staff description of orientation system.

SF-5

DNA if site does not provide staff for aquatic activities.

Does the site administration require that emergency procedures dealing specifically with near-drownings and other aquatic accidents be established in writing and be rehearsed periodically by site staff?   **Yes No**

Interpretation: Procedures and rehearsals should be specific to each aquatic area on site.

Compliance Demonstration: Visitor observation of written procedures; staff description of rehearsal.

SF-6

Does the site administration implement, or is there a written policy which is shared with user groups that requires them to implement, safety systems at all aquatic activities that enable lifeguards and lookouts to quickly account for all participants?   **Yes No**

Interpretation: The "buddy system" is a common example of a safety system for swimmers. It is not the only safe system, and others may be used to meet this standard. Tag boards and equipment check-out systems may be more appropriate for boating or other aquatic activities.

Compliance Demonstration: Staff description of system(s) used; visitor observation of written policy for user groups.

SF-7

DNA if site does not have a swimming pool.

If a swimming pool is used, are there procedures in practice that require:

    A. The following conditions be met:

        1. Access is controlled by a fence or other physical barrier,
        2. Water depths are clearly marked,
        3. Routine maintenance procedures appear to be in practice to address sanitation and safety concerns, and
        4. Pool rules are posted in a visible location?   **Yes No**

    B. Rescue equipment be readily available and in good repair?   **Yes No**

Interpretation: "Sanitation and safety concerns" include such things as chemical storage, covered drains, non-skid deck, ladders and diving boards in good repair, clear water, and absence of dirt, debris and algae.

Pool rules may include items such as no glass in pool area, no running, no diving in shallow end, swimming allowed only when guards are on duty, and so forth.

"Rescue equipment" should include at least reaching devices and a backboard.

Compliance Demonstration: Visitor observation of pool area and equipment; staff description of maintenance and sanitation procedures.

SF-8

DNA if natural bodies of water are not used for aquatic activities.

If a natural body of water is used for aquatic activities on site, are there procedures in practice that require:

A.   **The following conditions be met:**

   1. **Methods of controlling participant access are in practice,**
   2. **Known hazards are eliminated or activities near them are controlled,**
   3. **Facility equipment is regularly checked and maintained, and**
   4. **Separate areas are designated for aquatic activities?   Yes   No**

B.   **Rescue equipment be readily available and in good repair?   Yes   No**

Interpretation: Controlling participant access does not necessarily imply use of physical barriers, but may also include education, posting regulations, etc.

Hazards such as drop-offs, currents, and submerged objects should be eliminated when possible or clearly designated with warnings.

Facility equipment includes things such as docks, ladders, secured rafts, diving boards, etc. A system for safety checks and regular maintenance should be in place.

Areas for separate activities (e.g. swimming, waterskiing, boating, fishing) may be designated by physical markers, or by education, regulations, and/or scheduling.

Swimming areas should have a clearly defined shallow area for non-swimmers and defined diving area(s). Swimming areas for non-swimmers may be defined by ropes, buoys, booms, or deck markings; diving areas may be marked or posted, or designated in regulations.

"Rescue equipment" should include items such as backboards, ring buoys, reaching devices, or designated rescue boats, as appropriate to the activity.

Compliance Demonstration: Visitor observation of aquatic areas and equipment; staff description of procedures in use.

SF-9

DNA if persons in wheelchairs are not near bodies of water (natural or constructed).

Is there a requirement made known to user groups that seatbelts or ties be removed from all persons who are in wheelchairs while in watercraft or near bodies of water?   Yes   No

Compliance Demonstration: Staff description of procedures and method of informing user groups.

Site Approval

SF-10

DNA if no watercraft activities occur.

Is there a policy in practice, made known to user groups, that personal flotation devices (PFDs) are required to be:

A. **Safe for use as evidenced by:**

   1. **U.S. Coast Guard approval,**
   2. **Proper type, size and fit for each user,**
   3. **Buoyancy, as tested annually, sufficient to support designated weight, and**
   4. **A safety check given immediately prior to use?**   **Yes   No**

B. **Worn by all persons in small craft and in watercraft activities?**

                                                                    Yes   No

Interpretation: All PFDs used must be in serviceable condition (clasps, zippers, etc. working) and appropriate for the type of water and the activity. See Appendix (page 226) for a description of PFD types and uses.

Appropriate PFDs are to be worn by all participants and staff in canoes, rowboats, sailboats, etc. and on sailboards, water skis, etc.

Compliance Demonstration: Visitor observation of PFD use when possible; staff description of procedures for PFD usage.

SECTION SH — HORSEBACK RIDING

The Horseback Riding standards apply to all horseback riding activities including, but not limited to, English riding, western riding, trail riding, bareback riding, ring work, vaulting, and pony rides.

> Score the Horseback Riding section **ONLY IF** site provides horseback riding services to user groups, whether owned, rented, or leased animals and/or instructional services are provided.

SH-1

Are procedures being implemented which require that each horseback riding activity be led by an activity leader who has been trained to:

A. **Enforce established safety regulations?** Yes No

B. **Work with types of groups participating and provide necessary instruction?** Yes No

C. **Identify and manage environmental and other hazards related to the activity and the participants?** Yes No

D. **Apply emergency procedures related to the activity and the participants?** Yes No

Interpretation: If the horseback riding activity leader is not a site staff member, the site administrator must have assurances that the qualifications required by this standard are met.

Hazards in part C may include such things as trail conditions, temperament of horses, and behavior of participants (fear, excitement, endurance, etc.).

Compliance Demonstration: Director/staff description of implementation of the procedures; visitor observation of activities when possible.

SH-2

Are minimum ratios of horseback riding staff to participants established in writing and required to be in practice at each activity? Yes No

Interpretation: Ratios should be established in accordance with those recommended by authoritative sources and with the type of riding activities, types of user groups, and the area.

Compliance Demonstration: Visitor observation of written ratios; director/staff explanation of implementation.

SH-3

Is there a system in practice to:

1. **Evaluate and classify participants' riding ability, and**
2. **Assign them to horses, equipment, and activities commensurate with their ability?**   **Yes   No**

Interpretation: Evaluation does not necessarily imply a riding test. Participants may be interviewed and assigned to appropriate horses or activities until actual skill is demonstrated.

Even if assignments presume beginner or non-skilled level for everyone, individuals should still be evaluated to identify experience with the activity, comfort level, or fears that could affect their safety.

Compliance Demonstration: Staff description of system and procedures in use.

SH-4

Are safety regulations and emergency procedures specific to the activities:

A. **Established in writing?**   **Yes   No**

B. **Shared with all persons through orientation procedures prior to participation in riding activities?**   **Yes   No**

Interpretation: Safety regulations may include such things as requirements for helmets and boots, procedures for approaching horses, facility access and use limits, trail riding procedures, etc.

Emergency procedures include instructions on how to handle not only accidents such as a fall from a horse or injury from a kick but also emergencies such as a runaway horse.

Compliance Demonstration: Visitor observation of written regulations and procedures; staff description of orientation procedures.

SH-5

Does the site administrator implement procedures that require the following safety apparel be worn by participants and site staff:

A. **Shoes or boots that provide protection from:**

1. **Injury from being stepped on by horses, and,**
2. **If stirrups are used, feet becoming wedged into the stirrup (when stirrups are not specifically designed to prevent this occurrence)?**   **Yes   No**

B. **Long trousers?**   **Yes   No**

C. **Protective head gear constructed to minimize head injury in a fall, that fits the rider comfortably, does not obscure vision, and is secured by a strong chin strap?**   **Yes   No**

Interpretation: Shoes or boots that have firm, hard coverings offer protection far beyond tennis shoes or other soft-bodied shoes. A heel that prevents the shoe or boot from sliding too deeply into the stirrup can prevent the foot from becoming dangerously wedged.

This standard does not require the camp to use a particular kind of helmet. In consultation with authoritative sources, the camp administrator should determine the appropriate type of helmet based on the type and level of activity. Most horsemanship organizations (see Appendix, page 231) can supply lists of protective head gear that have undergone safety tests and have met minimum criteria for protection.

Compliance Demonstration: Visitor observation of horseback riding activity if possible; staff description of procedures in place.

SH-6

Does the site administrator train staff to implement a safety check of riding equipment prior to use, and is equipment that is not in good repair removed from service? **Yes No**

Director's Pre-Visit Evaluation

☐ Yes ☐ No

Compliance Demonstration: Visitor observation of equipment in use at riding activities; staff description of training received and procedures in use.

SH-7

Are stables, corrals, paddocks, and riding rings:

A. **Located away from living areas, with procedures in practice to control access?** **Yes No**

B. **Clean, free from accumulation of manure, and provided with a safe, clean, plentiful supply of water?** **Yes No**

Director's Pre-Visit Evaluation

A. ☐ Yes ☐ No
B. ☐ Yes ☐ No

Interpretation: "Away from" means that living areas (other than those for persons caring for horses) are located far enough from livestock to avoid increased flies, insects, undue odor, increased dust and dirt, etc.

Access may be controlled by such things as scheduling, education, or regulations, as well as with posted "off limits" signs and physical barriers.

In part B, water should be readily available, but should not create a safety hazard such as could be caused by having tubs of water inside the riding ring.

Compliance Demonstration: Visitor observation of stable and corral areas; staff description of procedures to maintain cleanliness and control access.

Part 4

Glossary

Glossary

Glossary

The following definitions apply throughout the standards. The information in parentheses indicates the standard number where this term first appears.

Activity leader: The staff member providing direct, on-site leadership at any program activity. (D-6)

Administrative personnel: Staff with supervisory and administrative responsibilities; may include positions such as camp director, assistant director, business manager, food service director, and health supervisor. (C-2)

Adventure/challenge activities: Include ropes course activities, spelunking, climbing, rappelling, initiative activities, and similar activities requiring spotting and/or belays. (D-21)

Aquatic activity: Any activity, whether recreational or instructional, occurring in, on, or near water. (F-1)

Aquatic area: The physical site of a specific aquatic activity. The aquatic area for swimming may be a pool, a lake, the ocean front, or other body of water. On a lake, there may be several aquatic areas such as one for swimming, another for boating, and another for waterskiing. (F-1)

Arrival and departure: Refers to what occurs on camp property as campers come to or leave the camp premises. (BT-3)

Associate visitor: A member of the American Camping Association who has completed at least twenty-one hours at training in order to assume responsibilities as a visitor, conducting camp accreditation visits. This individual shares the responsibility of a visit with a Lead Visitor.

Audit: A regular examination and verification of accounts and may be conducted either internally or externally. (SB-11)

Authoritative sources: Persons, organizations, etc. who have training and/or experience leading to expertise in a particular area. Examples include the American Red Cross in aquatics and first aid as well as individuals who have published or provided exemplary leadership in a particular area. (D-9)

Boardsailing: Also called sailboarding, windsurfing; operating a non-motorized, one-person sailing craft. (F-3)

Buildings: Permanent, enclosed structures that remain intact regardless of season. Tents and adirondack shelters are not considered buildings for the purposes of these standards. (A-11)

Camp or camping: A sustained experience which provides a creative, recreational, and educational opportunity in group living in the out-of-doors. It utilizes trained leadership and the resources of the natural surroundings to contribute to each camper's mental, physical, social, and spiritual growth.

Camp director: The individual on the campsite who holds the primary overall responsibility of the administration of program operations and support services (business, food service, health services, maintenance). These responsibilities may be delegated to other staff and the supportive functions shared by or coordinated by the site manager when applicable.

Counselor-support personnel: Auxiliary staff to aid special needs campers in daily living tasks. They generally do not have sole camper supervision responsibility and are often called aides or volunteers. They may be paid or unpaid. (C-5)

Counselors-in-training (CITs): Campers in leadership training programs. (C-4)

Day camp: A camp program that campers attend for an established period of time, returning to their homes at night, which provides creative, recreational and educational opportunities in group living in the out-of-doors. It utilizes trained leadership and the resources of the natural surroundings to contribute to each camper's mental, physical, and spiritual growth. It is principally oriented to providing such programming for children during school vacation periods.

Documented training and experience: Written evidence of competence in a leadership role. This may include records of previous leadership and/or training to instruct the activity, course completion certificates or cards, letters of reference, and/or written evaluation of previous successful leadership work. (Program, Specialized Activities sections)

Drugs: Includes all prescription medications as well as all over-the counter drugs which are potentially hazardous if misused (e.g. aspirin, cold tablets, etc.). (E-19)

Emergency accessories: Includes reflectors, fire extinguishers, or other supplies necessitated by weather conditions such as shovels and blankets. (BT-10)

Emergency exit: Does not imply a particular structure or evacuation device, but means a quick, safe, accessible alternative exit. Windows with screening could be considered emergency exits if occupants are informed of procedures for exit and could easily and safely escape through them. (*A-11)

Environmental hazards: May include those related to weather, terrain, or other conditions such as the presence of animals, poisonous plants, etc. (D-6)

Food contact surfaces: Anything that contacts raw food during preparation such as counters, cutting boards, knives, etc. (A-27)

Food handlers: Food service staff and any campers or program staff who regularly prepare food in decentralized living units. (A-27)

Food service utensils: Includes dishes, silverware and all other utensils used in the preparation or serving of food. (A-28)

General camp activities: Those activities that do not require special technical skills, equipment, or safety regulations other than general ones that apply throughout the camp. (C-4)

Handwashing facility: A supply of soap and fresh water, suitable for washing. It does not necessarily imply running water. (A-18)

Health care: Includes first aid, dispensing of medications, administration of prescribed medical treatment and health procedures as described in the Health Care Plan or Health Care Procedures and promotion of health and wellness practices in the camp. (Health Care Section)

Health care procedures: Less specific than standing orders and may include commonly accepted treatments for minor illnesses or injuries, general first aid guidelines, procedures for initial health screening, and identification of points at which professional medical treatment or advice should be sought. Such procedures should be developed, revised, or reviewed by a licensed physician. (E-6)

Health history: An annually updated record of one's past and present health status that is completed by the individual or by the parent/guardian if a minor. (E-8)

Health personnel: Persons employed to perform health-related functions and duties and may include the health manager, doctors, nurses, first aiders, and other persons charged primarily with health and/or first aid responsibilities.

Infirmary: A designated area for health care and supervision which provides shelter from the elements and has toilets and water supply for drinking and cleaning available in or next to facility for easy access. (E-20)

In-service training: Refers to training that occurs during the camp season while camp is in operation. (C-13)

Licensed medical personnel: Includes licensed physicians, certified or certification-eligible nurse practitioners, or other medical personnel licensed by the state. (E-11)

Lifeguard or guard: A staff member with the required certification to provide lifesaving and rescue skills. (F-2)

Lookout: Sometimes called "watcher" or "observer," may be any non-certified staff member assigned by and under the direct supervision of certified aquatic personnel, used in addition to those certified persons. (F-4)

Man-made hazards: May include public roads through camp property, construction activities on the camp site, abandoned wells, or other facilities on the site that may pose a risk. (B-2)

Medical waste: Such things as syringes, needles, or dressings wet with body fluids or blood. The use of barriers (masks and gloves), handwashing, sanitizing procedures and appropriate waste disposal should be considered in developing procedures in this area as appropriate to clientele served.(E-14)

Natural hazards: The presence on site of cliffs, poisonous snakes, wild animals, or other conditions of nature that may pose a risk to humans. (B-2)

Non-certified instructional assistants: Teaching assistants without current certification who are under the immediate supervision and direction of the certified instructor. (F-14)

Non-medical religious camp: A camp sponsored by a religious body whose church teachings concerning health are based on reliance upon faith rather than traditional medical intervention. The Christian Science Church is an example of such a sponsoring body.

Overnight/short trip: Trips, field trips, excursions, overnights of two nights or less. (D-13)

Participants: All persons involved in the camping operation including staff and campers.

Permanent sleeping quarters: Refers to structures, platform tents, covered wagons, etc. that are constructed in a fixed location and are used as primary residences for staff and campers. Temporary shelters such as tents used for overnight camping and backpacking would not fall under this classification. (A-22)

Pick up and drop off: Refers to picking up or returning a camper to his/her home or a central location near home. (BT-4)

Plan: A single document containing at least the information related to the topic specified in the standard.

Potentially hazardous (perishable) foods: Those foods that consist in whole or in part of milk or milk products, eggs, meat, poultry, fish, shellfish, edible crustacea or other ingredients (including synthetic ingredients) in a form capable of supporting growth of infectious or toxic microorganisms. Such food should be maintained at temperatures below 45 degrees F. or above 140 degrees F. (A-26)

Primarily serves campers with special needs: More than 50 percent of the campers enrolled for the camp season are special-needs campers.

Primitive camp: Those camps whose program is based on a philosophy centered on non-facility, utility-oriented principles. Generally, such camps have few permanent structures or facilities. (A-21)

Program activity: An individual event, class, or instructional period occurring under staff leadership or supervision that provides opportunity for recreational or educational participation by campers.

Program personnel: Staff directly involved in camp programming and camper supervision; may include such positions as unit supervisors, activity specialists, activity coordinators, and counselors. (C-2)

Regularly transport: Transportation is provided or arranged by the camp for scheduled or advertised camp activities or for transportation between camp and home. (Transportation standards, BT Section)

Rescue equipment: (In aquatics) Includes backboards, ring buoys, reaching devices, designated rescue boats, etc. appropriate to the activity. (F-12)

Short term staff: Staff (paid or unpaid) who are contracted for two weeks or less, excluding the training period. (C-7)

Site without facilities: Site that does not have buildings used for permanent sleeping quarters or substantial capital investment in structures. (A-2)

Small craft: Recreational boats up to 26 feet in length, such as canoes, kayaks, sailboats, rowboats, ski boats, rafts, etc. (Aquatics section, F Standards)

Special medical needs: Includes all disabling conditions which require special medical or health attention or care while the participant is in camp including chronic conditions such as insulin dependent diabetes or epilepsy, illnesses such as cancer, or physically disabling conditions such as spina bifida, etc. (E-16)

Special-needs campers: Campers with physical, medical, or behavioral characteristics that require special consideration in the camp setting. Examples include campers with physical disabilities, emotional disturbances, learning disabilities, mental retardation, or medical conditions such as diabetes, cancer, and asthma.

Staff: Includes all personnel, both paid and unpaid.

Staffed public facility: A facility not on the campsite where persons other than camp staff are responsible for the site and for supervision of the activity.

Standing orders: Specific treatments authorized by a licensed physician that are implemented by other licensed personnel. (E-6)

Support personnel: Those who provide services to the site other than activity programming and may include positions such as office work, maintenance, food service, aides or volunteers, or drivers.

Travel camp: A camp whose singular specialty is travel camping.

Travel camping: A program in which a group uses motorized transportation to move from one site to another for three nights or more, for experiences in different environments. Motorized transportation is normally a van, bus, or car, though it may also be a plane, boat, train, or a combination of those vehicles.

Trip camp: A camp whose area of program specialization is tripping, that generally has no permanent base camp.

Tripping or trip camping: a program in which a group of individuals move under their own power or by individually guided vehicle or animal (e.g. bicycle, horse, boat) and travel from one campsite to another for three nights or more (as differentiated from overnight camping).

Visitor: An individual trained and certified by the American Camping Association to conduct accreditation visits in the ACA Standards Programs.

Watercraft activity: Includes use of small craft (canoeing, sailing, rowing, kayaking, rafting, motorboating, etc.) as well as boardsailing, waterskiing, windsurfing, etc.

Glossary

173

Part 5

Self-Assessment of Additional Professional Practices for ACA Camp Directors

Signature of Reviewer: _____

Date of Last Review: _____

_____

_____

_____

INTRODUCTION

ACA Standard B-1 requires that the following "Self-Assessment of Additional Professional Practices" be completed. This document consists of practices which have been accepted by camping professionals as basic to camp operation.

Previous editions of *Standards With Interpretations* have included these items as standards which were individually scored in the accreditation process. As new items were added to the standards, the business practices and other items listed below were grouped into a new format and retained in this self-assessment process for directors. The entire self-assessment process is scored as one standard for ACA accreditation.

The intent of this document is to remind administrators of professionally accepted practices, and to encourage on-going self-analysis and growth in these areas. It is suggested that administrators identify steps to help their camps maintain a current, fresh approach to the administration of their operation. A "yes/no" or "met/not met" process is inadequate to encourage the camp to stretch beyond these minimum requirements. Therefore, options have been provided to identify recommendations for future action and other means to plan to move forward in these important areas.

The items below should be considered when starting a new camp, and they are also valuable reminders to current administrators. Some have been part of the recommended practices of the camping profession for over fifty years. Others have been introduced more recently. All have been updated to be consistent with current regulations and camp practices.

This assessment is to be used in conjunction with the accreditation standards contained in *Standards for Day and Resident Camps*. It is not designed to be used alone, but as a complement to the health, safety, and program quality focus of the standards in the accreditation program of the American Camping Association.

DIRECTIONS

Consider and assess your compliance with each item listed in this self-assessment tool, marking it "met" or "not met" as applicable. The **Considerations** will help you identify the intent or scope of the item to be assessed. **Additional considerations** suggest related areas that may assist you to stretch beyond simply meeting the minimum.

The right-hand column may be used for your notes, plans, ideas, or action steps. It is not ACA's expectation that there be notes under every item. It is suggested that as you continually evaluate your own operation, a number of these items would be addressed each year.

The ACA visitors will expect to see a copy of this self-assessment tool on the day of the visit. They will be looking to see that it has been used in your evaluation process. It is expected that several areas of growth or analysis will be in process at the time of the visit as an indication of your on-going commitment to self-improvement.

Self-Assessment of Additional Professional Practices

SITE

1. **Site or accessible areas provide natural resources that are used in camp program.**

   Considerations:

   The out-of-doors environment is utilized frequently to enrich campers' experiences at camp.

   Camp program and practices encourage responsible care and preservation of our natural surroundings.

   ☐ Met   ☐ Not Met

   Recommendations:
   _____

2. **Campers and staff receive instruction to control their impact on the environment and the site use demonstrates understanding of and concern for environmental protection.**

   Considerations:

   Is staff trained to understand the impact of program activities and their individual actions on the environment?

   Are program activities deliberately planned for campers to help them understand stewardship of the natural world?

   Are ecologically responsible practices being followed on the campsite?

   Has the camp reviewed and implemented recommendations concerning the use of plastics or non-degradable substances in camp?

   ☐ Met   ☐ Not Met

   Action Steps:
   _____

☐ Met   ☐ Not Met

Steps Requiring Action This Year:

_____

3. Appropriate insect/weed control methods are in effect, and only approved pesticides or herbicides are utilized on the property as identified by state/local codes.

Considerations:

What substances are banned in your jurisdiction?

Is the advice of local soil conservation officials periodically sought and followed?

Are appropriate insect control methods utilized in the dining hall?

Is the safety of persons and animals considered in decisions relating to control methods?

Additional considerations:

Are maintenance persons aware of banned substances or those that create problems for humans and animals?

☐ Met   ☐ Not Met

Action Steps:

_____

4. Erosion control methods are in practice where applicable.

Considerations:

Are appropriate control methods in effect on paths, around culverts and buildings, and elsewhere?

Who has the responsibility to regularly evaluate camp areas to determine where erosion may be creating unsafe conditions?

☐ Met   ☐ Not Met

Recommendations:

_____

5. Laundry facilities are available on site or nearby for campers and staff in long-term camps and for campers with special needs.

Considerations:

Are there campers with bladder control problems that may require frequent washing of bed clothes?

Sensitivity to staff and camper needs often separates the good from the excellent. How are you evaluating these needs and addressing persistent complaints/comments?

180

6. **Storage facilities are available for all supplies and equipment both during the season and off-season.**

   Considerations:

   Are equipment and supplies protected from unauthorized use?

   Is the camp's investment in supplies and equipment protected by safe and adequate storage?

   Does insurance coverage reflect the location of equipment both during the season and the off-season?

☐ Met   ☐ Not Met

Recommendations:
_____

7. **Adequate shelter for all campers and staff is provided during inclement weather.**

   Considerations:

   Is there adequate space for program to continue in spite of the weather?

   Has appropriate shelter been provided/identified for use in case of tornado, flood, or other severe conditions?

   What future needs can you predict?

☐ Met   ☐ Not Met

Recommendations:
_____

8. **Dining facilities have adequate space to allow freedom of movement at and between tables.**

   Considerations:

   Can the dining hall be vacated quickly in an emergency?

   Do persons with restricted mobility have freedom of movement in the dining hall?

☐ Met   ☐ Not Met

Recommendations:
_____

Self-Assessment

181

☐ Met ☐ Not Met

Action Steps:

9. The site provides separate facilities to provide privacy and freedom from campers for staff during their time off.

Considerations:

Is there a place for staff to "get away?"

What steps could be taken to improve the living accommodations and provision for staff living areas, lounges, and their ability to "get away" on their time off?

☐ Met ☐ Not Met

Recommendations:

10. Administrators using a non-owned site have a written agreement with the site owner specifying responsibility for the use of the site, facilities, equipment and services.

Considerations:

Is there a clear line of authority and responsibility for the above-named items?

Additional considerations:

When was this contract last reviewed by legal counsel?

What additional follow-up might be done with lease/rental groups to help you improve services?

☐ Met ☐ Not Met

Recommendations:

11. The camp has implemented a system to respond to special dietary needs of participants.

Considerations:

When and how do you discover special dietary needs?

Are you able and willing to accommodate them?

12. **Food records including menus, purchase records, inventories and numbers of persons served are maintained.**

☐ Met   ☐ Not Met

Changes Required: _____

Considerations:

Location of records: _____

_____

Who is responsible to maintain this information?

13. **Menus have been planned and/or approved by a nutritionist, dietician, or other person qualified to evaluate the nutrition and balance of the meals served.**

☐ Met   ☐ Not Met

Recommendations: _____

Approved by: _____

Date of last review: _____

Additional considerations:

Do menus include food items that reflect the cultural diversity and food preferences of your clientele?

14. **Food service staff wear appropriate hair covers as required by state/local regulations, and wear clean, neat, practical clothing.**

☐ Met   ☐ Not Met

Comments: _____

Considerations:

Local health departments are the source for current information on the hair cover requirement.

Additional considerations:

What training might be available from local health departments or colleges to train food service staff?

Self-Assessment

ADMINISTRATION

☐ Met   ☐ Not Met

Action Steps:

_____

15. **The camp has a Comprehensive Plan that is evaluated at least every 3 years to assess current conditions and project needs in each of the following areas:**

    a) **Site and facility development and/or management**
    b) **Program**
    c) **Market**
    d) **Finance and administration**
    e) **Environmental protection and preservation.**

    Considerations:

    Is there a master site plan?

    Is the camp's philosophy reflected in the above areas?

    Date of last evaluation:_____

    Additional considerations:

    What steps need to be taken in maintenance, program, and development to improve your camp's image and ability to serve your clientele?

☐ Met   ☐ Not Met

Recommendations:

_____

16. **The camp has implemented risk management planning that identifies possible operational financial risks, assesses how to handle those risks, and formulates a plan to handle them.**

    Considerations:

    Operational financial risks are those where property, equipment, and/or money might be damaged or lost. See the Appendix (page 204) for further information on risk management planning.

    When was your plan last reviewed by:

    Legal counsel? _____

    Insurance personnel? _____

17. **Parent/camp communication is facilitated through interviews, visitation days, newsletters, evaluation/suggestion, etc.**

    ☐ Met   ☐ Not Met

    Recommendations: _____

    Considerations:

    The purpose of communication may be to evaluate camp, provide information to parents, give opportunity for parents to interact with staff, etc.

18. **Procedures are in practice regarding the use and release of any and all personal information regarding campers and staff.**

    ☐ Met   ☐ Not Met

    Action Steps: _____

    Considerations:

    Do you obtain permission to release or print photos of individuals?

    Who has access to personnel records, financial records, medical records, and camper evaluations?

    To whom and under what conditions is information released to persons outside of the camp?

19. **Budgeting, bookkeeping and audit procedures consistent with good accounting practices are utilized annually.**

    ☐ Met   ☐ Not Met

    Action Steps: _____

    Considerations:

    Should your audit procedures be carried out internally or externally?

    Additional considerations:

    Are auditors' recommendations sought and followed concerning recordkeeping and other financial matters?

☐ Met   ☐ Not Met

Recommendations:

_____

20. Inventories of all facilities and equipment are reviewed and revised at least annually.

Considerations:

Are the inventories reviewed by camp administration in consideration not only of purchasing needs but also in light of insurance needs, equipment replacement schedules, depreciation schedules, and identification of equipment or supplies available for use?

Who is responsible for updating inventories?

☐ Met   ☐ Not Met

Recommendations:

_____

21. Arrangements for legal counsel have been made and such counsel is available as problems arise.

Attorney: _____

Phone:_____

Additional considerations:

Has the advice of legal counsel been sought concerning:
- review of application (camper and staff) forms and contracts?
- risk management planning?
- personnel policies and practices?

☐ Met   ☐ Not Met

Recommendations:

_____

22. The camp has identified appropriate laws, codes, and regulations affecting its operation including (but not limited to) areas such as wage and hour laws, sanitation codes, boat and vehicle registration and inspection, fire codes, plumbing codes, child abuse reporting regulations, and required operational permits and licenses.

Considerations:

Does the camp administrator/director:

a) participate in ACA meetings to stay current with legislation?
b) obtain a listing of laws applicable and make those requirements known to affected staff?

23. **Research projects involving persons in camp are in conformity with existing codes and federal regulations regarding protecting human subjects.**

☐ Met   ☐ Not Met

Recommendations: _____

Considerations:

Are such projects carried out in camp?

Is the researcher following appropriate procedures?

Do you have a contract with the researcher assuring that such protection will be provided?

PERSONNEL

24. **Each staff member is provided with a contract specifying salary or wages (if applicable), length of employment, benefits, and reference to job description and personnel policies.**

☐ Met   ☐ Not Met

Do contracts require further review at this time? If so, by whom? _____

Considerations:

Have staff contracts been reviewed recently by legal counsel?

25. **Each staff member is provided a job description defining duties and the position to which he/she is responsible.**

☐ Met   ☐ Not Met

Do job descriptions require further review at this time? If so, by whom? _____

Considerations:

Are they provided to both paid and volunteer staff?

Additional considerations:

Do staff review descriptions at the close of the season to suggest possible revisions?

Are performance appraisals based on identified duties and responsibilities?

☐ Met   ☐ Not Met

Action Required: _____

26. Each staff member is provided with or has access to an organizational chart.

Considerations:

Charts not only provide an overview of the entire staffing pattern, but also provide a clear picture of lines of responsibility and authority.

Does your chart reflect the current organization and makeup of your camp staff?

☐ Met   ☐ Not Met

Do personnel policies require further review at this time? If so, by whom? _____

27. Personnel policies are provided to all staff and include information on remuneration, time off, absence from work, health examinations and health histories, insurance, conditions of severance, performance evaluations, personal conduct, and any special conditions of service.

Considerations:

Personnel policies are also required by ACA's "Exemplary Ethical Practices for Camp Directors/ Owners."

Additional considerations:

Have personnel policies been reviewed by legal counsel?

☐ Met   ☐ Not Met

Recommendations: _____

28. In order to help encourage equal treatment of all children, the camp administration advises parents and staff that gratuities are prohibited.

Considerations:

Gratuities include monetary and/or expensive gifts.

Common professional practice identifies it as the camp's responsibility to appropriately remunerate its staff.

Additional considerations:

Have your reviewed salary ranges in similar camps and made efforts to update salary structures annually?

Have you instituted a graduated salary structure that recognizes experience, education and skills/ certifications?

29. The camp director has participated in at least one local or national ACA training program annually.

Date of sessions: _____

Topics: _____

Considerations:

In-service training and "networking" for the camp director, and for all camp staff, is valuable to the camp in keeping abreast of current trends and issues.

☐ Met   ☐ Not Met

Recommendations: _____

30. At least 20% of the camp administrative staff possess at least a bachelor's degree.

Considerations:

What efforts have been made by the camp administration to continually update the skill, training, and experience level of its staff?

☐ Met   ☐ Not Met

What changes are needed in your minimum staff requirements? _____

31. At least 50% of the camp's administrative and program staff are contracted for the entire season.

Considerations:

Continuity of staff and program is an important asset in a well-managed camp. There are many advantages to having staff members who are trained, experienced, and work together over an entire season.

Additional considerations:

How are part-time or short-term staff integrated with full-time staff?

☐ Met   ☐ Not Met

What changes are needed in your minimum staff requirements? _____

Self-Assessment

189

PROGRAM

☐ Met   ☐ Not Met

What action steps are required?

32. Contracts have been signed with all providers of program services such as aquatics, tripping and horseback riding that specify responsibility for meeting the intent of appropriate ACA standards.

Considerations:

Such contracts should identify items such as who is responsible to provide and maintain safety equipment or other gear used in the activity, responsibility for classifying and/or excluding campers from participation, establishing safety rules, providing emergency care in case of illness or injury, and other conditions established in the standards for the given activity.

Additional considerations:

Have such contracts been reviewed by the camp's legal counsel?

☐ Met   ☐ Not Met

Action Steps:

33. Campers participate in program planning in a variety of in-camp and off-season ways.

Considerations:

What deliberate methods have been implemented to identify and meet camper needs, interests, and preferences?

☐ Met   ☐ Not Met

What action steps are required?

34. There is flexibility in programming as evidenced by willingness to modify schedules and by the encouragement of spontaneous activities.

Considerations:

Staff are trained to respond to "teachable moments" and to modify schedules for weather or other reasons.

Additional considerations:

Staff and campers are involved in the periodic evaluation of camp program.

35. Campers choose daily some of the activities in which they participate.

Considerations:

Decision-making skills are important in the growth and development of campers. Opportunities for individual choice on a routine basis help campers practice decision-making skills.

Additional considerations:

What training could be provided to staff to help them assist campers in the development of skills such as decision making, relating effectively with others, and so forth?

☐ Met   ☐ Not Met

What action steps are required?

36. There are deliberately planned program activities designed to foster understanding of individual differences and group cooperation.

Considerations:

As our world "shrinks" and becomes a mosaic of individuals from varied backgrounds, it is important for the camping community to be proactive in developing skills of understanding and cooperation.

☐ Met   ☐ Not Met

What action steps are required?

37. There are deliberately planned program opportunities designed to help campers develop socially.

Considerations:

Staff are trained to design programs that encourage campers' social development.

☐ Met   ☐ Not Met

What action steps are required?

☐ Met   ☐ Not Met

Recommendations:

_____

38. Campers are free to practice their religious customs and to discuss spiritual matters in a manner that does not offend the rights and beliefs of others.

Considerations:

This statement does not require the camp to conduct religious services or provide religious instruction. Rather, it indicates that persons are free to practice their customs (e.g. prayer, recognizing religious holidays, etc.) or discuss spiritual topics in an open, non-forceful atmosphere.

Part 6

Appendix

Disclaimer

The forms in this manual are designed for use as samples only. Such forms should be carefully reviewed with the camp's legal counsel. They serve only as a guide for use in specific situations.

American Camping Association, Inc., disclaims any responsibility or liability which may be claimed to arise from, or to have arisen from, reliance upon such forms.

American Camping Association®
CAMP ACCREDITATION

Annual Statement of Compliance

American Camping Association Accredited Camp describes the operation of the site and the program of a camp by an owner/director. This may be sought by a camp operating on its own property or on the property belonging to someone else. The visitation requires establishing compliance with standards related to the camp site, and with standards related to camp program and operation, and it must occur while the full camp is in operation.

In order to apply for or maintain accreditation, a legal representative must sign the statement of compliance annually, and must agree to an on-site visit as determined by the Section but at least once every three years.

Statement of Compliance

1. I hereby concur with the definition of camping as set forth by the American Camping Association:

Camping is a sustained experience which provides a creative educational and recreational opportunity in group living in the out-of-doors. It utilizes trained leadership and the resources of the natural surroundings to contribute to each camper's mental, physical, social and spiritual growth.

2. I hereby confirm that the camp listed below is operating under the applicable federal, state and local laws, codes and regulations, and all required permits and licenses have been obtained.

The compliance with legal requirements of the jurisdictions within which a camp is located is the responsibility of the camp; enforcement is the responsibility of the appropriate government official. The American Camping Association does not consider itself a legal agency to enforce the law. Where the ACA Standard requires higher performance than the legal requirements, a camp must comply with the Standard.

3. If continuing my camp's accreditation, I affirm that the camp continues to meet the standards verified by the visitors on the day of the visit.

4. I understand that my camp accreditation may be withdrawn

a. if false information is knowingly provided to the visitors or the standards chairperson or his/her representatives; or

b. if it is verified that compliance with mandatory standards is not being continually maintained; or

c. if ACA has been notified by appropriate federal, state or local authorities that laws which significantly affect the health and safety of campers or staff have been violated, or ACA has documented reason to believe that such violations have occurred; or

d. at the discretion of the Section Board, following a Section Review and notification of the National Standards Board (NSB) prior to such action being taken. The camp has the right of appeal to the NSB in the event of such action. The NSB has the final and absolute authority in such matters.

5. My camp has complied and will continue to comply with all of the applicable mandatory standards for Camp Accreditation.
(Note: The mandatory standards are listed on the reverse side of this page.)

6. I affirm that I am willing to be held accountable for the provisions of the Code of Exemplary Ethical Practices for Camp Directors/Owners of the American Camping Association as established March, 1989.

> As the legally authorized representative of Camp _____ _____
> I do hereby affirm that we meet the requirements established in the Statement of Compliance above, and adhere to the mandatory standards for Camp Accreditation listed below. We wish to apply for or continue our camp accreditation.
>
> Dates of program being accredited from ___/___/___ to ___/___/___ which represent a gross operating income or expense (whichever is larger) of $_____
>
> _____
> **Signature**   **Date**
>
> _____
> **Position**

A separate form must be signed annually for *each* camp seeking accreditation.

over for mandatory standards →

*A-8

Are all firearms and ammunition in camp stored under lock?

Yes No

*A-9

Is there implementation of policies requiring that gas and liquid flammables, explosives, and poisonous materials be:
1. Stored in covered, safe containers that are plainly labeled as to contents,
2. Handled only by persons trained or experienced in their safe use, and
3. Stored in locations separate from food? Yes No

*A-11 Parts A and C

Are all buildings used by campers or staff for sleeping constructed or equipped with the following safety features:
*A. At least one emergency exit in addition to the main door or entrance? Yes No
*C. A direct means of emergency exit to the outside from each sleeping floor that does not have a ground level entrance?

Yes No

*D-19 Part D (and *G-11, D for Trip/Travel)

Has training been provided to campers and staff in written procedures that require:
*D. Persons using camp stoves and/or flammable liquids be instructed in their proper use and care and supervised until competency is demonstrated? Yes No

*E-5 Part A (and *G-4 for Trip/Travel)

To provide first aid, does the camp require that staff with the following qualifications be on duty in camp at all times when campers are present:
*A. Licensed physician, or registered nurse, or emergency medical technician, or paramedic, or a staff member currently certified in American Red Cross Standard First Aid (minimum requirement), Medic First Aid, or the equivalent?

Yes No

*E-8

Has the camp administration implemented a policy requiring signed health histories that ask for all of the following to be on site for all campers and all staff:
1. Description of any current health conditions requiring medication, treatment, or special restrictions or considerations while at camp,
2. Record of past medical treatment,
3. Record of immunizations, including date of last tetanus shot, and
4. Record of allergies? Yes No

*E-13

Is there evidence that emergency transportation is available at all times for medical emergencies, provided by either:
1. The camp, or
2. Community emergency services with whom prior arrangements have been made in writing? Yes No

*F-2 Part A (and *F-21, A for public facilities)

Is there a policy in practice that each swimming activity be guarded by a staff member who is:
*A. Certified — Holds one of the following:
1. American Red Cross Lifeguard Training
2. YMCA Lifeguard, or
3. Lifeguard BSA, or
4. Royal Lifesaving Bronze Medallion, or
5. Equivalent certification? Yes No

*F-3 Part A (and *F-21, B for public facilities)

At each aquatic activity, other than swimming, is there a policy in practice that a staff member be on duty who is:
*A. Certified — Holds one of the following:
1. American Red Cross Lifeguard Training, or Emergency Water Safety, or
2. YMCA Lifeguard, or
3. Lifeguard BSA, or
4. Royal Lifesaving Bronze Medallion, or
5. Instructor rating in the appropriate craft, or
6. Equivalent certification? Yes No

*F-5 Part B (and *F-21, C for public facilities)

Is there a policy in practice requiring that a staff member be present and accessible at each separate aquatic location or facility (pool, lake, river, etc.) who holds the following current certification(s):
*B. Cardiopulmonary Resuscitation for the age level served from the American Red Cross, the American Heart Association, or the equivalent? Yes No

*F-11 Parts A and B

Is there a written policy in practice which establishes procedures for staff use of aquatic activities that specifies:
*A. For swimming — Certified guards (as in F-2) are present at all times, and procedures specify when guards or lookouts must be out of the water? Yes No

*B. For activities other than swimming — Qualifications for use, safety regulations, and times when facilities and equipment may be used by staff; and if certified personnel are not present, a checkout system is utilized? Yes No

*F-15

Do procedures require that a staff person with current Scuba Instructor rating from the Professional Association of Diving Instructors (PADI), National Association of Underwater Instructors (NAUI), Scuba Schools International (SSI), YMCA, or equivalent certification be present whenever scuba diving occurs?

Yes No

*G-6 Part B

Are all campers and staff required to participate in pre-trip orientation that includes at least:
*B. Information and training on how and where to obtain medical and/or emergency assistance on the trip?

Yes No

*G-15

Is there a policy in practice requiring that all aquatic activities be guarded/supervised by:
1. For aquatic trips, where the primary activity or mode of travel is in/on the water, a staff member who:
   a. Is certified in American Red Cross Lifeguard Training, Emergency Water Safety, Instructor rating in the appropriate craft, or the equivalent, and/or
   b. Has documented skills and training in water rescue and emergency procedures specific to the location and the activity; and/or
2. For travel or backpacking trips, where aquatic activity is incidental, a staff member who is certified in American Red Cross Lifeguard Training, Advanced Lifesaving, Emergency Water Safety, or the equivalent?

Yes No

American Camping Association®
SITE APPROVAL

Annual Statement of Compliance

American Camping Association Approved Site describes the facilities and services offered to another camp director or program director. This designation is only applicable to camps that rent or lease their facilities to other groups who retain the responsibility for their own program. The visitation requires establishing compliance with standards related to the camp site, and to services offered to user groups, and it should occur while the site is in use by a user group.

In order to apply for or maintain site approval, a legal representative must sign the statement of compliance annually, and must agree to an on-site visit as determined by the Section but at least once every three years.

Statement of Compliance

1. **I hereby concur with the definition of camping as set forth by the American Camping Association:**

   Camping is a sustained experience which provides a creative educational and recreational opportunity in group living in the out-of-doors. It utilizes trained leadership and the resources of the natural surroundings to contribute to each camper's mental, physical, social and spiritual growth.

2. **I hereby confirm that the camp listed below is operating under the applicable federal, state and local laws, codes and regulations, and all required permits and licenses have been obtained.**

   The compliance with legal requirements of the jurisdictions within which a camp is located is the responsibility of the camp; enforcement is the responsibility of the appropriate government official. The American Camping Association does not consider itself a legal agency to enforce the law. Where the ACA standard requires higher performance than the legal requirements, a camp must comply with the standard.

3. **If continuing my camp's site approval, I affirm that the camp continues to meet the standards verified by the visitors on the day of the visit.**

4. **I understand that my camp's site approval may be withdrawn**

   a. if false information is knowingly provided to the visitors or the standards chairperson or his/her representatives; or

   b. if it is verified that compliance with mandatory standards is not being continually maintained; or

   c. if ACA has been notified by appropriate federal, state or local authorities that laws which significantly affect the health and safety of campers or staff have been violated, or ACA has documented reason to believe that such violations have occurred; or

   d. at the discretion of the Section Board, following a Section Review and notification of the National Standards Board (NSB) prior to such action being taken. The camp has the right of appeal to the NSB in the event of such action. The NSB has the final and absolute authority in such matters.

5. **My camp has complied and will continue to comply with all of the applicable mandatory standards for Site Approval.**
   (Note: The mandatory standards are listed on the reverse side of this page.)

6. **I affirm that I am willing to be held accountable for the provisions of the Code of Exemplary Ethical Practices for Camp Directors/Owners of the American Camping Association as established March, 1989.**

As the legally authorized representative of Camp _____
I do hereby affirm that we meet the requirements established in the Statement of Compliance above, and adhere to the mandatory standards for Site Approval listed below. We wish to apply for or continue our site approval.

Dates of season being accredited from ___/___/___ to ___/___/___ which represent a gross income or expense (whichever is larger of $ _____

_____
Signature   **Date**

_____
Position

A separate form must be signed annually for *each* camp seeking site approval.

over for mandatory standards →

Appendix

Mandatory Standards for Site Approval

*SA-13

Are all firearms and ammunition owned by site owner/operator or site staff stored under lock?   **Yes   No**

*SA-14

Is there implementation of policies requiring that gas and liquid flammables, explosives, and poisonous materials be:
1. Stored in covered, safe containers that are plainly labeled as to contents,
2. Handled only by persons trained or experienced in their safe use, and
3. Stored in locations separate from food?   **Yes   No**

*SA-16 Parts A and C

Are all buildings used by site staff or user groups for sleeping constructed or equipped with the following safety features:

*A. At least one emergency exit in addition to the main door or entrance?   **Yes   No**

*C. A direct means of emergency exit to the outside from each sleeping floor that does not have a ground level entrance?
   Yes   No

*SB-6

Is there evidence that transportation is available at all times for any medical emergencies of user groups provided by either:
1. The site, or
2. Community emergency services with whom prior arrangements have been made in writing, or
3. The user group, as evidenced by a written policy requiring the group to provide their own emergency transportation?
   Yes   No

*SB-23 Part A

To provide first aid, does the site administration require staff with the following qualifications to be on duty at all times when user groups are present:

*A. Licensed physician, or registered nurse, or emergency medical technician, or paramedic, or an adult currently certified in American Red Cross Standard First Aid (minimum requirement), Medic First Aid, or the equivalent?   **Yes   No**

*SF-1

Is a policy in practice that either the site administration provides, or there is written evidence that each user group is required to provide, persons who hold one of the following current certifications to guard each <u>swimming</u> activity:
1. American Red Cross Lifeguard Training,
2. YMCA Lifeguard,
3. Lifeguard BSA,
4. Royal Lifesaving Bronze Medallion, or
5. Equivalent certification?   **Yes   No**

*SF-2

Is a written policy in practice that requires <u>each aquatic activity other than swimming</u> be supervised as follows:

*A. For youth groups — The site administration provides or there is written evidence that the youth group is required to provide a person holding:
1. American Red Cross Lifeguard Training, or Emergency Water Safety,
2. YMCA Lifeguard,
3. Lifeguard BSA,
4. Royal Lifesaving Bronze Medallion,
5. Instructor rating in the appropriate craft, or
6. Equivalent certification?   **Yes   No**

*B. For all-adult groups or for families with the parent(s) present and supervising —
1. Same as in part A, <u>or</u>
2. All-adult groups or families are oriented to written procedures requiring that:
   a. PFDs be worn by all persons at all times,
   b. Safety regulations be followed, and
   c. A designated checkout system be utilized?
   Yes   No

Written Documents Required of Camps Seeking Camp Accreditation

STANDARD	TOPIC	STAFF ASSIGNED
A-1	Fire and law enforcement contact letter	_____
A-3	Approval of water supply	_____
A-4	Blueprints/charts of utility and sanitation lines	_____
A-24	Documentation of food service supervisor training/experience	_____
A-26	Refrigeration temperature charts	_____
A-28	Dishwasher temperature charts	_____
B-1	Self-Assessment documentation	_____
B-2	Risk management materials	_____
B-3	Safety regulations and emergency procedures	_____
B-4	Incident/accident reports	_____
B-6	Search and rescue procedures	_____
B-7	Procedures for safety in public places	_____
B-8	Emergency communications plan	_____
B-9	Procedures on release of minors and verification of absentees	_____
B-10	Policy on camper/staff personal equipment, vehicles and animals	_____
B-12	Insurance coverage	_____
BT-5	Transportation information for parents	_____
BT-7	Vehicle accident procedures	_____
BT-9	Safety procedures for transporting campers and staff	_____
BT-11	Transportation policies on health information and supervision	_____
BT-12	Authorization from owners of private vehicles	_____
BT-14	Vehicle mechanical evaluation	_____
BT-15	Policy on vehicle safety checks	_____
BT-17	Training records and driver procedures	_____
C-2, C-4, C-5, C-6	Chart of staff	_____
C-3	Documentation of work histories or references	_____
C-4	Supervision procedures/ratios	_____
C-11	Behavior management procedures	_____
C-12	Staff organization chart or list	_____
D-1	Goals and objectives	_____
D-8, D-13, D-21, D-28, D-32, D-38, and D-42	Documentation of activity supervisor skill and training	_____
D-9, D-14, D-22, D-29, D-33, D-39, and D-43	Operating procedures for specialized activities	_____
*D-19	Camping procedures	_____
D-27	Documentation of ropes course maintenance	_____
E-1	Health Care plan	_____

Appendix

E-4	Certification/license of camp health manager or personnel on-call/on-site daily	_____
*E-5	Certification/license of first aid personnel	_____
E-6	Standing orders or health care procedures	_____
E-7	Policy on additional first aid personnel needed	_____
E-8, E-9	Health histories	_____
E-10	Permission-to-treat forms	_____
E-11	License of personnel screening or written screening instructions	_____
E-12	Health examination forms	_____
*E-13	Arrangements for emergency transportation (if necessary)	_____
E-14	Staff health care procedures	_____
E-16	Approval/ratios for special medical needs-health care staff	_____
E-17	Information for campers and staff	_____
E-18	Health log and record forms	_____
F-1, *F-2, *F-3, *F-5, F-14, *F-15, and F-17	Aquatics — Documentation of certification, skill, and experience	_____
F-4	Aquatics — Guarding ratios	_____
F-6	Aquatics — Safety regulations	_____
F-7	Aquatics — Emergency and accident procedures	_____
*F-11	Aquatics — Staff use policy and procedures	_____
F-16	Aquatics — Pool rules posted	_____
G-1, *G-4, *G-15	Trip/Travel — Documentation of certification, skill, and experience	_____
G-2	Trip/Travel — Staff/camper ratios	_____
G-5	Trip/Travel — Procedures for participation	_____
G-6	Trip/Travel — Safety regulations and emergency procedures	_____
G-10	Trip/Travel — Itinerary	_____
*G-11	Trip/Travel — Camping procedures	_____
G-13	Trip/Travel — Equipment maintenance procedures	_____
G-16	Trip/Travel — Aquatic activity procedures and ratios	_____
H-1, H-3	Horseback Riding — Documentation of certification, skill, and experience	_____
H-4	Horseback Riding — Staff/camper ratios	_____
H-5	Horseback Riding — Safety regulations	_____
H-6	Horseback Riding — Accident and emergency procedures	_____

Written Documents Required of Camps Seeking Site Approval

STANDARD	TOPIC	STAFF ASSIGNED
SA-1	Comprehensive plan	_____
SA-3	Fire and law enforcement contact letters	_____
SA-5	Approval of water supply	_____
SA-6	Blueprints/charts of sanitation and utility lines	_____
SA-30	Dishwashing/storage procedures	_____
SA-34	Menus and food records	_____
SB-1	Risk management materials	_____
SB-2	Rules, regulations and emergency procedures for user groups	_____
SB-3	Information for user groups	_____
SB-4	Written agreement with user groups	_____
SB-5	First aid and emergency services information	_____
*SB-6	Arrangements for emergency transportation	_____
SB-7	Policy for user groups on firearms, flammable materials and poisons, and power tools	_____
SB-9	Vehicle regulations for user groups	_____
SB-10	Insurance coverage	_____
SB-13	Job descriptions	_____
SB-14	Employment agreement	_____
SB-15	Personnel policies	_____
SB-16	Staff organization chart	_____
SB-17	Vehicle mechanical evaluation	_____
SB-18	Policy on vehicle safety checks	_____
SB-21	Transportation safety procedures	_____
SB-22	Policy on passenger safety orientation	_____
*SB-23	Certification/license of first aider	_____
SB-24	Staff health care procedures	_____
SB-25	Standing orders or health care procedures	_____
SB-26	Health log and accident reports	_____
*SF-1, *SF-2, and SF-3	Aquatics — Evidence of certification/license	_____
SF-4	Aquatics — Safety regulations	_____
SF-5	Aquatics — Emergency and accident procedures	_____
SF-6	Aquatics — Policy requiring use of safety systems (if required)	_____
SF-7	Aquatics — Pool rules posted	_____
SH-2	Horseback Riding — Staff/participant ratios	_____
SH-4	Horseback Riding — Safety regulations and emergency procedures	_____

Architectural Barriers Checklist

The following checklist is intended to give examples of basic design features that will help make camp facilities accessible to persons with limited mobility. For the purposes of the chart below, we are addressing the needs of persons with physical disabilities, since those are most likely to affect the camp site. For the purpose of the ADA, camps must also consider needs of persons with hearing impairments, emotional disturbance, developmental delays, and so forth.

For more comprehensive guidance, refer to the "Americans With Disabilities Act Accessibility Guidelines for Buildings and Facilities" (ADAAG). Note that ADAAG standards were developed for adult dimensions and may require some modification for children.

ADAAG standards refer mainly to buildings, toilets, bathing facilities, and parking. They do not include guidelines for recreational facilities, which were under development at the time of this publication. Information on ADAAG is available from the US Architectural and Transportation Barriers Compliance Board, 1111 18th Street, NW, Suite 501, Washington, D.C. 20036-3894. Phone: 202-653-7834 v/TDD. Fax: 202-653-7863.

The Americans With Disabilities Act of 1990 (ADA) requires that all public accommodations make "reasonable accommodations" for persons with disabilities. Information on ADA is available in the *Camp Director's Primer to the Americans With Disabilities Act of 1990,* available from the ACA Bookstore. 800-428-2267.

NAME OF UNIT

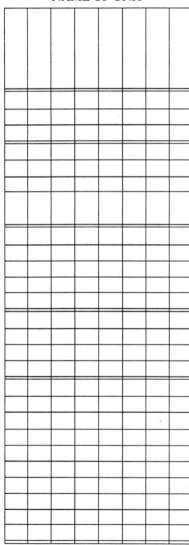

GENERAL GUIDELINES

PARKING
- 1 accessible 96" wide space per 25 spaces in parking areas
- with 60" access aisle for cars or 96" wide access aisle for vans

WALKWAYS AND PATH OF TRAVEL IN BUILDINGS
- 36" wide for one-way traffic, 60" wide for two way traffic
- stable, firm, slip-resistant surface
- gradient not greater than 1' rise in 20'
  (Running slopes greater than 1:20 must meet ramp requirements)

RAMPS
- incline no more than 1' in 12'
- slip-resistant surface
- handrail 34-38" above ramp on each side of ramp
- landing (min. 60") at each end of ramp

DOORS AND DOORWAYS
- 32" opening by single effort
- 5' level clearance in direction door swings
- threshold flush or less than ½"

BATHROOMS
- toilet stall 5' x 5' x 8' with 32" door opening and grab bars on each side of toilet
- urinals with rim at 17" max. above floor
- toilet with top of seat 17-19" from floor; minimum 48" from lip of seat to opposite wall
- sink rim/counter no higher than 34" from floor
- clearance of 29" under sink
- hot water pipes wrapped or removed from obstructing chair
- bottom edge of mirrors and dispensers no higher than 40" from floor
- faucets lever or push operated
- shower stall 3' x 3' minimum, with clear floor space of at least 3' x 4'

Other considerations: curb ramps, signage identifying accessible facilities set no higher than 60" from floor, signage for persons with visual impairments, and audible and visual smoke alarms.

Sample Temperature Charts

Refrigeration Unit Temperature Chart

Location_____

Week Dates	Day	Time	Temp.	Recorder	Action
	Sun.				
	Mon.				
	Tues.				
	Wed.				
	Thurs.				
	Fri.				
	Sat.				
	Sun.				
	Mon.				
	Tues.				
	Wed.				
	Thurs.				
	Fri.				
	Sat.				

Dishwasher Temperature Chart

Location_____

Week Dates	Day	Time	Wash Temp.	Rinse Temp.	Recorder	Action
	Sun.					
	Mon.					
	Tues.					
	Wed.					
	Thurs.					
	Fri.					
	Sat.					
	Sun.					
	Mon.					
	Tues.					
	Wed.					
	Thurs.					
	Fri.					
	Sat.					

Charts on this page may be photocopied for camp use.

Helps in Risk Management Planning (Standard B-2 and SB-1)

Introduction

Risk is an uncertainty or probability concerning the loss of resources. Risk Management Plans are systems to identify, reduce, prevent, or control the loss of resources associated with the camp.

Risk management planning is referred to in three locations in these standards. For accreditation: standard B-2 and item 16 in the Self-Assessment (page 177); and for Site Approval: standard SB-1. The entire educational process involved in accreditation takes one through many risk reduction steps. The completion of the accreditation process addresses risk management planning, but does not in and of itself result in a Risk Management Plan.

Risk management is an integrated approach to dealing with the uncertainty of loss. It includes areas such as health and safety (many of which are identified in the standards) as well as business and financial concerns (a few of which are addressed in the Self-Assessment). A full Risk Management Plan will involve input from legal, financial, and insurance counsel, your camp board or owners, and other professionals providing advice on the camp's operation.

Steps in meeting standard B-2

(Note: For brevity, the references which follow indicate accreditation standards. There are similar requirements in Site Approval in most instances.)

This standard requires an overall look at your camp operation <u>once you have completed</u> developing materials for the other standards in the accreditation process. Those things developed for other standards need not be repeated in the documentation provided for this standard.

A. Identification of health and safety concerns and possible emergency situations

<u>Elsewhere</u> in the standards, you have established procedures for general health concerns (Health Care Plan, E-1), fire detection in sleeping quarters (A-11), procedures for missing persons and intruders (B-5 and 6), communication procedures (B-8), campers/staff possession of personal equipment (B-10), etc.

<u>Now</u> you should evaluate the five categories listed under letter A of standard B-2 and develop a list of <u>reasonably foreseeable</u> situations specific to your camp from these five categories that have not been addressed in other standards. The definitions and some examples of each are listed in the interpretation to the standard.

B. Specify measures to reduce, control, or prevent risks

First, note that not all of the reduction steps listed as #1-4 under part B of this standard will apply to each of the risks you have identified. However, for each reduction step, you should consider any of the risks you identified under A (above) that is applicable.

For instance, **safety regulations** (part B, #1).

Identify the <u>general camp safety regulations</u> that are needed to address any of your natural hazards (stay away from the cliffs unless your counselor is with you), man-made hazards (this is a public road — look and listen before you cross it), etc.

When considering the "conduct of campers and staff" (part A, #5), it is appropriate to address regulations dealing with concerns related to drugs, alcohol, smoking, fighting, always travelling with a "buddy," please wear shoes at all times, etc.

When you complete this section, you should have a list of general safety regulations that are in addition to any you have previously developed for specific activities such as aquatics, horseback riding, and so forth.

Everything you listed as a possible risk in part A will not necessarily require safety regulations.

Continue to identify risk reduction steps for each of the items #2-4 under part B: **methods to control access, protective devices, and camper/staff training needed.** Identify steps here for any of the list from "A" that would benefit from having protective devices, or training, etc.

C. Establish emergency procedures.

Again, look at the list you developed for "A." Which of those items may require the establishment of emergency procedures? "Disasters" is an easily identifiable category. Therefore, establish plans (as appropriate to your camp) for things such as:

Evacuation of the dining hall in case of fire

Evacuation of the camp in case of fire, flood, tornado, earthquake, etc.

Feeding campers/staff in case of loss of dining hall, or extended loss of power

Not all of your "A" list will require emergency procedures. However, those that do should be listed here, with appropriate procedures developed.

General Reminders

The completion of this standard does not constitute a Risk Management Plan. It does help you address one step in a limited plan — the step of **reduction.**

Risks may also be handled in at least three other ways:

Transfer — placing that risk or portion of the risk in the hands of another party such as an insurance company, or by developing a contract with another party to assume that risk.

Retention — retaining the risk and accepting the consequences of the loss. Generally, risks are only retained when the loss is not very likely to happen and not very costly when it does happen.

Avoidance — removing the risk entirely. For instance, re-routing a county road so it does not go through your camp will help you avoid a risk.

Risk reduction is perhaps the most important method because it is needed even if transfer or retention is used.

Resources available to help in your risk management planning include:

***Management of Risks and Emergencies,** Camp Fire, Inc., Kansas City, Missouri
***Legal Liability and Risk Management for Public and Private Entities**, Betty van der Smissen
  YMCA Risk Management Program, YMCA, Chicago, Illinois

Available from ACA Publications. Call 1-800/428-CAMP.

Summary of Required
Safety Regulations and Emergency Procedures

Safety regulations and procedures to deal with emergencies are required throughout the Camp Accreditation and Site Approval standards. Most are required to be in writing and included in staff and/or camper orientation and training.

Required for Camp Accreditation

1. **Safety Regulations**

    General — B-2 and B-3 (written)

    When campers are with the public — B-7 (written)

    Related to personal sports equipment, vehicles, and animals — B-10 (written)

    To control vehicular traffic on the campsite — BT-1

    Policy on hayrides/trucks — BT-2

    In vehicles — BT-9 (written)

    For day camp arrival and departure — BT-3

    For day camp pick-up and drop-off — BT-5 (written)

    For target sports — D-9 (written)

    For overnights/short trips — D-14 (written)

    For adventure/challenge activities — D-22 (written)

    For gymnastics — D-29 (written)

    For use of motorized vehicles — D-33 (written)

    For bicycling — D-39 (written)

    For other specialized activities — D-43 (written)

    For aquatic activities — F-6 (written)

    For staff use of aquatic facilities — *F-11 (written)

    For trip/travel programs — G-6 (written)

    For horseback riding — H-5 (written)

2. **Emergency Procedures**

    General — B-3 (written)

    Steps to deal with intruders — B-5

    Search and rescue procedures — B-6 (written)

    Emergency communications plan — B-8 (written)

    Vehicle accident procedures — BT-7 (written)

    In case of vehicular breakdown or passenger illness — BT-17 (written)

    For target sports — D-9 (written)

    For overnights/short trips — D-14 (written)

    How to get emergency assistance on out-of-camp trips — D-17 (written)

    For adventure/challenge activities — D-22 (written)

    For gymnastics — D-29 (written)

    For operation of motorized vehicles — D-33 (written)

    For bicycling — D-39 (written)

    For other specialized activities — D-43 (written)

    First aid/emergency procedures — E-14 (written), and E-15

    For aquatic accidents and emergencies — F-7 (written)

    For emergency situations on trips — G-3, and *G-6 (written)

    For aquatic emergencies on trips — G-16 (written)

    For horseback riding — H-2, and H-6 (written)

Required for Site Approval

1. **Safety Regulations**

    General — SB-1 and SB-2 (written)

    Policies on firearms, flammables and power tools — SB-7 (written)

    For vehicles on the site — SB-9 (written)

    Policy on hayrides/trucks — SB-8

    In vehicles — SB-21 and SB-22 (written)

    For aquatic activities — SF-4 (written)

    For horseback riding — SH-3 (written)

2. **Emergency Procedures**

    General — SB-1 and SB-2 (written)

    Disaster and emergency assistance procedures — SB-3 (written)

    Arrangements for emergency transportation — *SB-6 (written)

    For transportation emergencies — SB-22 (written)

    First aid/emergency procedures — SB-24 (written)

    For aquatic accidents and emergencies — SF-5 (written)

    For horseback riding — SH-4 (written)

Accident/Incident Report Form   FM 01

Appendix G

Developed by the *American Camping Association*
(Fill out 1 on each incident or person)

Camp Name _____ Date _____

Address _____
        Street & Number   *City*   *State*   *Zip*

Name of person involved _____ Age _____ Sex _____ ❑ Camper ❑ Staff ❑ Visitor
                   Last   *First*   *Middle*

Address _____ Phone _____
        Street & Number   *City*   *State*   *Zip*   *Area/Number*

Name of Parent/Guardian *(if minor)* _____

Address _____ Phone _____
        Street & Number   *City*   *State*   *Zip*   *Area/Number*

Name/Addresses of Witnesses *(You may wish to attach signed statements.)*

1. _____

2. _____

3. _____

Type of incident   ❑ Behavioral   ❑ Accident   ❑ Epidemic illness   ❑ Other (describe)

Date of Incident/Accident _____ Hour _____ ❑ a.m. ❑ p.m.
                       Day of Week   *Month*   *Day*   *Year*

Describe the sequence of activity in detail including what the (injured) person was doing at the time _____

_____

_____

_____

_____

_____

Where occurred? *(Specify location, including location of injured and witnesses. Use diagram to locate persons/objects.)*

Was injured participating in an activity at time of injury?   ❑ Yes ❑ No   If so, what activity? _____

Any equipment involved in accident?   ❑ Yes ❑ No   If so, what kind? _____

What could the injured have done to prevent injury? _____

_____

Emergency procedures followed at time of incident/accident _____

_____

_____

By whom?_____

Submitted by _____ Position _____ Date _____

Appendix

Medical Report of Accident

Were parents notified? ☐ Yes ☐ No   By ☐ Writing ☐ Phone ☐ Other _____

By whom? _____ Title _____ When _____
                                                                                    Time   Date

Parent's Response _____

_____

Where was treatment given?   ☐ At Accident Site ☐ Camp Health Service ☐ Doctor's Office ☐ Hospital

If treatment was given at camp, where? _____

   By whom? _____ Date _____

   Treatment given _____

   Was injured retained overnight in camp health service? ☐ Yes ☐ No   If so, when? _____

   Treatment given _____

   By Whom? _____ Title _____

   Date released from health service _____

   Released to   ☐ Camp Activities ☐ Home ☐ Other _____

Treatment given elsewhere than camp? ☐ Yes ☐ No   Where? _____

   By whom? _____ Date _____

   Was injured retained overnight in hospital? ☐ Yes ☐ No   If so, which? _____

   Where? _____ Date _____ ☐ Out-patient ☐ In-patient

   Name of physician in attendance _____

   Date released from hospital _____

   Released to   ☐ Camp ☐ Health Service ☐ Home ☐ Other _____

Comments _____

_____

_____

Persons notified such as camp owner/sponsor, board of directors, etc.

Name	Position	Date
_____	_____	_____
_____	_____	_____
_____	_____	_____

Describe any contact made with/by the media regarding this situation _____

_____

Signed _____ Position _____ Date _____

Insurance Notification   Date

1. ☐ Parent's Insurance   By ☐ Parent ☐ Camp   _____
2. ☐ Camp Health Insurance   _____
3. ☐ Worker's Compensation   _____
4. ☐ Camp Liability Insurance   _____

CHILDREN'S CAMP INSURANCE CHECK LIST

PROPERTY	Do Have	Do Not Have	No Action Needed

BUILDINGS & CONTENTS

a) Basic Causes of Loss	_____	_____	_____
b) Broad Causes of Loss	_____	_____	_____
c) Special Causes of Loss	_____	_____	_____
d) Deductible; $250 is standard; $500 and $1,000 available	_____	_____	_____
e) Replacement Cost Coverage	_____	_____	_____
f) Blanket Coverage on Building & Contents	_____	_____	_____
g) Current Appraisal	_____	_____	_____
h) Coinsurance Compliance	_____	_____	_____
i) Signs	_____	_____	_____
j) Earthquake & Flood-Difference in Conditions	_____	_____	_____
k) Property of Others in Your Control	_____	_____	_____

CAMP EQUIPMENT FLOATER

a) Broad Causes of Loss	_____	_____	_____
b) Special Causes of Loss	_____	_____	_____
c) Deductible	_____	_____	_____
d) Computers and Audio-Visual	_____	_____	_____

BUSINESS INTERRUPTION

a) Camper Fees	_____	_____	_____
b) Extra Expense	_____	_____	_____
c) Other Income	_____	_____	_____

AUTOMOBILE

a) Limits of Liability — $1,000,000 Single Limit BI & PD	_____	_____	_____
b) Uninsured Motorist and Underinsured Motorist Increased Limits	_____	_____	_____
c) Nonowned, Hired and Borrowed Autos	_____	_____	_____
d) Leased Autos/Additional Insureds	_____	_____	_____
e) Autos Furnished by Employees	_____	_____	_____
f) Medical Payments	_____	_____	_____
g) No Fault	_____	_____	_____
h) Comprehensive	_____	_____	_____
i) Collision	_____	_____	_____
j) Towing/Private Passenger Vehicles	_____	_____	_____
k) Drivers Operating Records Checked	_____	_____	_____

Provided courtesy of Markel Rhulen Underwriters and Brokers, Glen Allen, Virginia.

Appendix

PROGRAM CHECK LIST

	Do Have	Do Not Have	No Action Needed
GENERAL LIABILITY			
a) Occurrence Form	_____	_____	_____
b) Limits of Liability — $1,000,000 CSL BI & PD	_____	_____	_____
c) Aggregate/Cap on Liability Limits	_____	_____	_____
d) Products Liability	_____	_____	_____
e) Independent Contractors Liability	_____	_____	_____
f) Sexual Abuse Liability	_____	_____	_____
g) Malpractice Including Camp and Individual Doctor, Nurse or EMT	_____	_____	_____
h) Personal Injury Liability Including Employee Coverage	_____	_____	_____
i) Advertising Liability	_____	_____	_____
j) Contractual Liability	_____	_____	_____
k) Saddle Animal Liability	_____	_____	_____
l) Fire Legal Liability	_____	_____	_____
m) Owned Watercraft	_____	_____	_____
n) Nonowned Watercraft under 26 ft.	_____	_____	_____
o) Additional Insured Employees/Volunteers	_____	_____	_____
p) Host Liquor Liability	_____	_____	_____
q) Excess Camper Medical	_____	_____	_____
r) Other Exposures or Business	_____	_____	_____
UMBRELLA (CATASTROPHE) LIABILITY			
a) Drop Down Feature	_____	_____	_____
b) "Pay On Behalf Of" vs. Reimbursement Clause	_____	_____	_____
WORKERS' COMPENSATION			
a) Executive Officers of Corporations Excluded (where permitted by State Law)	_____	_____	_____
b) Employers Liability Increased Limits	_____	_____	_____
c) Non-Occupational Benefits Law (DBL)	_____	_____	_____
d) Other States Coverage	_____	_____	_____
CAMPER MEDICAL COVERAGE			
a) Benefit Maximum Adequate? (Minimum $1,000 per camper)	_____	_____	_____
b) Staff Included?	_____	_____	_____
c) Primary or Secondary Coverage?; Deductible?	_____	_____	_____
DIRECTORS & OFFICERS LIABILITY (Nonprofit)			
a) Directors Covered?	_____	_____	_____
b) Officers Covered?	_____	_____	_____
c) Prior Acts Included?	_____	_____	_____
CRIME INSURANCE			
a) Coverage for Employee Dishonesty	_____	_____	_____
b) Loss of Money & Securities (Inside & Outside)	_____	_____	_____
PERSONNEL			
a) Key Man Life Insurance	_____	_____	_____
b) Major Medical Insurance	_____	_____	_____
c) Pension/Profit Sharing	_____	_____	_____
d) Disability	_____	_____	_____
e) 24 Hour Accident Insurance (Business & Pleasure)	_____	_____	_____

Personnel Chart

The qualifications required by various standards have been categorized below. *Each* staff member should be included on such a chart to help visitors and directors determine compliance with standards C-2, C-4, C-5, and C-6.

Name	Positions/Age Group	Age	Education	Leadership Experience

Staff Pre-camp Training Topics

The following topics are required by the Camp Accreditation standards to be included in staff training. Generally, this will be accomplished during "Pre-camp Training." The list is provided as a help to camp directors in preparing training schedules, and it will be supplemented by other training and activities, according to the needs of individual camps.

1. Safety regulations and emergency procedures

General camp safety regulations and rules (B-2 and B-3)

Emergency procedures — fire drills, storm procedures, general care of injured, etc. (B-2 and B-3)

Training to enforce safety regulations, work with groups, identify activity hazards, and apply appropriate emergency procedures (D-6)

Procedure for reporting incidents and accidents (B-4)

Procedure for dealing with possible intruders (B-5)

Search and rescue procedures for persons lost, missing or runaway (B-6)

Regulations and practices for supervising campers when intermingled with the public (B-7)

Emergency communication plan and procedures (B-8)

As applicable:

Procedures in case of accident during transportation (BT-7)

Bus safety procedures and group management (BT-8 and BT-9)

Training for vehicle drivers (BT-17)

Day camp arrival and departure safety procedures (BT-3)

Program activity safety regulations (D-9, D-14, D-22, D-29, D-33, D-39, D-43, F-6, G-6, and H-5)

2. Programming and camper/staff interaction procedures

Goals and objectives for camper development (D-1)

Responsibilities when supervising campers (C-4)

System to care for special needs of campers (C-9)

General practices for effectively relating to campers (C-10)

Behavior management policies and techniques (C-11)

Appropriate staff/camper and staff/staff behaviors (C-11)

Training for supervisors (C-12)

3. General procedures

Required general maintenance routines — cleaning, reporting maintenance problems, etc. (A-7)

Training to monitor program equipment (D-7)

Responsibilities for first aid and health care (E-14)

As applicable:

Proper handling of flammable or poisonous materials — kerosene, cleaning agents, etc. (*A-9)

Proper handling and use of power tools (A-10)

Food preparation and storage procedures (A-24 through A-29)

4. Program activity procedures (D, F, G, and H standards)

<u>All staff</u> need to be oriented to overall regulations and procedures for participation in each available program activity, whether participating with groups of campers or not. Orientation/training/information may include topics such as eligibility, ratios, safety signals or systems used, equipment or area restrictions, and leadership requirements.

<u>Staff with leadership responsibilities</u> for program activities will need to learn and/or review **all** applicable standard requirements in that particular area. Skills of program activity leaders (both "generalists" and activity "specialists") may be documented during pre-camp, as staff learn or review the specific skills needed to implement program with campers.

Some standards specifically require that skills be demonstrated (see *D-19, D-24, D-31, F-2, F-3, F-8, and *G-11). Others require training and supervision specific to the activity, area, and participants (see D-6, F-2, F-3, F-7, G-3, G-6, and H-2).

Camper Training Topics

Some standards for Camp Accreditation require specific training/orientation for campers. Instruction for staff will include specifics on how the following topics will be covered with campers (as applicable):

General:

General camp safety regulations and emergency procedures (B-3)

Steps to deal with possible intruders (B-5)

Regulations and practices when intermingled with the public (B-7)

Day camp arrival and departure safety procedures (BT-3)

Handling flammable or poisonous materials (*A-9)

Related to program activities:

Handling power tools (A-10)

Target sport safety signals (D-12)

Orientation for overnights/short trips (D-16)

Water, food, dishwashing, and stove-use procedures on overnights and trips (*D-19 and *G-11)

Safety orientation for adventure/challenge activities (D-23)

Spotting and belaying instruction and supervision (D-24 and D-31)

Safety orientation for motorized vehicles (D-34)

Safety orientation for bicycling (D-41)

Aquatic safety regulations (F-6 and F-23)

Preliminary training for watercraft (F-19 and G-19)

Trip/travel orientation and how to get emergency help (*G-6)

Training to recognize and deal with hazardous water (G-17)

Horseback riding safety regulations (H-5 and H-15)

Sample Statement of Goals and Objectives
for Camper Development
(Standard D-1)

GOALS describe the general purpose or intent of the camp experience and provide overall direction in camp development. The goals shown below are camp program goals. Other goals will be expressed in the Comprehensive Plan (Self-Assessment requirement for Accreditation, Standard SA-1 in Site Approval) as related to site development, market, finance and administration, and environmental protection and preservation.

Example: It is the goal of our camp to —

- encourage each camper to develop new skills and work toward improving her performance at a given task.

- develop in each camper an appreciation for the natural surroundings including a concern for ecology, and a desire to help preserve our environment.

- help each camper gain a deeper understanding of and appreciation for their own skills and abilities.

- encourage the development of leadership skills in campers of all ages.

OBJECTIVES provide a more specific description of the areas and levels of growth and development which campers will achieve as a result of their camp experience. One example for each of the above goal areas is listed below. Often, camps will have several objectives related to each general program goal. The objective should be stated specifically, so that staff can tell when the objective has been attained.

Examples:

1. *Skill development* — Each camper will master at least three skills not previously performed in the areas of horsemanship, aquatics, or outdoor living.

2. *Appreciation of the natural surroundings* — Each camper will participate in the planning and carrying out of an activity which will provide for action in environmental protection, improvement projects, or appreciation of nature.

3. *Appreciation of their own skills and abilities* — Each camper will satisfactorily complete adventure/challenge programs where they exercise leadership and group and individual problem-solving roles.

4. *Leadership development* — Each camper will assume the role of group leader at least three times during the camp session.

Sample Outline of Health Care Plan (E-1)

The purpose of developing a written Health Care Plan is for the administrative and health staff to systematically evaluate the health care needs of their camp. Those needs will vary depending on the age and medical condition of the participants, the type and duration of activities, the proximity of professional medical treatment facilities, and the number and qualifications of the health care staff.

This outline represents a starting point for the development of the camp's plan. Specific standard numbers have been noted in parentheses where applicable. The plan should be developed in consultation with and reviewed by the camp physician.

I. HEALTH CARE NEEDS OF PARTICIPANTS
  A. Typical health care needs of campers
  B. Typical health care needs of staff

II. RESPONSIBILITY AND AUTHORITY OF CAMP STAFF IN HEALTH CARE
  A. Health Care Staff
    1. Number and qualifications of persons (E-4, E-5, E-16)
    2. Job Descriptions (E-4)
    3. Define whether person(s) is (are) on site or on call (E-4)
    4. Housing provided
  B. General camp staff
    1. Responsibility (limits) in providing first aid (E-14)
    2. Locations where first aid-certified persons should be present (E-7)

III. GENERAL ROUTINES FOR CAMP HEALTH CARE AND SANITATION
  A. Policies concerning written health record requirements for campers/staff
    1. Health history — content and frequency (E-8, E-9)
    2. Health examination — content and frequency (E-12)
    3. Parent permission for emergency care (E-10)
    4. Record retention policy (E-18)
    5. Health record log (E-18)
  B. Procedures for health screening (E-6, E-11)
    1. Who administers?
    2. When?
    3. Communication of significant findings to counseling and program staff (C-9)
    4. Pre-/post-trip screening (who? when? what?) (G-7)

  C. First aid (E-5, E-7, E-14, E-15; also F-5, G-4, H-3)
    1. Who administers?
    2. Qualifications of persons administering
    3. Location of first aid supplies (BT-10, E-7)
    4. Record keeping (E-18)
    5. Standing orders/procedures (E-6)
    6. Training of all staff (E-14)
  D. Emergency medical care (E-1)
    1. Who administers?
    2. Qualifications of persons administering
    3. Provision and procurement of emergency transportation (E-13)
    4. Standing orders/procedures (E-6)
    5. Training of all staff (E-14)
    6. Written records to accompany persons off camp grounds (BT-11, D-18, G-8, E-15)
    7. Communication with parents/guardians (B-8)
    8. Procedures for documentation of such care (accident reports, etc.) (E-18)
  E. Daily medical care
    1. Who administers? (E-3)
    2. Hours?
    3. Record keeping (E-18)
    4. Standing orders (E-6)
    5. Medications policies (storage, dispensing, etc.) (E-19)
    6. Communication with parents/guardians (B-8, E-17)
  F. Routine health care
    1. Who is responsible for supervision? (E-3)
    2. Monitoring of personal hygiene
    3. Supervision of orders for daily medications (E-19)
    4. Supervision in infirmary (E-21)

G. Supervision of overall camp practices
  1. Sanitation facilities/practices (E-3)
  2. Food service facilities/staff (A-24)
  3. Tripping/travel/out-of-camp programs (D-16 & 17; G-4 & 6)
  4. Grounds
  5. Living accommodations
  6. Program areas

IV. RECORDKEEPING
  A. Health history, and health examination forms (resident camps) (E-18)
  B. Daily medical log (E-18)
  C. Accident reports (E-18)

V. PROVISION OF SUPPLIES AND EQUIPMENT
  A. Health care facility and supplies (E-20)
    1. Location
    2. Equipment/accommodations
    3. Supplies to be available
  B. Supplies to be used by all staff (E-14)

VI. AGREEMENTS WITH MEDICAL PERSONNEL, HOSPITALS, EMERGENCY CARE PROVIDERS
  A. Camp physician
    1. Location — off-site and on call, on-site
    2. Qualifications
    3. Procedures for obtaining and updating standing orders/health care procedures including approval of screening procedures (E-6, E-11)
  B. Hospital/emergency facility (E-1, #5)
    1. Agreement for residential health care
    2. Agreement for emergency health care
  C. Professional therapy (when provided)
    1. Who administers?
    2. Qualifications
    3. Who refers?
    4. Parental permission/report
    5. Confidentiality

Sample Outline
Standing Orders/Health Care Procedures

The outline which follows identifies a minimal list of policies that should be covered by standing orders/procedures. The specifics should reflect the location, clientele, program, and staff of the camp to which they apply.

The orders reflect the medical responsibility of the camp physician. The camp's Health Care Plan (E-1) should indicate the responsibility for the implementation of these orders.

I. HEALTH SCREENING

    A. Who may conduct it?

    B. Content of screening

    C. Record keeping of screening

    D. Timing of screening

        1. arriving campers

        2. arriving staff

        3. campers and staff pre-/post-trip

II. ROUTINE HEALTH/MEDICAL TREATMENT

    A. Standing orders for basic treatments such as cuts, infections, sprains, elevated temperatures, diarrhea, sore throat, etc.

    B. Identification of points at which professional medical advice/treatment should be sought.

III. EMERGENCY PROCEDURES

    A. Acceptable first aid procedures

    B. Points at which professional medical treatment should be sought

    C. Hospital/emergency care treatment locations

Health History and Health Examination Forms

A "health history" reflects information about an individual filled out by that person or his/her parent/guardian. Since persons may be seen by a number of different physicians at clinics, in school, or as families move, medical professionals see the family as the best source of information on illnesses, allergies, immunizations, etc. The ACA standards require a health history for all campers and staff in day and resident camps (standards *E-8 and E-9).

A "health examination" reflects results established by licensed medical personnel such as doctors or licensed nurse practitioners. The ACA standards require a health examination for resident campers and staff within the two years prior to camp attendance. The camp may obtain either a copy of the examination form itself, or a form from the doctor indicating that an examination had been conducted within the past two years and indicating any special treatments or considerations about that individual's participation in camp activities (standard E-12).

While the standard requires the health examination to be conducted within the two years prior to camp attendance, some camps require the examination within other time frames (annually, within 6 months, within 3 years, etc.). According to medical advice, the important concept is that persons be seeing a physician for an examination on a regular basis. The camp is generally interested in the recommendations of the physician in light of camp participation, not necessarily the results of particular tests done in that examination. Camp administrators should review with their camp physician and legal counsel the precise information needed in light of clientele served and other factors.

Camps may gather this information on a single form, or on multiple forms. ACA publishes several kinds of forms and formats to assist camps in this process. A sample combined Health History and Health Examination/Record form follows. The following copyrighted materials are also available from the ACA Publications Department (1-800/428-CAMP):

	Paper 8 x 11	Card 5 x 8
Combined Health History and Examination/Record (for children and adults)	FM08	
		FM 06 female
		FM 07 male
Camper Health History Form	FM 11	FM 14
Physician's Health Examination/Record	FM 12	FM 13

Health History and Examination Form
for Children, Youth and Adults
Attending Camps
Form FM 08

Developed and Approved by the
American Camping Association
with the American Academy of Pediatrics

Mail to the address below by _____ (Date)

Information on this form is not part of the camper or staff acceptance process, but is gathered to assist us in identifying appropriate care.
(This side to be filled in by parents/guardian of minors or by adult campers/staff members themselves.)

Name _____ Birthdate _____ Sex _____ Age _____
         Last   First   Initial

Parent or Guardian *(or Spouse)* _____

Home Address _____ Phone _____
         Street & Number   City   State   Zip   Area/Number
Business _____ Phone _____
         Street & Number   City   State   Zip   Area/Number

Second Parent or Guardian or Emergency Contact _____

Home Address _____ Phone _____
         Street & Number   City   State   Zip   Area/Number
Business Address _____ Phone _____
         Street & Number   City   State   Zip   Area/Number

If not available in an emergency, notify

Name _____

Address _____ Phone _____
         Street & Number   City   State   Zip   Area/Number

Health History
(Check. Give approximate dates.)
_____ Frequent Ear Infections
_____ Heart Defect/Disease
_____ Convulsions
_____ Diabetes
_____ Bleeding/Clotting Disorders
_____ Hypertension
_____ Mononucleosis

Diseases
_____ Chicken Pox
_____ Measles
_____ German Measles
_____ Mumps

Allergies (Dates not needed)
_____ Hay Fever
_____ Ivy Poisoning, etc.
_____ Insect Stings
_____ Penicillin
_____ Other Drugs
_____ Asthma
_____ Other *(Specify)*
_____
_____

Operations or serious injuries *(dates)* _____
_____

Chronic or recurring illness or medical condition _____
_____

Dietary restrictions _____

Current medications *(send with instructions)* _____

Other diseases _____

Name of dentist/orthodontist _____ Phone _____

Name of family physician _____ Phone _____

Do you carry family medical/hospital insurance? ☐ Yes ☐ No

If so, indicate: Carrier _____ Policy or Group # _____

Suggestions on health related information for camp personnel _____
_____
_____

For Female

Has this person menstruated? _____ If not, has she been told about it? _____

If so, is her menstrual history normal? _____ Special Consideration _____

Important — This Box Must be Completed for Attendance*

This health history is correct so far as I know, and the person herein described has permission to engage in all prescribed camp activities except as noted. **Authorization for Treatment:** I hereby give permission to the medical personnel selected by the camp director to order X-rays, routine tests, treatment; to release any records necessary for insurance purposes; and to provide or arrange necessary related transportation for me/or my child. In the event I cannot be reached in an emergency, I hereby give permission to the physician selected by the camp director to secure and administer treatment, including hospitalization, for the person named above. The completed forms may be photocopied for trips out of camp.

Signature of parent or guardian or adult camper/staffer _____

Witness _____ Date _____

I also understand and agree to abide with the restrictions placed on my camp activities.

Signature of minor or adult camper/staffer _____ Date _____

If for religious reasons you cannot sign this, then the camp should be contacted for a legal waiver which must be signed for attendance.

Name

Date Examined

Cabin or Tent

Year

Appendix

Immunization History

Required immunizations must be determined locally. Please record the date (month and year) of basic immunizations and most recent booster doses.

Vaccines		Year of Basic Immunization	Year of Last Booster
Diphtheria Pertussis (Whooping Cough) Tetanus	} DPT*	1 2 3	1 2
or			
Tetanus Diphtheria	} TD*		
or			
Tetanus			
Oral Polio (Sabin)* TOPV			
Injectable Polio (Salk)			
Measles (hard measles, red measles, Rubeola)			
Mumps			
Rubella (German measles, 3-day measles)			
Other			
Tuberculin test given _____ (most recent)			
Haemophilus influenza b (HIB)			
Hepatitis B			

Health Care Recommendations by Licensed Physician

I have examined the above camp applicant within the past two years.   Date Examined _____

In my opinion, the above's condition ☐ does ☐ does not preclude his/her participation in an active camp program.

Height _____   Weight _____   Blood Pressure_____

The applicant is under the care of a physician for the following condition(s)

_____

_____

Current treatment (include current medications)_____

_____

Explanation of any reported loss of consciousness, convulsion, or concussion_____

_____

Does applicant have epilepsy? ☐ Yes ☐ No   Does applicant have diabetes? ☐ Yes ☐ No

Recommendations and Restrictions While at Camp

Any treatment to be continued at camp _____

_____

Any medication to be administered at camp (specific dosages)_____

_____

Any medically prescribed meal plan or dietary restrictions _____

_____

Any allergies (food, drugs, plants, insects, etc.) _____

_____

Activities to be encouraged or limited _____

_____

Additional Health Information _____

Licensed Physician's Signature _____

Address_____ Phone _____
         Street & Number   City   State   Zip Code   Area/Number

Date of Form Completion _____   *By_____
                                          *Initial if completed by nurse or physician's assistant.

Sample Request for Waiver of Health Examination and Immunization Requirements for Religious Reasons

The form below is designed to be used by <u>camps who have individual campers or staff members</u> attending whose religious beliefs preclude medical treatment. Camps serving only participants with such beliefs will normally utilize health history forms and health supervision practices approved by that religious sponsoring body. The camp's legal counsel should review/approve any form used.

State law generally permits such an exemption by state departments of health, in the absence of an emergency or epidemic of disease, when the parents are members of a religious body whose religious beliefs are in conflict with requirements for vaccination or immunization. Check with your legal counsel if you have questions.

Release and Application for Exemption From Physical Examination and Immunization Requirements

It is respectfully requested that _____ be exempted upon religious grounds from the physical examination and all immunization requirements required for attendance at the camp. To the best of my knowledge and belief, (he/she) is and has been in normal good health and is free from all communicable or contagious diseases.

Should _____ manifest any condition where there appears to be reasonable grounds for suspecting the presence of a communicable or contagious disease, I agree that a physical examination may be performed. Also, I agree that if any such disease is found, _____ will comply with the regular quarantine or isolation procedures of the camp and of the community.

It is further understood that, should an emergency arise, I will be notified immediately. However, in the event that we cannot be located immediately, the authorities of the camp may take such temporary measures as they deem necessary.

I release and forever discharge the camp and each and every one of its officers, directors, partners, shareholders, employees, agents, insurers, affiliates, successors in interest, attorneys, or any other person or persons associated with any or all of them or any variation in the name of any or all of them who might be liable (the "Release Parties") from all causes of action, suits, claims, demands, or any other damages or costs associated with actions taken by the Released Parties relative to the health, sickness, and treatment of _____.

I further understand and acknowledge that I make this release in full accord and satisfaction of and in compromise of any current or future disputed or alleged claims or causes of action relative to the health sickness, and treatment of _____ against the Released Parties.

I represent and acknowledge that I have read and understand this agreement and release and warrant that all statements made herein are true to the best of my knowledge. I further warrant and acknowledge that I am of legal age, legally competent to execute this agreement and release, and accept full responsibility therefore.

_____   _____
       Date   Signature of Parent/Guardian

_____
    Street   City   State   Phone

Certification of Church Membership

I hereby certify that _____ is a member in good standing of

_____ and that _____ is a pupil in Sunday School.

_____   _____
       Date   Signature of Authorized Church Representative

_____   _____
  Parent/Guardian   Name of Applicant

_____
     Christian Science Church or Society

Guidelines for Camps Primarily Serving
Persons with Special Medical Needs (E-16)

DIABETES

Medical Staff Levels Required

If the camp serves 25 or more persons with diabetes (at any one time), the following ratios of health care professionals to all persons in camp with diabetes must be met in order to be in compliance with E-16A:

A. One Registered Nurse in residence for every 30 persons (or less) with diabetes;
B. One Licensed Physician in residence for every 100 persons (or less) with diabetes; and
C. One Registered Dietician with daily on-site availability for every 100 persons (or less) with diabetes.

Sample Medical Management Plan Outline

Using diabetes as a model, the components of a written philosophy of health care management should include, briefly:

A. Identification of the population served (diabetes in children)
B. Determination of special needs (insulin, diet, exercise)
C. Enabling activities (that help promote good control of blood sugars to facilitate optimal growth and development)
D. Rationale (for those management approaches to promote good control of blood sugars and elimination of symptoms of hyperglycemia and hypoglycemia)

Sample Information for Parents/Participants

As children with diabetes mellitus have lost the ability to produce their own insulin, it becomes necessary for them to have daily insulin injections. The actions of the insulins in the body require careful planning of food intake and timing of exercise. The balancing of these components will facilitate the child's enjoyment of the camp experience.

We strive to keep the blood sugars as normal as possible using these management approaches:

1. A minimum of 1-3 insulin injections per day.
2. Three meals and 3 snacks will be served daily calculating carbohydrate, protein and fat intake. The American Diabetes Association Exchange List will be used for these calculations. All serving portions will be measured and/or weighed.
3. Exercise schedules will be balanced with food intake and insulin levels.
4. Monitoring and recording sugar levels as checked with blood and/or urine samples.
5. Changes from the home management routine, as recommended by the camp medical team, may occur due to changes in activity patterns.
6. Psychosocial concerns will be addressed through camp activities, such as nap sessions, cabin interactions, and group projects to promote an increase in adaptive behaviors with camp experiences.

Camping Programs that Include Persons with Diabetes

The underlying principle, conceptually, of camping programs should be that these are CAMPS for CHILDREN who happen to have DIABETES, in that order of priority, thus it should be assured that the children have fun. The emphasis should be that these children can participate in all camp activities. While it cannot be ignored, diabetes should not be the overriding issue for these children. The camping experience offers the parents a respite from the daily dealings with diabetes while allowing the children to have a vacation from their parents. The camping experience assists in the teaching of children with diabetes independence and self-discipline in their approach to their condition and their approach to life.

Many children attending camp require some level of supervision in carrying out their daily care. This will also include diabetes management for the person with diabetes. Coordination of care at camp with home management can be facilitated by obtaining the following information from parents or the camper prior to camp:

1. Current insulin type and dosage
2. Food plan and times of day to eat (including snacks)
3. Symptoms of low blood sugar and usual methods of treatment
4. Areas of diabetes care to be assumed by the individual
5. Areas of diabetes care to be assumed by the camp, such as insulin administration, sugar and ketone checks, diet selection, record keeping and balance of snacks and exercise.

For additional information, contact your local American Diabetes Association or American Diabetes Association, National Center, 1660 Duke Street, Alexandria, VA 22314, 1-800/232-3472.

ASTHMA

Camps that primarily serve children with asthma should refer to *Guidelines for the Operation of Camps for Children with Asthma*, published by a consortium of children's asthma camps and available through Penny Gottier, American Lung Association, 1829 Portland Ave., Minneapolis, MN 55404, 612/871-7332.

Aquatic Certifications in Selected Countries

For the purpose of scoring ACA standards, the following list is provided to help camp administrators identify certifications from other countries that may qualify aquatics staff members. This list is based on information available at the time of publication, and is not necessarily complete. Since requirements for certification change, staff members should always be required to demonstrate the requisite skills for an aquatics position.

	Lifesaving/Lifeguarding	Swimming Instruction	Boating
Canada	RLSS-Canada Bronze Medallion and Scuba Bronze Medallion Bronze Cross Award of Merit National Lifeguard Service Award	Canadian ASA Teachers Award CRCS Instructor	RLSSC Boat Rescue Award CRCS Small Craft Instructor
United Kingdom	RLSS-UK Bronze Medallion and Pool Bronze Medallion	ASA Preliminary Teachers Award	RLSS Boat Rescue Award
Australia/ New Zealand	RLSS-Australia/New Zealand Bronze Medallion and Pool Bronze Medallion Surf Bronze Medallion Sub-Aqua Bronze Medallion	Aust Swim Teaching Certificate	RLSS Canoe Bronze Medallion and Boating Bronze Medallion
Finland		Swimming Instruction Diploma from Finnish Association for Swimming Instruction and Life Saving	
Holland	Swim Level E or F plus Lifesaving Level 5 or 6		
Germany	DLRG Gold Award	DLRG Instructor	DLRG Small Craft Rescuer

RLSS: Royal Life Saving Society
CRSC: Canadian Red Cross Society
ASA: Amateur Swimming Association
DLRG: Deutsche Lebens Rettungs Gesellschaft

Considerations for Establishing Lifeguarding Ratios (F-4 and SF-1)

The safety of campers in the water is a critical concern to Camp Directors and all waterfront staff members. Many have asked that ratios of lifeguards (persons certified in Lifeguard Training or the equivalent) and lookouts (staff members assisting lifeguards in observing participants in the water) be established.

As stated in the interpretation to Standard F-4, there are many variables affecting the establishment of "safe" ratios. In previous editions of *Standards with Interpretations*, the ratios of 1 lifeguard per 25 participants and 1 lookout to 10 participants were required.

In varying from this ratio camp administrative personnel should take the following into consideration:

Environmental Hazards

Tides, currents, wind conditions
Glare — visibility of surface
Bottom conditions — rocks, weeds, mud, dark
  (can't be seen clearly)
Air and water temperature
Shoreline — straight vs. undulating
Water traffic — other boats, activities
Weather
Turbidity — cloudiness of water for any reason

Experience and Qualifications of Guards

Maturity and judgment of guards
Experience of staff with this type of aquatic area
Knowledge and experience of staff with activities
  being guarded
Location of guards — Are they roving? Elevated
  above the water level? Able to see all areas?

Skill Level of Swimmers

Age — particularly with reference to their ability
  to follow directions clearly and quickly
Number of persons per square foot in the water
Physical condition/ability of persons in water
Disabilities — such as impaired hearing or sight,
  mental retardation, or seizure disorders

Degree of Risk of Activity

How far are guards from campers?
Is there other activity nearby (boats, skiers, divers,
  etc.)
Degree of control by guards/instructors
  (instructional activities with a great deal of
  control vs. recreational activities where many
  different things are happening at once)
Can people stand or is water depth over their
  heads?
Is swimming skill of participants known to guards?
What equipment is available to assist in rescue?

Types and Uses of Coast Guard-Approved
Personal Flotation Devices
(Life Jackets)

The term "Personal Flotation Device" (PFD) covers a range of devices, from cushions that provide only a small degree of safety, to jackets that can keep your head out of the water even if you're unconscious.

Standards F-18, F-24, G-18, and SF-10 require that U.S. Coast Guard approved PFDs which are of the proper type, size and fit be worn in watercraft activities. Most camps use Type II and Type III PFDs. Check labels for recommended uses and limitations.

Type I   **Offshore Life Jacket**

Best for open, rough or remote water, where rescue may be slow in coming. Will float most people face-up, even if unconscious. It has a minimum buoyancy of 22 pounds (adult), which means it can support even heavy adults. Highly visible, but bulky and cumbersome.

Available in two sizes to fit most children and adults.

Type II   **Near Shore Life Vest**

Good for calm, inland water, or where there is good chance of fast rescue. Will support some wearers face-up if unconscious, and provides good flotation at low cost. It has 15.5 pounds of buoyancy, and is less bulky than a Type I, but less comfortable than a Type III. Not suitable for either rough or cold water.

Available in Infant, Child-Small, Child-Medium, and Adult sizes.

Type III   **Flotation Aid**

Good for calm, inland water, or where there is good chance of fast rescue. Generally the most comfortable type for continuous wear, allowing freedom of movement for water skiing, small boat sailing, fishing, etc. It has 15.5 pounds of buoyancy, but wearer may have to tilt head back to keep face out of water. Not for rough water.

Available in many individual sizes from Child-Small through Adult.

Type IV   **Throwable Device**

A broad category of PFDs designed to be thrown to a person in the water. It must have a buoyancy of 16.5 pounds for rings, or 18 pounds for cushions. Cannot be worn, and should only be used where help is nearby. It not acceptable to meet ACA standards for "being worn."

Type V   **Special Use Device**

Only for special uses or conditions. Varieties include work vests, deck suits, boardsailing vests, and hybrid PFDs for restricted use.

Recommended Wilderness Ethics for ACA Camps

As camp people we have a unique opportunity to teach youngsters and adults to care for and respect, to feel at ease in, and to come to love the natural world around them. We should always seek to go through the woods and forests, the deserts, and canyon lands and across the mountains so no one will know we have passed that way. We should seek to instill a reverence for all living things and, where possible, point out their interrelationships. Procedures consistent with this philosophy would include the following:

1. Water

Bathing, laundry, and scrubbing pots/pans should be done well back from the shores of streams or lakes. If soap is used, a good biodegradable soap (not detergent) such as Ivory* is recommended, with rinsing by bucket or wash basin.

2. Campsites

Choose locations well back from lakeshores, streams, and trails (100 yards where practicable) and away from fragile vegetation, or known animal habitats or breeding grounds. Never cut boughs or poles or put nails into trees or dig trenches around tents. A general rule — don't use the same campsite more than one night, and when breaking camp, leave no evidence that you were there.

3. Fires

Stove cooking is recommended (required) in increasing numbers of areas. If a fire is built, use an existing site if one is there, or if none is available, remove topsoil in an open area (never against trees or rocks and don't circle with rocks). Never leave unattended. To extinguish, sprinkle with water and stir until cold. Scatter ashes over a wide area or bury. Restore topsoil. Leave no tell-tale evidence. Conserve wood. Use small down wood only — do not use axes/saws or break off branches from living or dead trees. Picking plants and flowers or collecting natural objects is discouraged.

4. Sanitation

Individual toilets should be dug four to six inches deep at least 100 yards from any drainage and not in a potential camping spot. Burn toilet paper (or carry out) and cover hole with dirt, not rocks.

5. Garbage

Pack out all garbage including plastic bags and foil, tin cans, and tabs. Orange peels are not readily biodegradable. Foil will not burn. Left over food, fish heads, entrails, etc., should be burned or packed out (never buried).

6. Trails

Where marked trails exist, stay on them; don't cut across switchbacks or corners. Be careful not to kick loose rocks, and NEVER throw them. Give horses the right-of-way by stepping well off the trail but in clear view and waiting quietly for them to pass. If hiking cross-country, don't blaze trees or leave other signs.

7. Pack Stock

Inquire about local regulations. Do not overgraze. One day in a given meadow is generally maximum. Do not graze or tie horses near trails or campsites or within one-fourth mile of a lake. Carry supplemental feed whenever possible.

Note: It is recognized that particular wilderness areas may be under the jurisdiction of locally administered federal and state agencies having specific policies regarding campsites, fires, and sanitation. In the event that defined policies exist, they should be followed.

Other brands include Campsuds, Dr. Bronner's, Bio Suds, Sutter's Camp Soap, etc.

ADOPTED: JUNE 1980.

Sample Comprehensive Plan Outline

The Comprehensive Plan (SA-1, and Self-Assessment item 15) is an all-encompassing plan which sets forth all aspects, including the master site plan and the master program plan which are based upon a statement of goals.

The following outline indicates those elements which should be included in the Comprehensive Plan of a camp:

I. The Philosophy of the Sponsoring Organization or Individual(s)

II. Statement of Camp Goals and Objectives

III. Assessment of Current Conditions (or information about "where we are now") in the areas of

A. SITE/FACILITIES

What is the condition of the camp site (location/natural setting/etc.) as well as all buildings (structure/utilities/maintenance/etc.)? How do present conditions relate to the master site plan?

B. PROGRAM

What activities are being offered now? How are they being received? How is it structured?

C. MARKET

Who are the clientele or personnel utilizing the program?

D. ADMINISTRATION AND FINANCE

What is the current support system for the facility and program, including but not limited to staff, equipment, camper recruitment/registration? What are the factors relating to camp expenditure or income?

E. ENVIRONMENTAL PRESERVATION

What conditions are noted in drainage and erosion control? How is the natural environment being protected/cared for?

IV. Projections of Future Development (or "where we want to be by when") in the areas of

A. SITE/FACILITIES

What changes, if any, are needed and are they included in the master site plan?

B. PROGRAM

What will the program consist of and how will it be structured?

C. MARKET

Who are the potential clientele and what is the plan to reach them?

D. ADMINISTRATION AND FINANCE

What will the future operational needs be? What financial resources will be needed and how will they be obtained?

E. ENVIRONMENTAL PROTECTION AND PRESERVATION

What steps should be taken to preserve the natural environment of the camp for future generations? What steps can be taken in the next five years to improve/maintain water quality and other environmental surroundings?

V. Periodic Review Planned and Modifications Made as Needed

Organizations Offering Additional Resources

American Camping Association, Inc.
5000 St. Rd. 67 N.
Martinsville, IN 46151-7902
Phone: 317/342-8456
Fax: 317/342-2065

Resources: *Camp and Program Leader Catalog, Camping Magazine, Computer Listing of Training Events*, CampLine, national conference, local sections, training workshops, Certified Camp Director program, Outdoor Living Skills program.

I. RELATED PROFESSIONAL ASSOCIATIONS

American Alliance of Health, Physical Education, Recreation and Dance
1900 Association Dr.
Reston, VA 22091
Phone: 703/476-3490

Resources: Publications, magazines, and conferences for health, recreation, and/or physical education interests.

Association for Experiential Education
2885 Aurora Ave., Suite 8
Boulder, CO 80303-2252
Phone: 303/440-8844

Resources: Publications service, journal, conference, jobs clearinghouse.

Canadian Camping Association
1806 Ave. Rd., Suite 2
Toronto, Ontario, Canada M5M 3Z1
Phone: 416/781-4717

Resources: *Canadian Camping Magazine*, national conferences and skill schools, publications service.

Christian Camping International
P.O. Box 62189
Colorado Springs, CO 80962-2189
Phone: 719/260-9400, Fax: 719/260-6398

Resources: Magazine, national conventions, leadership development institutes, workshops.

National Recreation and Park Association
3101 Park Center Dr., 12th Fl.
Alexandria, VA 22302
Phone: 703/820-4940

Resources: Publications, magazines, and conferences for health, recreation, and/or physical education interests.

International Association of Conference Centers
243 N. Lindbergh Blvd.
St. Louis, MO 63141-7851
Phone: 314/349-5576

Resources: Magazine, directory, workshops, and annual conference.

International Association of Conference Center Administrators
199 Greenfield Ave.
San Rafael, CA 94901
Phone: 415/456-5102

Resources: Annual conference, quarterly publication, personnel referral.

Ontario Camping Association
1806 Avenue Rd., Suite 2
Toronto, Ontario, Canada M5M 3Z1
Phone: 416/781-0525

Resources: Information on children's camping, Province of Ontario, Canada.

II. SPECIAL PROGRAM ACTIVITIES

AQUATICS

American Canoe Association
7432 Alban Station Blvd., Suite B 226
Springfield, VA 22150-2311
Phone: 703/451-0141

Resources: Safety literature, film library, magazine.

American Red Cross
17th and D Streets, N.W.
Washington, D. C. 20006
Phone: 202/639-3329

Resources: Instructors, courses, and materials in swimming, boating and first aid.

American Water Ski Association
799 Overlook Dr.
P.O. Box 191
Winter Haven, FL 33884-1671
Phone: 813/324-4341, Fax: 813/325-8259

Resources: Waterski program for camps, booklets, manuals.

Council for National Cooperation in Aquatics (CNCA)
P.O. Box 351743
Toledo, OH 43635
Phone:

Resources: Magazine, training conferences, and cooperative programs from national organizations.

National Organization for River Sports
314 N. 20th St.
Colorado Springs, CO 80904
Phone: 719/473-2466

Resources: *Currents* magazine; whitewater information.

NAUI (National Association of Underwater Instructors)
4650 Arrow Hwy., Suite F-1
P.O. Box 14650
Montclair, CA 91763
Phone: 714/621-5801

Resources: Training programs and instructor certification.

PADI (Professional Association of Diving Instructors)
1251 E. Dyer Rd., Suite 100
Santa Ana, CA 92705
Phone: 714/540-7234

Resources: Training programs and instructor certification.

SSI (Scuba Schools International)
2619 Canton Court
Ft. Collins, CO 80525-4498
Phone: 303/482-0883

Resources: Training programs and instructor certification.

National Water Ski Association
P.O. Box 141
Odessa, FL 33556
Phone: 813/920-2160

U.S. Sailing Association
P.O. Box 209
Newport, RI 02840
Phone: 401/849-5200, Fax 401/849-5208

U.S. Coast Guard
2100 2nd St. S.W.
Washington, D.C. 20593-0001
Phone: 202/267-1077

Resources: *Currents* magazine; whitewater information.

ARCHERY

American Archery Council
604 Forest Ave.
Park Rapids, MN 56470
Phone: 218/732-3879

Resources: Youth archery program for camps.

National Archery Association
1750 E. Boulder St.
Colorado Springs, CO 80909
Phone: 719/578-4576

Resources: Archery instructor certification courses.

National Field Archery Association
31407 Outer I-10
Redlands, CA 92373
Phone: 714/794-2133

Resources: Magazine and youth archery program information.

CHALLENGE/ROPES COURSES

Cradlerock Outdoor Network
P.O. Box 1431
Princeton, NJ 08542
Phone: 609/466-1644

Project Adventure, Inc.
P.O. Box 100
Hamilton, MA 01936
Phone: 508/468-7981

Resources: Trains staff, constructs and inspects ropes courses.

Signature Research and Marketing
1979 Moody Hollow,
Hiwassee, GA 30546
Phone: 404/896-1487

ENVIRONMENTAL CONCERNS

National Wildlife Federation
1400 16th St., N.W.
Washington, DC 20036-0001
Phone: 703/790-4415

Resources: Nature study activity guides, nature periodicals, conservation education publications.

HORSEBACK RIDING

The Association for Horsemanship Safety and Education
P.O. Box 188
Lawrence, MI 49064
Phone: 616/674-8074

Resources: Four-level riding instructor's training with certification program with manuals. Covers both English and Western riding. Guidelines for camp riding programs. Job placement service. Insurance Program. Group buying program for helmets.

Horsemanship Safety Association, Inc.
517 Bear Rd.
Lake Placid, FL 33852
Phone: 813/465-1365

Resources: Riding Instructor Certification clinics and manuals. Lectures, developing/improving riding programs, and publications.

The United States Pony Clubs, Inc.
893 S. Matlack St., Suite 110
West Chester, PA 19382-4913
Phone: 215/436-0300

Resources: Newsletter, teaching aids, publications, list of protective headgear, clinics.

TRIP CAMPING

American Mountain Guides Association
P.O. Box 4473
Bellingham, WA 98227
Phone: 206/647-1167

Resources: Accreditation and certification programs.

Appalachian Mountain Club
5 Joy St.
Boston, MA 02108
Phone: 617/523-0636

Resources: Publish and sell trial guides and maps for the Northeast.

III. SPECIAL POPULATIONS

American Diabetes Association, Inc.
1660 Duke St.
Alexandria, VA 22314
Phone: 800/232-3472, 212/683-7444

Resources: National camp exchange program.

American Lung Association
1740 Broadway
New York, NY 10019
Phone: 212/315-8700

Resources: Asthma camp guidelines.

Epilepsy Foundation of America
4351 Garden City Dr.
Landover, MD 20785
Phone: 301/459-3700

Muscular Dystrophy Association
3561 E. Sunrise Dr.
Tucson, AZ 85718-3204

National Easter Seal Society
70 E. Lake St.
Chicago, IL 60601
Phone: 312/726-6200

Resources: Publications dealing with camping and recreation for persons with disabilities.

National Hemophilia Foundation
110 Greene St.
New York, NY 10012
Phone: 212/219-8180

IV. NATIONAL ORGANIZATIONS SPONSORING CAMPING

Boys and Girls Clubs of America
771 First Ave.
New York, NY 10017
Phone: 212/532-4949

Resources: Technical assistance, training workshops, and publications.

Boy Scouts of America (National Office)
1325 Walnut Hill Ln.
P.O. Box 152079
Irving, TX 75015-2079
Phone: 214/580-2000

Resources: Technical, management, program
ideas, audiovisual presentations and
equipment. Reference material available.

Camp Fire, Inc.
4601 Madison Ave.
Kansas City, MO 64112-1278
Phone: 816/756-1950

Resources: Management of risks and
emergencies, *Outdoor Book*, training model
in outdoor living.

Girl Scouts of the U.S.A.
420 Fifth Ave.
New York, NY 10018
Phone: 212/852-8000, Fax: 212/852-6515

Resources: Publications, program ideas,
camping guidelines.

Girls, Incorporated
30 E. 33rd St.
New York, NY 10016
Phone: 212/689-3700

Jewish Welfare Board
15 E. 26th St.
New York, NY 10010
Phone: 212/532-4949

**National 4-H Administrative Staff
  Extension Service**
USDA — Science & Education Administration
South Building, Room 3860
Washington, DC 20250-0900
Phone: 202/720-5516

YMCA of the U.S.A.
101 N. Wacker Dr., 14th Fl.
Chicago, IL 60606
Phone: 312/977-0031

Resources: Staff training, long-range planning.

YWCA
726 Broadway, 5th Fl.
New York, NY 10003
Phone: 212/614-2700

V. RELIGIOUS ORGANIZATIONS WITH CAMPING PROGRAMS

American Baptist Board of Education
P.O. Box 851
Valley Forge, PA 19481

Baptist Brotherhood Commission
Royal Ambassador Division
1548 Poplar
Memphis, TN 38104
Phone: 901/272-2461

Resources: Camp materials and campcraft
training.

Camp Cherith National
(Pioneer Ministries)
Box 788, 27 W. 130 St. Charles Rd.
Wheaton, IL 60189-0788
Phone: 708/293-1600 ext. 311

Resources: Camp Bible study curriculum plus
training tools and resources for camp boards,
directors, staff and campers-in-leadership
training.

Catholic Youth Organization
910 Marion St.
Seattle, WA 98104
Phone: 206/382-4562

Church of Jesus Christ of Latter Day Saints
76 N. Main
Salt Lake City, UT 84150
Phone: 801/531-2141

Resources: Camp manual, Campcrafter
certification program.

Church of the Brethren
1451 Dundee
Elgin, IL 60120
Phone: 312/742-5100

Resources: Slide-tape presentation on the
Biblical theological basis of church camping.

Episcopal Church Center
Office of Religious Education
815 Second Ave.
New York, NY 10017
Phone: 212/867-8400

Resources: Newsletter, resource and consultant
referrals.

Federation of Jewish Philanthropies
130 E. 59th St.
New York, NY 10022
Phone: 212/980-1000

Evangelical Covenant Church of America
5101 N. Francisco Ave.
Chicago, IL 60625
Phone: 312/784-3000

Resources: Counselor training materials, filmstrip library.

Evangelical Lutheran Church in America
8765 W. Higgins Rd.
Chicago, IL 60631
Phone: 800/638-3522, 312/380-2560

Reorganized Church of Latter Day Saints
P.O. Box 1059
Independence, MO 64051
Phone: 816/833-1000

The Salvation Army
615 Slaters Ln.
P.O. Box 269
Alexandria, VA 22363
703/684-5500

Resources: Manuals on resident and day camping; guidelines for staff training and recruitment.

Seventh Day Adventist
NAD Church Ministries
12501 Old Columbia Pike
Silver Springs, MD 20904-1608
Phone: 301/680-6426

Southern Baptist Convention
  Baptist Sunday School Board
Church Recreation Department
127 Ninth Ave., N.
Nashville, TN 37234
615/251-3825

The United Church of Christ
Hoot Hill, 15 Crawley Falls Rd.
Brentwood, NH 03833
Phone: 603/642-8758

General Board of Discipleship
  United Methodist Church
P.O. Box 840
Nashville, TN 37202
Phone: 615/340-7200

Resources: Toward excellence in church camping; camp leadership guide and others.

Jewish Community Center Association
15 E. 26th St.
New York, NY 10010
Phone: 212/532-4949

Jewish Theological Seminary
  National Ramah Division
3080 Broadway
New York, NY 10027
Phone: 212/678-8881

Lutheran Church — Missouri Synod
  Board of Youth Services
1333 S. Kirkwood Rd.
St. Louis, MO 63122
Phone: 314/965-9000

Presbyterian Church U.S.A.
100 Whitherspoon St.
Louisville, KY 40202-1396
Phone: 502/569-5000

VI. OTHER AGENCIES

American Academy of Pediatrics
141 Northwest Point Blvd.
P.O. Box 927
Elk Grove Village, IL 60009-0927
Phone: 312/288-5005

American Nature Study Society
5881 Cold Brook Rd.
Homer, NY 13077
Phone: 201/948-4646

Bunacamp
P.O. Box 49
S. Britain, CT 06487
Phone: 203/264-0901

Resources: International counselors.

Appendix

233

Camp America
102 Greenwich Ave.
Greenwich, CT 06830
Phone: 203/869-9090

Resources: International counselors.

Camp Counselors U.S.A.
26 Third St.
San Francisco, CA 94103
Phone: 415/777-0702

Resources: International counselors.

Centers for Disease Control
U.S. Department of HHS
Public Health Service
Atlanta, GA 30333
Phone: 404/262-6649

International Student Center
38 W. 88th St.
New York, NY 10025
Phone: 212/787-7706

Resources: International counselors

National Fire Protection Association
Batterymarch Park
Quincy, MA 02269
Phone: 617/770-3000

National Rifle Association of America
1600 Rhode Island Ave., NW
Washington, DC 20036
Phone: 202/828-6000

National Safety Council
1121 Spring Lake Dr.
Itasca, IL 60143-3201
Phone: 708/285-1121

Association of Camp Nurses
8504 Thorsonveien N.E.
Bemidji, MN 56601
218/586-2556

OBIS (Outdoor Biology Instruction Strategies)
Delta Education, Inc.
P.O. Box M
Nashua, NH 03061

NOLS (National Outdoor Leadership School)
288 Main St.
Lander, WY 82520
Phone: 307/332-6973

Resources: Outdoor training.

WEA (Wilderness Education Association)
2 Winona Ave., Box 89
Saranac Lake, NY 12983
518/891-2915

YMCA International Camp Counselor Program
356 W. 34th St.
New York, NY 10001
Phone: 212/563-3441